Accidental Journey:
An Owner's Guide to a Broken Body

by Gayle Andrew and Jess Kielman

Deep Blue Press
P.O. Box 449, Lenox, MA 01240
© 2010

Accidental Journey
An Owner's Guide to a Broken Body

For additional copies:

Deep Blue Press
P.O. Box 449
Lenox, MA 01240

jess.kielman@gmail.com
www.deepbluepress.com

Cover design by Jess Kielman
Technical Assistant, Joe Wilk
Front Cover photo by Dave Rash
Back Cover photo by Jess Kielman

BISAC Subject Headings:
HEA036000 HEALTH & FITNESS / Pain Management
BIO026000 BIOGRAPHY & AUTOBIOGRAPHY / Personal Memoirs
SEL021000 SELF-HELP / Motivational & Inspirational

Dedication

This book is dedicated to all those who prayed, rescued, nursed, healed, and helped rehabilitate Gayle, our son, and our family. You were an integral part of this "accidental" journey.

To the Reader

If you are reading this book because you or someone you love has been hurt, this is my way of extending a hug to you. I have worked hard to help you navigate your new life, and I want you to know that I have great empathy for what you are facing. With my embrace, know that I understand that nothing will ever be the same, but everything will be okay.

Gayle Andrew

Acknowledgements

We wish to thank Matt Came, our son Devin's best friend, who devoured our first three chapters while on the way to a soccer game. Your enthusiasm helped us to know that we were on to something. Thanks to our first editor, Nancy Boxer, and Victoria Wright, our second editor, who not only continued the editing process but also encouraged us to take that final leap towards publication. Thanks to our friend and fellow author, Jerry Posner, who recommended Victoria. Thanks to our NYC friend, Dr. Beth Ross, who read the first completed manuscript. Because you were new to the details of our story, telling us that you couldn't put it down and that it should be made into a movie helped us know that the book had value beyond our family and close-to-home friends. We are grateful to our daughter, Rebecca, for reading and editing with our family's needs in mind, and to her husband, Glenn Dickerson, who insisted that we work to write a stronger ending. Deep appreciation goes to all those who gave so much of their time and thoughtfulness when answering the many challenging questions of our interviewing process. We believe your interviews create the depth and dimension that sets our book apart from others.

Special Thanks

There are always people who go the extra mile, who make an extra effort to do their job with heart. We thank Trish and Janet for making doctor visits run smoothly with humor, compassion, and a personal touch. You always make us feel like family. And to Roberta and Sandra, two wonderful PTs, for being extra inventive, compassionate, and loving.

Table of Contents

A Sunday in June

by Gerry Binder

Thunder, lightening, heavy rain
nothing short of a downpour.
So the morning went.
By afternoon it cleared.
The sun came out.
The clouds lifted.
Earth settled down
to a pleasant Sunday.

The phone rang.
The spoken words
shattered our world.
A terrible car collision.
Lives turned inside out.
Bodies broken. Tears
and fears and prayers
so many prayers.
Now we wait.

Doctors, nurses work
to restore our loved ones.
We hold one another
to calm our fears
to dry our tears.
And we pray, "Please, God,
please, bring back our peace.
Bring back our quiet day."

Chapter 1: Going Before the Judge

The young man sat stiffly upright as the judge spoke. He knew, as did everyone else in the courtroom, that the woman facing him wouldn't be in a wheelchair if he hadn't fallen asleep driving his father's new truck. She wouldn't need the IV line trailing her, the IV that brought back memories of fluids dripping into his own arm that first terrible night in the hospital. He cringed as he looked over to his parents. It was not the first time since that horrible day that he had witnessed their disapproving silence. Did he know that he almost killed a woman and her young son, they had asked repeatedly. It had been so upsetting that not a soul had been able or willing to tell him if they'd survived those first couple weeks. He pushed away the lingering pain in his ankle and jaw as he continued to torment himself. *If only I had stopped to close my eyes for a few minutes before driving home*, he thought. *If only I'd stopped partying earlier the night before. If only…*

He stared, shamefaced, at the floor. His lawyer nudged him. *Look up. They'll think you're a bad person if you won't even acknowledge the woman you crippled.* But it was so hard to watch. Her partner was wheeling her in front of the judge, brushing awkwardly against the lawyer's table on the way. The wheelchair seemed so big with the leg supports both extended. Pain meds gave the woman's eyes a slightly unfocused look. He knew that look. He'd seen it in the mirror those first few weeks. Then he heard her clear her throat once, then again, looking around, frowning slightly as she spotted him. *Oh, man, she's going to crucify me. She should crucify me. I caused all this.* He fought back tears.

The woman in the wheelchair kept looking, not at the judge, not at the lawyers, but right at him. His lawyer poked him, again. *Stare back at her, kid, your fate is hanging by a thread.* God, could it get any worse than this? Men were staring at him as if he were the only deer they were being allowed for the hunting season, and they'd be hauling out their rifles any minute. He could hear people sniffling, see them blotting their eyes. Even his own mother was pulling out a tissue. God, now that woman was unfolding several pieces of paper. He could see her trembling. Now she was speaking to the judge but looking straight at him!

"Your honor?"

"Yes?"

"I know I am supposed to address this to you, but may I have your permission to address Lionel?" Her voice was small and raspy.

The judge smiled and said, "That would be fine, Ms. Andrew."

The woman nodded, glanced back at her papers, then began. "My name is Gayle Andrew." Her voice was barely more than whisper. Suddenly the buzzing courtroom grew silent. People were craning forward to hear her speak.

"I and my twelve-year-old son, Devin, are the two people that you crashed into on June 3, 2001, changing our lives forever. Most of the bones in my body were broken or fractured. One nurse took the time to count 123 breaks and fractures, which she discovered was a new record. I need assistance with even the most simple things in life: bathing, brushing my teeth, getting dressed, eating. Going to the bathroom is a major event. I was planning to begin a new career, but now I am uncertain when I will be able to do that. My new cross-country skis will sit unused, perhaps forever.

"I have missed six months of my son's life. I could not be there for him when he was hurt and needing me. His nose and toes were broken, his wrist and his ankle, too. He remembers most of the accident. The horror of watching his mother barely holding on to life, the pain within his own body, the panic of believing that the car was on fire. Trying to free me from the clutches of the crushed car, the stress of separation as I was medevaced[1] to Albany while he remained behind. This accident has changed him in ways that I still am discovering. He had to attend his graduation in a wheelchair; of course I could not attend. He missed the soccer playoffs and will be unable to play for another six months.

"All of my family and friends' lives have been affected. The worry, the time spent in caring for me, cheering and encouraging me, the expense of travel and

---

[1] Taken by medical helicopter

hotel stays, the inconvenience of sleeping on chairs in my hospital room, the workdays missed, all have been extremely stressful. My partner, Jess, was waiting for me to come home on June 3rd, but instead the Williamstown police called, telling her that Devin and I had been in a serious accident. Doctors told her that I might not make it. My parents, ages 79 and 82, stayed at the hospital, believing that I could die at any time. Jess missed three weeks of work to sit beside me, and had to reduce her work schedule to take care of me. She had to convert our home for the wheelchair, building a long ramp to get me into the house. Our dreams, hopes, and desires as well as our budding business have been put on hold. She now takes care of me and is exhausted most of the time. Just two nights ago my knee swelled and felt like it was on fire. I was put on IV antibiotics again, and she had to set the alarm for meds every two hours. We have missed vacations with the children. My 21-year-old stepdaughter, Rebecca, moved into her first apartment. I have yet to see it, because it is on the second floor.

"Lionel, I hope you realize how much pain you have brought to so many people. Whatever the court decides today, I hope you take it with good grace. I hope you can find within yourself the courage to grow from this experience. Just as I am trying to make the best of a bad situation, I hope that you do the same."

The silence continued for several long moments after she was finished. Her partner, standing behind her, quietly wheeled her back. The judge glanced at each of the lawyers in turn, but they had nothing more to add.

He straightened his papers, folded his hands, and cleared his throat. He was about to deliver the sentence. It was a serious matter and jail time was clearly merited. But he hesitated. It was as if he were looking for help with his decision. He rubbed his palms in an attempt to stave off the inevitable. *This was just a kid, for God's sake. He'd seen plenty of kids come through the court system. Would this one be any different?*

Finally he spoke. "I am reluctant, but I must include jail time in my ruling." As he looked around the room, the victim caught his eye. Her arm trembled with the effort to move, yet shyly she raised her hand as if she were in school.

"May I speak?" she asked the judge.

"Yes. Please."

"This young man was not out to get us. He wasn't drunk. When he got behind the wheel that day, he made a poor decision. He chose to drive while tired. No good can come from sending him to jail."

The judge nodded, unlocked his fingers, and abruptly pushed his chair back. It made a loud, grating sound. He stood and before leaving the room, he whispered to the bailiff. Court was recessed so that he could consider the victim's request. Lionel's mother was in tears. She looked at her son, but he made eye contact with no one. His head hung in shame and resignation. He thought he deserved jail time. *Throw away the key!*

Gayle's eyes shut. She was in pain. It had been an effort to leave her hospital bed at home to come here today. It had hurt transferring from her bed to the wheelchair. And it was still frightening to go anywhere in a car. Her mother and father sat close, whispering. Her partner reached around the wheelchair to rub her neck. It seemed like everyone was fighting tears or holding their breath. The bailiff walked up to the victim and quietly asked a question. When she nodded, he smiled briefly, then addressed the court, "You are all asked to leave except for Gayle Andrew and Lionel White. His honor wishes that they have time to talk."

Apprehension filled the room. Gayle's parents and partner were the last to leave. It was an interminably long fifteen minutes before the bailiff announced that everyone should return to the courtroom. Another ten minutes passed before the judge entered and took his seat. He clasped his hands and spoke directly to Lionel. "After much deliberation, I have decided that your license will be revoked for a period of six months. You will serve no jail time, however, I am going to do something that has not been done before in this court. Lionel White, you will serve one hundred community service hours." With that he turned his gaze to Gayle. "And those community service hours will be given directly to Gayle Andrew."

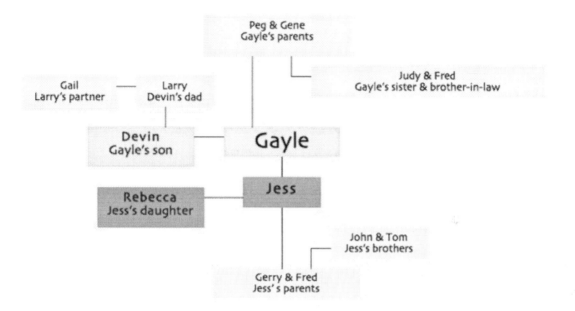

Chapter 2: Jess's Story

I was filling in for someone at work that Sunday. A stroke of luck, because if I had not, Devin might have died. It was obvious looking at the picture that appeared in the local newspaper. I would have been in the front seat next to Gayle, and Devin would have been in the back seat behind his mother. But there was no more back seat. Looking at the photo, none of us could believe that my partner and son had been a part of all that tangled metal and shattered glass. No one could believe that anyone could have survived. It was months before I could bear to look at the picture again; over a year before Gayle could take her first look at it.

I was waiting at home with dinner ready when I got the call from the Williamstown police. Gayle and Devin were in an accident, they told me. "A fender bender?" I asked. "No. You need to get to the hospital right away."

Her ex-husband, Larry, was there with his partner, confusingly also called Gail. Larry was trembling. His face was sunken and colorless. A nurse asked if I was Jess, then brought me quickly to Gayle. Her body was covered, offering no hint of the extensive wreckage underneath. She was worried about Devin and asked how I thought he was.

I found him next to her with a curtain separating them. He was pale and looked small. People were moving quickly around us. Gayle's parents, Peg and Gene, had just arrived, and I found myself bouncing from person to person getting and giving information. We were told that Gayle would be medevaced to Albany, but since Devin had no internal injuries, he would be staying where he was. I felt ripped in two.

I returned to Gayle's side. The nurses had to get her ready, and one of them asked me to leave. Gayle looked at me with a sad look in her eyes. "Baby, I'm not sure I'm going to make it," she whispered.

I wanted to hold her hands but they were under the sheet. Instead I stroked her hair. "You're going to be fine, honey," I assured her. "Everything will be all right." As I said the words, I felt them to be true, but I had no way of knowing.

Certainly I wanted them to be true. I bent down close to kiss her. I promised I would see her in Albany.

Then I went to Devin and kissed him, saying, "I'm going to Albany to be with your mom. I'll take good care of her. Grandma and Grandpa and your Dad and Gail are staying here for you." He smiled weakly and I was gone. I called my daughter, Rebecca, and asked her to come with me. She was eighteen at the time and quite shaken by the news. I went home and gathered an odd collection of clothes and other supplies while waiting for her to arrive. In the meantime, I started making phone calls. I was surprisingly calm. There were a lot of arrangements that needed to be made.

Waiting for Rebecca and her boyfriend in the driveway, I heard a deep, rhythmic sound. *Thud, thud, thud*. Helicopter, I thought, and looked up to see it lifting, hovering for a few moments before flying away. My heart was in my throat. How could this be happening? There I was on the ground while my beloved Gayle was tied to a stretcher, high above, racing across the sky to Albany.

Although we arrived at the hospital by eight-thirty, I did not get to see Gayle until midnight. It took considerable convincing to get Rebecca to leave my side, but I wanted her and her boyfriend to find an affordable motel and get some rest so they would be ready to relieve me later. Gayle was in the hall outside of x-ray before being taken to surgery. She was surprisingly alert and speaking almost like normal. It was not until they took her away to prepare her for surgery that I was told how serious things were. I will never forget what the surgeon said. "When even one long bone breaks, the chances are great that the patient can die. Gayle has five." The hours that followed were excruciating. I paced, I fidgeted in several different chairs, I tried to read a magazine. Nothing relieved the agony of limbo. The not knowing, the strange surroundings, the loneliness, the uncertainty of Gayle's fate, all stretched out endlessly. Surgery went for four hours but I was not allowed to see her until seven-thirty the next morning. I may have been strung out with fatigue, but when I was finally allowed in and could see for myself that she was still alive, a sense of rightness descended upon me. Nothing was okay, but everything was manageable. She was still alive.

I was not allowed to stay very long before they reclaimed her. There were endless medical procedures they still had to do. In any case, we couldn't talk, couldn't comfort each other, for they had put her into a drug-induced coma. We could sit by her side for a while. Then we would have to leave. While in the waiting room, another visitor told me she was keeping a journal. She explained that when her father woke again, she was sure he'd want to know all the details of his life in the ICU. Besides, it would keep her mind busy with something more constructive than worrying. And so I was inspired to begin a journal for Gayle. Here are some excerpts.

Sunday, June 3rd
"He who has a why to live for can bear almost any how."
- Friedrich Nietzsche

That was the first card I pulled from the pouch that Rebecca had made for you when we found out you had cancer in your hand, but that's another story. Someone here in the waiting room suggested that we keep a journal during your stay. I don't know if you will ever want to read this, but it's as much for me as it is for you. It keeps me from going crazy when they won't let me sit in the room with you.

On Sunday afternoon while you were on your way to Devin's school, a 17-year-old boy from Worthington was returning from a lunch in Williamstown and lost control of his Dodge Dakota truck on Route 7 in Williamstown. He apparently struck one vehicle without doing much damage at all, then careened off, slamming into you and Devin. I was at work filling in for one of the other women. I had called at three to see how things were going at home, and you said you were heading up to school to look for Devin's French book. The accident occurred at quarter past four.

I got the call from the Williamstown Police at quarter to six. I had started to worry a half hour earlier, and was about to call around to see if you were at your folk's house or something. My heart sank as the officer said that you had been involved in an accident.

One of the nurses got me in to see you and Devin as quickly at possible. You whispered in my ear, "They say I'm going to make it, but I'm not so sure." I stroked your hair and insisted, "You're going to be fine! I'm psychic, remember!"

It's odd what goes through your head at moments like this. Back at home I changed into my lucky polo shirt, the yellow pullover you love to look at, and the earrings that Devin gave me. But did I pack any other clothes? Or even underwear? No! But I did put in contact lens stuff, my toothbrush, a nearly empty tube of toothpaste, and a hairbrush. I made a bunch of phone calls: my mother to visit Devin in the hospital and take care of our dog, Lisa and Ed to take care of Larry and Gail, Ellie to take care of your folks, Cherie to take care of work, and Ann to pull together prayer groups. Becca would take care of me and her boyfriend would take care of her. As we sat in the car waiting for him to arrive, we saw the helicopter carrying you.

"Bye, honey. I'll be with you soon," I said. That was the first time I cried. But not the last by a long shot.

Becca called around and found us a hotel. They left at around eleven to get some sleep. She didn't want to go, but I insisted and assured her that I would call when there was anything to report. An hour after they left, Dr. Max Alley came out and explained that there could be many surgeries ahead for you. Then I was alone. I paced, sat, watched TV, walked outside in the nearly full moon—which often increases bleeding—tried not to worry, and prayed. Dr. Max found me at 11:45 and told me where to wait so that I could see you between scanning and surgery. He sat with me while I blubbered on about how upset your hand surgeon, Bill Morgan, would be to know that you'd been so injured. "I'm Bill Morgan-trained!" he said with pride. What wonderful words! I will never forget them. They made me feel that you were being watched over.

Monday, June 4th

"How a person masters his fate is more important than what his fate is."
- Wilhelm von Humboldt

At midnight they wheeled you out and left you in the hall outside of surgery. I got to stroke your hair and kiss your forehead for five minutes. It was hard to see you in so much pain, but you looked pretty good, given what you were going through. You weren't sure you were going to make it, you murmured again, but I kept reassuring you that everything would turn out okay. All too soon you were whisked away. I felt lost and alone. Strangers were going to try to put you back together. Knowing that thought is energy, I reminded myself that you deserved better than my worry and tears. Tears of empathy I could accept, but the tears over what might be, I fought back.

You were in surgery until 4 AM. Max came out to report on your progress. He gave me your anklet and rings, telling me it might be a while before they would let me see you.

Wait. Watch TV. Pace. Stare into the ICU. Cry. Wait. Sleep ten minutes. Pace. At 7 AM, a nurse came out. She must have seen the look on my face. "Are you all right?"

"Yes," I said, crying.

"It won't be much longer," she assured me.

At 7:30 they let me in. What a relief to see your face and know that you had made it this far. Becca returned at 9ish. Your folks were here with Ellie by 9:30. It was a long day of watching and waiting.

The first surgery was to clean up the gash in your left arm. There were no other major flesh wounds. You had a broken left leg bone; they put pins and a rod in to stabilize it. Both knee caps and the pelvis were shattered. They put a screen around one or both kneecaps. They pinned and plated your right foot. That was all you could tolerate for now. Max explained that your pelvis might heal on its own. Hip surgery is too major after such a trauma, and there is usually only about a one month window to do it in, he explained. Oh, honey, there was so much information. I hope I got it all correct.

To be admitted into the ICU, family and friends had to call on a special phone to see if it was okay to go in. Many phone calls later, we were allowed in to sit with you. Our favorite nurse, Callie, said we could put up pictures, a balloon or two, no flowers, and later we could bring in a tape recorder. I took Devin's soccer picture out of my checkbook and taped it over your head on the metal traction bar. I kept telling you that Devin was fine. He had a broken ankle and a broken wrist, both of which were set and casted. You were unconscious, but I wanted to be sure that you knew what had happened to Devin, and that I loved you.

Becca went home to take care of things, visit Devin, and get me fresh clothing. Grandpa and Ellie went home after supper to rest. He was a mess! Your mom and I took the shuttle back to the hotel at 10:30 PM. It was hard to leave you, but they said that you were stable, and we'd better get some rest. We were reluctant to leave, but they assured us we could call at any hour. We called at midnight and later at 6:00 AM. Both times you were sedated and still stable.

Tuesday, June 5th
"The art of life lives in a constant readjustment to our surroundings."
- Okakura Kukuzo

This morning they decided you were in good enough condition for more surgery. Max explained that we had a week-long window to work on your legs and arms, so we figured you must be doing well to be heading into surgery again so quickly.

The first call from anyone outside of the immediate family was from my boss, Cherie, that afternoon. It was wonderful to hear the concern and love in her voice. She said she got my message and everything at work would be taken care of. She wanted updates on your condition. And if there was anything anyone could do—meals for Becca and Devin, a car while we're here—we shouldn't hesitate to ask.

When we got back to the hotel, there was an email from someone at work.

They were paying my hotel bill for the first five nights. What a wonderful place!

I called Becca, who told me all about Devin: who had called him, who had visited, how well he was doing. Then she cracked me up, saying, "I thought you guys only had two friends in the whole world! The phone is ringing off the hook. And with the number of people who want to bring flowers and plants, you could open a small nursery. Can you believe someone called at eight in the morning? Good God!" It felt so good to laugh. She said even the Williamstown police wanted to know how you were, and if there was anything they could do. Mel and Richard called to offer help. Mel told Becca that they shut down their whole building for a few minutes of prayer. Ann had called every synagogue, church, and prayer group in Berkshire County.

Your surgery went well, all four hours of it. Earlier, they put in a vena cava filter to stop the fat globules that are released with the blood when you break long bones. Those clots can travel through the heart and go to the lungs, causing an embolism. At least that what I remember the surgeon said. Now they were going to be setting your right elbow and both wrists. They were surprised when they checked your shoulder. What they thought was a fracture turned out to be a dislocation. Any little piece of good news is what we focus on right now. Your mother and I were already in the surgical waiting room, but your dad joined us later with Ellie and Linda. Ann and Becca came together, and then my mother, Fred, John, and Tom were there. I think that's eleven. Yup! Eleven! As soon as the surgeon came up to tell us you were done and doing well, everyone started saying their goodbyes and soon most everyone was gone. Becca was torn. She wanted to stay; she wanted to go. I left it up to her. She decided to stay, but while we were saying goodbye to Ann, she said she wanted to see you one more time and then go. Poor thing.

Okay, so the quote thing. All the while I'm with you, I'm struggling with how to communicate. Sure, after a few weeks, you were nodding "yes" and "no" to simple questions: Pain? Can't breathe? Are you upset? But I wanted to get more complicated messages from you somehow. Becca had brought pictures of Devin, a tape player, and tapes. She added the white satin pouch of sayings that she'd made for you when you were going through cancer. Along with the quotes there are also a few jokes. She printed them on her computer, cut them up into small pieces, then laminated each one so that they would last.

So what I would do is close my eyes, focus deeply, and ask your high self to communicate with me. Before the cards came I simply repeated over and over silently to you, "Whatever your destiny is, I will support your choices." So now I had a tool. I reached in and got the quote I put at the beginning of each journal entry. The first day was, "He who has a why to live for can bear almost any how." Everyday I would find your message. I also used it for my own guidance and will share that with you, too.

Wednesday, June 6th

"What is dumber than 2 brunettes that tried to build a house
at the bottom of the ocean?
The 2 blondes that tried to burn it down!"
- Web Joke

I guess today is supposed to be a bit lighter. That's the first time one of Becca's jokes came out of the bag. Not much good or bad today. We connected a lot with Annette, an older woman from Miami who reminds me of my Grandma Gillon. We also chatted a lot with her granddaughter, Molly, who is studying for the law boards at the end of July. Your folks and I really enjoy them. They are the mother and daughter of Glenn, a few doors down from you, who was thrown from a horse at his farm. When the two of you are well again, we'll be going for a visit. Did I tell you that all the gloves here are purple?

Thursday, June 7th

"Cherish your visions and your dreams, as they are the children of your soul and
the blueprints of your ultimate achievements."
- Napoleon Hill

I waited too long to write anything for this day, but I did save the quote. Can't really remember anything except you slept a lot. I spend a lot of time wondering why, then just affirming that you know best what to do. I will respect and support whatever you need in your life, with or without understanding.

Friday, June 8th
"Success is a state of mind."
- Joyce Brothers

Friday was uneventful. The only good news was that you were tolerating liquid food, the white nutritious stuff. Unfortunately, it goes through a tube down your nose. Fortunately, you probably aren't aware of that nasty thought. There was no bad news. Your dad brought your mom home till Sunday. I keep stroking your hair and humming a Cris Williamson lullaby, "Like a ship on the ocean. Like a mother and child. Like a light in the darkness. I'll hold you awhile. We'll rock on the water. I'll cradle you deep. And hold you while angels sing you to sleep."

I only hope that when I'm humming, you are hearing angels instead of me. Don't want to bring on a migraine. Sometimes I change to a healing chant so I don't drive you crazy with the same thing over and over.

Saturday, June 9th
"You have to have faith that there is a reason you go through certain things. I can't say I'm glad to go through pain, but in a way one must, in order to gain courage and really feel joy."
- Carol Burnett

I didn't pull a card from the bag of quotes until later in the evening because you had such a good day. Your mom and I went for a walk around three. Two blocks from the hospital we discovered what looked like a little park, then gravel walking paths and flowers, then a pond reflecting a building. It turned out to be a beautiful, brightly painted outdoor theater in Washington Park. Out the back door was the pond, where people were fishing. We discovered a tree that looked like the tree on your Integrative Acupressure sign. I put my arms around it and asked it to make your bones strong again. I'm pretty sure your mom thought I was nuts. There was a wading pool with a huge rock waterfall and a sculpted Zeus on top. When you're better, we'll take you there. Callie, our favorite nurse, told us that they have a spectacular tulip festival on Mother's Day weekend. I put it in the reminder calendar for next year.

On the way back to you, we stopped for ice cream and a couple of scratch tickets. I won two dollars but lost it to your mom in a bet that her second ticket would be a winner. It wasn't, so she got my two dollars. It was good to take a giggle break. I keep reminding myself how important it is to stay well, rested, and take time to exercise so that I can go the distance with you. I'm still on my diet, hoping to be 150 pounds by the time you leave the hospital and go into rehab.

Your friend Jerilee tried to get in to see you, but they were doing something and she had to get to the airport to pick up her son. It was such a pleasant surprise to see someone from home, someone who loves you so much! I gave her a thorough update. She left us with a basket filled with fruit and goodies. I gave your malted milk balls to the nurses. Mel told me to give them treats and be sure to say who they're from. Mel insists that gets you better care, so I handed them over with little compunction. But I didn't offer the dark chocolate raspberry espresso bar. No way!

Since you had such a uneventful day, we thought we might take our first early night. But at 7:30, when we were thinking of leaving, you started to fuss. By eight, you were in so much pain, struggling with reflux and coughing, that there was no way we were going. We asked you questions to figure what was going on. You were amazing, how you were able to communicate with head nods and expressions. I had my hand on your chest to comfort you and felt a rattle. The nurse came in and I told her about the rattle. That helped her to figure out that you needed the suction put back on your chest tube. For some reason you started to build fluid in the chest cavity after they thought you were nearly done. Good thing they hadn't pulled the tube prematurely.

Your mom and I were getting angry that the chest x-ray was taking so long, but by 9:30 it was finally done. It took them until 10:00 before it was seen by a doctor. In the meantime, you had us both in tears with all the pain you were in. On several occasions, your blood pressure got dangerously high. At your worst, it was 183 over 92.

I called to see how Devin made out. He told me they took him to the soccer game and he was made an honorary captain. They wheeled him to the center of the field for the coin toss, then gave him the official coin to keep. He was pretty pleased about it. Unfortunately, his team got creamed—8 to 1! I reminded him that they're still pretty shook up about his injuries. I gave him a slightly modified version of your problems so as not to worry him more than necessary. But I didn't want to tell him how wonderful you were, either. He'd know I was lying through my teeth. I try to keep my morning email updates on the chipper side while still giving him accurate information.

Your chest x-ray was normal, so they decided to put the suction on your chest tube again. By 11:00, they removed enough fluid that you were down to 120 over 60. We went to the hotel and collapsed. At midnight I called and you were fine. At 1:30 Becca called. We talked a little about the trouble you had, but that it was resolved. Then she couldn't contain herself. She had opened the mail. Richard and Mel sent a check for a rather large amount "to cover the extra cost of gas and phone and unexpected stuff." We were both in tears. She said someone from work had called offering help, and your chiropractor lit candles for you at the outdoor sanctuary on Route 20. I told her that he also paid for two nights of our hotel stay. We ended the conversation uplifted by the generosity and compassion around us.

Sunday, June 10th
"In the middle of every difficulty lies opportunity."
- Albert Einstein

I called at 6:30 and you were okay, so your mother and I took leisurely showers and I emailed Devin his morning update. We got there at 8:30 and you seemed better. I could hear only a small rattle. By noon the rattle was gone. Today was the first day you didn't have rosy cheeks, though. You were a bit yellow. The nurse said she'd that she had noticed and was going to take some blood for testing. She explained that the body shoots off all kinds of fat globules that the liver has to deal with. Also you haven't had a bowel movement of any kind yet, so she was going to try a suppository. If that didn't work, she'd give you an enema. Honey, I'm praying you poop soon!

It's 3:30 and you've been in and out of excruciating pain with nausea and difficulty breathing. Your mom and I are feeling helpless. We don't know whether you'd be better off if we left or not. It seems your mother is looking to me for answers and I don't have any. It has now been one week since the accident. Perhaps your body is reacting to that. While I was trying to figure out what to do, the nurse told us we had to leave for a while. I hate when that happens, but I know that there are things we probably shouldn't witness. While waiting to be called back in, I drew an extra card from the pouch hoping to ease my angst.

*"Life is eternal and love is immortal and death is only a horizon
and horizon is nothing save the limit of our sight."*
- Unknown

That's the message I got for myself. I remember you saying you weren't sure you were going to make it, so it's not like I haven't tried to ready myself for that possibility. Since Sunday my mantra has been: Whatever is your destiny, I will support you in your decisions. So, after reading that at 4:15 PM, I broke down and went back to the hotel room to cry and perhaps sleep. Unfortunately, the key wasn't activated and I had to go back down to the lobby. I was tired, frustrated, and really trying hard to keep a stiff upper lip, but two of the women at the desk grabbed me and dragged me into their office for hugs and more tears. They were so nice. The key was fixed and I went to my room to crash. At 6:45 I woke, feeling more in control again. On the way back to the hospital, I realized that I had lost it, one week to the minute. Watching you in such unimaginable pain, not being able to speak, and us not knowing what to do is a nightmare. Your mother, father, Ellie, and Linda went home shortly after I left. I called and your mother said she also broke down. When I saw you later, you seemed better and the nurse said you had a very small bowel movement. Oh, thank goodness!

Monday, June 11th

"The human spirit is stronger than anything that happens to it."
- C. C. Scott

I woke at five and couldn't sleep any longer. Half an hour later I called the hospital. You had settled in a bit but were resisting the tubes. "Take it out!" you told them. You must have made hand gestures, because you couldn't speak and you were still in a drug-induced coma. Your nurse, Deb, understood enough and checked. Sure enough, there was a leak. She told me how impressed she was with your awareness and ability to communicate. They anesthetized your throat and replaced the tubes with little pain or difficulty, she told me. I hope it's true.

Today was blessedly uneventful. Your pain was somewhat manageable with all the meds they were giving you. The respiratory people came at 11 to change apparatus and do some breaths with the big purple hand breather. That was the worst pain that I witnessed that day. I was with you from 7:45 till noon, off and on. Larry came at 9:30 for an hour or so. He said Devin was pretty certain he could go to graduation, so Becca and I will be going to keep an eye on him and show support.

While you slept, I closed my eyes and imagined walking with you in the rain in the beautiful park near the hospital. I tried to feel your hand in mine. Did you see the mamma duck and her seven babies? I showed you some incredibly beautiful private homes on the outskirts of the park that I had found the day before. Weren't they wonderful? I hope you felt the peace of my imaginings.

Honey, I really want to stay fit through all of this. I know that much will be expected of me when you are well enough to go home. At night when I'm at the hotel, I practice lifting the computer in Becca's backpack in case I have to lift you. I'll need stronger arms. I know I'm strong, but I need to get stronger.

I stayed from 1:00 to 2:30, then went for a rest. Every TV show I tried to watch put me to sleep, so I just turned it off and got serious about sleeping. At 4:30 I woke very hungry. I went down to the restaurant in the hotel and had my first real meal since the accident. It was weird eating without you. I don't like it, but I'm trying to do "normal" things. I ordered a steak with extra vegetables, and yes! I had a glass of wine. I felt guilty drinking it without you, but after two or three sips, I got over it. What a great glass of wine. I closed my eyes and imagined you there with me having a glass with me. Did it taste good? I know you prefer white wine, so forgive me for ordering you red. Hey, I'm stressed! And I hate to say that the steak and asparagus were delicious. Almost as good as mine. I promise to make all your favorite foods when you are home. You *will* go home, I promise!

Tonight's my last night at the hotel unless I'm really tired some night during your stay here. We really can't afford much more because I'm not working yet. It's a long lonely drive home, but I know you'll be upset if I deplete our savings so soon. I'm sure I'll be okay. If I get tired, you can be sure I'll stop and rest. I'll leave after seeing you in the morning. I will go home and spend time with Becca, Devin, and Ginger. Maybe I'll mow the lawn and put in some flowers. We'll see what I have energy for. Kids come first, then Ginger, then the yard. I'm sorry you're missing the garden. Except for the weeds, it's beautiful right now.

While I was gone, Ryan[2] came to visit. He left a card on your table. I read it to you and taped it up on the wall with all the others. You're getting quite a gallery going. Your mom and dad are coming in the morning. Devin will be coming with Larry in the afternoon. He has a doctor's appointment and will head to you right after. At least that's Larry's plan. He's still so shook up by all this and paying a lot of attention to Dev. Gail says he's sleeping in a chair next to his bed in their living room. I'll be back Wednesday morning. I'm not working till

---

[2] Larry's son by his first marriage.

after what would have been our vacation. I'm so sad for the timing of this. We so needed that vacation, and Devin was looking forward to seeing his friends there. Remember them? They got along so well. But no self pity. Ever onward. And there's really not a lot of spare time to feel sorry for myself. You keep us all pretty occupied. But the nights are difficult. It was easier when your mom stayed in the hotel with me, but I'll manage. I miss you so much. I try not to hold the tears back. I know that it's better to grieve than get all stressed and tired from trying to "be strong".

Your night nurse was Leah. She's very pleasant and capable. She involves us a lot in your care, even if it's just sliding your boot on and off. The boot keeps your right foot from swinging out too much. She explained that you've been taking as many as 12 breaths a minute on your own. They watch to see how much you breathe over the machine. Isn't that great? She also said you had a fairly gentle night. You certainly deserve a gentle night. And thank God for drugs! I left at 10 PM after you settled in from having another chest x-ray. Tomorrow they'll have to get you off your bed and onto their table for another x-ray to check your low back. I won't be there for it, but your mom and dad will be. I love you.

Tuesday, June 12th
"You never know when you're making a memory."
- Rickie Lee Jones

Today I left the hotel. I was a little sad to leave. It's been something like a safe haven when I'm not with you. And I'm a little concerned about all the driving. Maybe I'll get a winning scratch ticket and be able to stay a few more times. Yah never know!

I didn't get to the hospital until 8:20, but they made me wait before they let me in to see you. Your folks got there at 8:45 and when your dad called on the special phone, they let us right in. Can you believe it? Oh well, maybe they were just done with you when he buzzed in. When we got into your cubicle, you were agitated about something. We could not figure out what you needed. By 9:30 you settled down, so we figured it was pain. I headed home for my first "normal" day since the accident. It's important to get back to the kids and keep the sense of family alive.

Dev was at the doctor's, so I couldn't make plans with him yet. I lay down on the back porch and let our pup Ginger maul me a while. No French kissing though. I have my standards, as you are well aware. She was so happy to see me. I held her and told her you were okay. Becca was taking a shower, so I got off the floor and puttered around the kitchen, putting things where they belong, cleaning the dining-room table and making a bouquet from the garden. I wanted the comfort of making things look like home for all of us.

Larry brought Devin home from the doctors and it was exhausting. Apparently the doctor was a little rough putting on a new cast, so the poor guy went down for a nap. The doc said to let the leg rest a few days, so the trip to see you is off for now. I felt sad, and yet a bit relieved. It would have been an ordeal for all of us. I think he's still nervous about being in a car. I mowed the lawn and had a beer in the shower. The weeds are *wild*, but the yard looks great. The new lawn that I put in is growing; so is the spot where I took out the bush in the front. Your dad finished the rest of the seeding for me, since I've been busy watching over you. I finished gluing and painting the new door insert and will caulk it tomorrow. I know we didn't need to change the door, but you had mentioned before all this that you didn't like being in the front hall with the windows in the door. So they're gone. I think you'll like the new color.

Larry called and said Dev woke from his nap and wanted to come over. Becca and I ordered a couple of pizzas and settled in for several rousing rounds of Go Fish, complete with a lot of boisterous swearing on Devin's part. I let it ride. It seemed innocuous compared to all the other things happening, and anyway, it's a good method to disperse some anger. We laughed a lot. When the pizza arrived, we put on Star Wars. Larry showed up at nine, just as it was ending. The three of us were sprawled out on the couch together. That got a big smile from Larry. I know it was good for him to see a glimpse of normal. I know the three of us enjoyed it. It certainly was weird not having you with us, but we tried to put it out of our heads and have a good time. It was good to feel like a family, even if only for a while. After Devin left, which was also weird, Becca and I took Ginger for a night walk. We stopped in on Colette. Remember I used to know her when she owned a health food store? I wanted to make sure she knew about the accident. She offered to do whatever I needed, so I told her if she likes to weed, even a half hour would make a dent in our jungle.

While we were walking the last block towards the house, Becca got a little sad. She said she wished we could have had Devin longer so that things felt more back to normal. We talked about her promise to take him to the ocean when he's up to it. He told her he's really sad about missing the Cape. He asked me how long it might be before you came home. Anywhere from two and a half months (wonder woman estimate) and four months (lots of setbacks), I said; we have no way of knowing. All in all, it was a good day, but I missed you so much. I ache for you.

Becca and I are heading up to bed soon. I think it will help her to relax, with me sleeping here more. She told me she vector splattered (our phrase for losing composure) with her boyfriend last night.

I called the hospital twice, once after Devin left and once again around midnight before falling asleep. I guess you had a relatively easy day. They took the chest tube out in the morning, the breathing tube out in the afternoon and took x-rays of your lower back to see if you will be able to sit up. You were told not to try talking for another day. Shit, you're amazing! A week and a half without talking alone would certainly have done me in! I'm going to leave at 9:00 AM tomorrow to come and see you. I love you. I'll see you in the morning, baby.

Wednesday, June 13th

"Without order nothing can exist - without chaos nothing can evolve."
- Unknown

I got in at about 9:00. Your folks were there before me. Judy and Fred showed up, and then Devin, Larry, and Gail. Of course they only let a couple of us in at a time. Devin told me in the waiting room that you asked if he was angry.

He told me about the accident and how he saw the whole thing. He said you swerved so that the truck would hit you more than him. I was struck with how matter-of-fact and grown-up he sounds. I don't like it. I hope Larry keeps taking him to therapy for a while.

When they brought your supper, I noticed that no one had used the info that I gave them about your allergies. Judy was spoon feeding you chicken soup. I said you were allergic, but she said they strained all the chicken out of it. I tried to be gentle, telling her that you could have a bad reaction even to the broth. She thought about that and agreed that it wasn't worth the risk.

I have to remind myself that everyone cares for you in their own way, and I am angry with the hospital for disregarding the allergy list I gave them. What's the point? You were cutely agitated about wanting to go home. "Just let me stand for a few seconds. I'll be a good girl." Then you insisted there was a little girl in the room playing marbles. Your nurse was acting like a know-it-all saying it was just the drugs talking. I'm sure they have their influence on your mind, but I hated her for being so dismissive. I hope Mel is right about the nurses and the "bribes" I bring. This one's not a favorite. Who's to say there wasn't a little girl in your room? *We* believe in ghosts! But then maybe you're seeing yourself at that age. Perhaps that would be comforting.

Thursday, June 14th
"Better to light a candle than bemoan the darkness."
- Chinese Proverb

You had a tough day today. I couldn't get there till 11:00, between taking all the phone calls, finding the necessary paperwork, and going to the lawyer's office. Judy was fussing over you and engaging you, so I kept quiet. You look so tired. I was upset again today because they had given you whole milk instead of Lactaid[3]. The nurse didn't seem to know what it is, so I just let it all go.

You had a most blood pressure elevating bowel movement, hardly worth

---

[3] A special milk product for lactose-intolerant people.

all the effort but nonetheless important. You managed to eat a whole spoonful of Jell-O plus a bit of overcooked spaghetti with sauce and mushy zucchini. Thank goodness they're still sustaining life through the IV! By 1:30 you were *finally* nodding off. I went for a walk. An hour later you were still sleeping, so I took a nap in the waiting room. I woke at 4:00 and called in. You were still sleeping, so I ventured out to price a new microwave at Home Depot. The old one is acting funky. You were awake when I got back at around six. The creepy nurse was there and wagged her finger at me, warning me, "Now you can visit with her, but if I see you fussing with her, I'm going to ask you to leave." That really annoyed me since I wasn't "fussing" with you. You would have been proud of me. I just smiled and assured her I would behave myself.

Ann showed up half an hour later and you didn't really recognize her so we went to the waiting room and chatted about all the churches, synagogues, and the like that she went to or called asking for prayers. God and her angels are certainly busy with you! I thought it best not to disturb you again, so I left, reluctantly, at 7:30. From home I emailed everyone, then called Devin. He went to the awards ceremony at school and was in a great deal of pain. He'd had a good therapy session with Ariel, and I noticed his voice wasn't so tight and squeaky. That's good! No walk tonight with Ginger; I'll have to take her in the morning. She's staring up at me with those pitiful eyes. Sorry, girl. I'm too tired!

Friday, June 15th

"I'm not afraid of storms, for I'm learning how to sail my ship."
- Louisa May Alcott

It was a long day. We got up early for Devin's graduation. Larry was running late, so Becca and I went ahead to save seats. It didn't really matter because things started late there, too.

It was so hard to drive past the place where your accident occurred. Twice I had to do it! There were short skid marks on your side, but none on Lionel's side of the road. You must have tried to stop, so it's obvious that you saw the accident about to happen and tried to stop it. I can't imagine your horror.

And it was hard being at Dev's graduation without you. I have so many mixed feelings. Mrs. Bernard gave me a great big hug, and so did Mrs. Filio. Devin looked pale but wonderful in his hot pink leg cast with the hotter pink carnation sticking out the top. He sat in the wheelchair, only getting up for the prayer and the singing. Daniel made a scene climbing over everyone to sit next to him. You would have loved watching that. Daniel seemed a little protective, too.

I was surprised that no mention was made of Devin's courage in coming to the graduation, or that his mother was in the hospital fighting for her life. It made me mad more than disappointed. In a school that small, you'd think that there would be some recognition of such a traumatic event that happened to one of their students. Becca was mad, too, and ranted about it part of the way home then got very quiet. Her silence concerns me. She's in so much emotional pain, and needs to talk to you. But you can't help her. The day was difficult, hard to be away from you, but it's where we needed to be. Could you feel me holding your hand?

Saturday, June 16th
"Success is a state of mind."
- Joyce Brothers

Today wasn't your best day. I don't like the care here on 4E. I'm not sure what kind of a wing of the hospital it is, certainly nothing like ICU. I'm afraid that they let you leave there too soon. I can rarely find a nurse or CNA in the halls when I need something or have a question. It's frightening to go from such extreme care to such neglect.

I reserved a room at the Quality Inn, and by the time everything was set up for your hip surgery tomorrow, it felt good not to have to drive that long road home.

Larry and Gail brought Devin for a visit. You truly brightened when you saw him. The trip was hard, but he seemed happy that he made it. He's still struggling with getting in a car, as you can imagine, in spite of all his sessions with Ariel.

While Devin and Larry went to the cafeteria, Gail told me how wonderful Larry has been, staying at Devin's side day and night. She told me how the accident affected him, how shaken he was and still is. She told me that Larry seems to be touching Devin all the time. We agreed that sometimes tragedy can focus people on what is most important to them. I think she's pleased with how this has brought things out in Larry that may benefit their relationship as well as Devin's. And it's obvious that he still loves you so much. He struggles along with the rest of us seeing you in such bad shape.

Sunday, June 17th

A ninety-year-old man was asked to what he attributed his longevity.
"I reckon," he said with a twinkle in his eye, "It's because most nights I went to bed and slept when I should have sat up and worried."

At 5:20 Sunday morning they changed their minds and decided to do your hip surgery on Monday. You had an infection which they thought was in your leg, but by that afternoon they figured out that it was in the urinary tract. That's much easier to deal with. Your folks, and Becca, had come early for the surgery, and I was there from the day before. It was hard to be all geared up, with hotel rooms and all, just to find it rescheduled. Oh, well!

You were struggling to breathe, but the nurses didn't seem to think there was a problem. Larry and I stared in disbelief and began looking around to make sure things were plugged in, etc. Finally, he noticed that the cap on the water for the oxygen wasn't screwed on right causing a leak in the system. Sweet Jesus, it's frustrating! I hate the care you're getting on this floor.

Monday, June 18th

"Patience is a bitter plant, but it bears sweet fruit."
- German Proverb

Your folks and I got up at 5:15 to see you before they took you in for surgery. I let Becca sleep. Your breathing sucked, and we were a bit surprised they took you anyway. The docs know best. At least we hope they do! They've gotten you this far. By 7:00 we were nervously settled in the surgical waiting area.

It wasn't until 8:45 that Dr. Hospodar informed us they had decided not to operate. They didn't want to risk it, because you were breathing poorly and your white blood count was up again. It's only an optional surgery, anyway, to stabilize your hip so that you are less likely to experience arthritis.

It turned out that your lung collapsed again and you had to be put on a full ventilator. They moved you to the second floor Cardiac Care Unit, where things were better, but still not as good as ICU. I miss Callie and Leah and Tim!

At ten, I emailed everyone while Becca showered. After that we went back to the hospital. It was a long day with all the resting, struggling, resting, and struggling some more.

Tuesday, June 19th

"Change your thoughts and you change your world."
- Norman Vincent Peale

Well, my sweet, it was a hell of a rollercoaster ride for us today. I was about to drive over the mountain when your mother called. The hospital had tried to get me but they must have dialed a wrong number or tried calling me at the hotel. She said you were having emergency gall bladder surgery. So I cried and prayed, said affirmations, calmed and panicked and calmed myself some more. When I got there at 10:45, I checked in at the surgical waiting desk. After twenty minutes, someone came and said you were still in your room. I could scream! I flew up the stairs trying not to get angry about the poor communications. When I got there they had you off your pain meds to determine whether you really needed the surgery. So I went out in the hall to see if I could reach your parents in time. With no real emergency, there was no reason to come all that way, but they didn't answer; they were already on the road. By the time they arrived, I'd been told that the test wasn't until three. I couldn't believe they were going to keep you off pain meds that long—five hours! Your folks and I thought our heads would spin clear off our shoulders. You were struggling with the pain, agitated, and frightened about the test. You were trying so hard to tell us things, but we couldn't get the majority of what you needed to say. We tried to calm you as much as we could— lots of cold cloths, stroking, and "I love yous".

They took you for the test at three. We were exhausted, so we went to the parking lot, put our seats back and took naps. Your mother said she actually slept a bit. So did I. A bird on the fifth-floor fence woke me. It was just like the one we have had at our feeder at home. And the same one that my friend Richard emailed me a picture of just the other day. Weird, huh?

By five you were back in your room, and they were drugging you up again. The test was inconclusive, and now they're saying there won't be any surgery tomorrow. Who knows. We'll just play it by ear. Your folks left at 5:30. I sat with you till you were thoroughly settled and sleeping deeply. I'm waiting for the shift change at eleven. I didn't like the way the night nurse talked to me last night and again this morning when I called to check on you. Maybe if I meet her, things will go better. If not, I'll bring her chocolate. What if she doesn't like chocolate? Oh, well, I'll just have to put out a contract on her. Don't *mess* with my Gayle!

You'd be pleased. Larry took Ginger to the hairdresser's. She was so filthy and shaggy. She misses you! I'm hoping you are still settled and sleeping well. You had a long damned day!

Wednesday, June 20th

*"Nobody trips over mountains. It is a small pebble that causes you
to stumble. Pass all the pebbles in your path and you will
find you have crossed a mountain."*

- Unknown

Today was my second day off. I used it well. I slept late, went for two walks, mowed the lawn, had a beer, cleared my desk, made phone calls, emailed everyone, and had the kids for spaghetti and *two* movies this time. We watched "bar" movies at my request. Becca wanted us to see *Coyote Ugly*, so I added Tom Cruise's *Cocktail*. Both movies were a ton of fun. Devin loved the part where Tom Cruise juggles the bottles. Becca and I were sure he was going to try it when no one was around. Larry came at 9:30 to take him back. It was good to be together, and hard to let him go.

There was one really sappy part in *Coyote Ugly* that got me teary. Both kids leaned in for hugs when I said, "I miss Gayle." I guess I could have held it in, but I didn't. I may as well set a good example. Devin's been stuffing his emotions, I know it, and that's not good.

Your Mom called three times to tell me what kind of a day you had. White blood cell count was up. Your breathing wasn't great. And the care was mediocre. But you did get a lot of rest.

Thursday, June 21st

"What's the difference between a man and a battery?
A battery has a positive side."

Welcome, Summer! And goodbye, gall bladder!

I picked the quote above, twice, so I guess that's it for today. I expected something more serious, given the seriousness of the day. But perhaps you are doing better than I think. Or maybe you're mad at some guy. Or perhaps you're battery needs charging. Alas, I am too tired to find the deeper meaning. I'll give that some thought later perhaps.

I got there at about ten and they had me signing stuff again. It was time to take out your gall bladder. Your skin was still pretty yellow and your urine brown.

They let me follow to the operating room door. Dr. Hashim did this one. He was very sweet. He lowered the side of the bed saying, "That should make it easier to kiss her."

I checked your astrology forecast, which is disgusting all summer long, but there was a pleasant window from 1:00 to 3:30 today. Can you believe they began on you at 1:30 and by 2:30 it was done. Larry got there at 2:00 and sat with me. Dr. Hashim said they managed it all with full laparoscopy, didn't have to make any major cuts, but it was quite enlarged and inflamed, and had leaked a little. They cleaned it and sewed you back up. Bada bing, bada boom! It's supposed to give you considerable relief.

Okay, so there was something funny; at least your mother got a kick out of it. After I kissed you goodbye, Dr. Hashim started to give me the bum's rush. With a wave of his hand he said, "Time to say goodbye to your daughter." Daughter! Hey, you're the one who got hit by a truck and is about to have a burst gall bladder! And he thinks you look better than me! I told everyone in the waiting room, expressing grave indignation, and your mother exploded in laughter. Well, as you can imagine, that made everyone else laugh. Oh, well! I guess the stress is making me look like crap!

I figured it would take at least an hour and a half to get you stitched, out of recovery, and re-intubated, so Larry went with me in search of a backpack briefcase. We found an Office Max, where I bought an awesome one for fifty bucks. By the time we returned, you had just gotten settled and were fast asleep. Larry left at four, and I left at eight. You slept most of the time. I'm glad you're back in ICU. Those nurses are *so* much better.

When I got home, Becca had vacuumed, washed our sheets, and placed flowers all over the house. Earlier in the day, she drove to the office of our local newspaper and raised holy hell for writing that you were in critical condition but not saying anything about Devin. People were calling thinking Devin had died, and the family wasn't allowing the paper to say anything. Their coverage the next day was *perfect*, and she felt fabulous about being able to blow off some steam.

Friday, June 22nd
"Success is a state of mind."
- Joyce Brothers

Today I slept late, made blueberry pancakes for Becca, weeded till I got blisters, did paperwork, paid a few bills, and dealt with some legal stuff. You will be happy to know that when I write checks, I print. Becca says you'll have a fit if you can't read my writing. Isn't she protective? And practical!

When I got there at 3:00 you were sleeping, sleeping, and sleeping. Your folks left at 5:00 and I stayed till 7:30. You were coughing a lot and said your head and neck hurt. You needed a unit of blood. Your color was better, your urine is in the dark yellow range instead of brown. You smiled a few times when you woke, especially when I asked if you still wanted a red front door. Your nurse Rhonda asked a lot of questions about the accident. She's a sweetie.

Saturday, June 23rd
"You have within you right now, everything you need to deal with whatever the world can throw at you."
- Brian Tracy

You looked just okay to me today, but I didn't get to see you much. Big Bad Bernice kicked me out, so I went to Sam's Club and Home Depot to get some basics. At Home Depot I bought the red paint for the front door, a new handle, and brass numbers. Actually it's a deep fuchsia kind of red. Very good feng shui! If it's wrong, we'll change it when you get home.

So I was in town for six hours, but only got to see you for 45 minutes. No doctors! Nothing! You woke a bit from 8:00 on, and didn't like it when I said I was going to leave. Finally, at 9:45, you seemed less edgy. I told you I really should go and you nodded your approval. I hated leaving, but I was tired. It's only an hour-long drive, but it seems like two some nights.

Sunday, June 24th

*"Though no one can go back and make a brand new start, anyone
can start from now and make a brand new ending."*
- Unknown

I called at six and you were fine. Rhonda said your blood count was up one point, she'd upped your pain meds and helped you cough a few times, but mostly you slept. Yesterday's short Tarot reading said you'd be better by Wednesday. Let's hope our guides are right.

I stayed home to get a lot of stuff done. The garden looks better, and the door now opens in. I cried, feeling sorry for myself because so many of our family and friends have disappointed me. So, of course, what happened next was that two clients called, Lynette and Maria. Lynette was sweet and supportive, and Maria told me, "I've been through a similar thing. I'm praying every day." I broke down, sobbing. Maria just listened and said all the right things. I was grateful, to say the least. And the timing couldn't have been better. She wanted a reading "when you're doing better" but I told her I'd like to do one for her soon. I explained that I was nervous about maybe having "lost it". She said she would be honest, so we set it up for later tonight.

Your folks said Bernice kicked them out, too, saying you needed your sleep. Your mom thought you looked a bit better. They were there all day and got to see you four times for a total of about half an hour. Your father doesn't have as much of a problem doing what the nurses tell him to do. And when it comes to tears, your Dad's the one to let them come. I'm constantly impressed with them as a couple and as individuals. They are so different.

Devin had plans with Michael, so I picked Becca up at 6:30 from work and we had pasta at Over The Rainbow. I wanted to splurge a little because we've been so stressed and she's been so helpful. Then I did the reading for Maria, and it was spot-on. She spent a long time telling me how wonderful it was, saying, "You still got it, my friend!" That made me feel great. I guess I don't have to worry about going back to work and not being able to perform.

Becca was sad and cried tonight. There's no one else that she can talk to the way she talks to you. I guess we've both temporarily lost our best friend. Sounds like there are some lessons here, but I'm too tired to figure them out. Goodnight, sweet love.

Monday, June 25th

"Family...a group experience of love and support."
- Marianne Williamson

Becca and I got to you by 10:30 that morning. Monica was your nurse for the day. She's a little like the weekend nurses but smaller and nicer. I told her I hadn't seen a doctor in four days. While Becca and I visited, a woman doctor introduced herself and apologized for not speaking with anyone in a few days. She answered my questions and then gave permission for us to use homeopathic remedies and flower essences as soon as the tubes are out. She said I could put vitamin E oil on anytime but not where there were still open wounds. I was so impressed with her knowledge of homeopathy. Most doctors either freak or are simply dismissive. Allis, the Oriental ortho resident, said you were on the schedule for hip surgery again Wednesday but the time hasn't been set yet.

I thought you looked better, softer, less frightened but still a bit disoriented. They're pulling back on the pain meds and today you are breathing without the help of the respirator for longer periods of time. It's good that you are trying to breath on your own again. I guess the surgery was a setback. You smiled so wonderfully at us when we walked in, and again when I told you Devin was coming later for a visit.

After I rubbed some vitamin E oil on your closed scars and massaged your arms, you went right to sleep. You haven't been sleeping well, but I think you do better when one of us is in the room with you. The hell with the weekend nurses; I'll have one of the doctors put in an order allowing family in the room while you're sleeping. That Bernice has to go!

We left for lunch; when we came back you looked like a sleeping baby. We stayed another hour, but you didn't budge. We left a little earlier than planned so that we could buy a new microwave. With all the nuking Becca and I have been doing, the old machine finally bit it. Some of the moms from Devin's school brought food, so we've been doing a lot of reheating.

On the way home I called Cherie to see if I was on the schedule for my first night back. She said that my Guided Imagery lecture was a go. I told her that if all went well, I'd like to restart the feng shui lecture and begin the private sessions so that all our hard work doesn't go to someone else. She agreed that it was the least they could do. She went on about how wonderful you are, "What a kind person Gayle is. She's our angel! What a trooper she is! God bless her, I've never met such a gentle soul!"

I went up to the meditation room early to get centered before the lecture. It felt good to be back—weird but good. A guest and her daughter recognized me outside the dining hall. She was sweet and mentioned that she heard I was having some personal difficulties. I started to tell her what happened, but she already knew.

"How did you find out?" I asked.

"Oh, we have our sources," she replied in a pleasant drawl and both of them put their arms around me. "We've been praying since we found out." The generosity of people outside of our immediate circle never ceases to amaze me. We are truly blessed.

Tuesday, June 26th

"Treasure the love that you receive above all. It will survive
long after your gold and good health have vanished."
- Og Mandino

Well, my darling girl, I won't be with you today. Hi ho, hi ho! I hope I don't break down too many times. I managed to tear up only twice, leading the Guided Imagery session last night. Wish me luck, as I will you. I hope you continue to improve today and are super-strong for your surgery tomorrow. I am *so* scared!

But I will rein that in and think only positive thoughts.

I didn't cry at all. I felt really good about you today, almost back to normal! Your folks said that you laughed and joked and made very funny faces. Apparently your pain is not so great and you're down off the drugs by a lot. I can't wait to see you.

Clare, a massage therapist from work and the woman we had dinner with two days before the accident, gave me a huge hug. I got another hug from Cherie, and I had seven half-hour sessions at work and about six guests showed up for the lecture. It could have been a better turnout, but I guess it's respectable for the summer. Overall, it was a decent day. Ann, a massage therapist who was also seriously injured in a car accident, brought me some supper, and I got yet another hug. It was a wonderfully huggy day. I was done at 7:00, came home, and ate Ann's polenta and sauce with sausage and peppers and a glass of wine. So much for my diet. I ate on the front porch. Lovely food, but there was no one to clang forks or glasses with. No one to look lovingly upon. No one to snuggle in bed with either. Soon, sweetheart, soon!

Wednesday, June 27th

"Without order nothing can exist - without chaos nothing can evolve."
- Unknown

I pulled that saying before. It makes sense.

It's surgery day again today. Your folks came at nine to pick me up. I had figured on driving but Grandpa insisted. So I sat in the back with my laptop and worked on an astrology calendar for a client and occasionally chatted some with them. They were in a good mood.

You were amazing. You made animated faces, big nods. And you wiggled from head to toe when I told you your niece Cori Lynn was pregnant. You even wrote a bit on the dry erase board to tell Monica what you wanted. My God, you even had a bowel movement!

Dr. Hospodar came in after surgery to give us the details of how things went with your right knee. It was hard for us to hear all of what he told us. All his warnings about what could happen, though it probably won't, scared us. When he left, we were silent for a few moments. Finally, your father summed up our feelings when he said, "I kept waiting for him to tell us the good news."

At the time, we were all devastated. Eventually we realized that his little speech was like the warning on the drug sheets from the pharmacist. The truth of the matter is that your right leg was pretty much crushed, and it needed a lot of trussing. It sounds as though it will be an inch or more shorter than the other. The knee was shattered, and they have very little hope for it ever being good again. It will probably always be unstable. But then he doesn't know what a good healer you are. Your hip developed too much scar tissue to allow surgery to be done safely. It, too, will probably always hurt. He reiterated that with lots of physical therapy and determination, you may be able to walk. He doubts that you'll ever run again. We'll see.

Your folks left soon after seeing you back to your room. They were pretty wrung out. I didn't know whether I should stay at the hotel or go home. Becca has to go to work early, so Larry said he'd stay and give me a ride home if I needed to let Becca take the car. He called home to see how Devin was and told him about your surgery. I was still undecided about staying or leaving. The nurse assured me that you would be heavily sedated and that I may as well leave. The ride home with Larry was a tough one. We talked about how hard it was going to be to maneuver the wheelchair in our house and my thoughts about buying a ranch. I was pretty overwhelmed but didn't recognize it until he said, "Well, maybe you don't have to think about all that now." I broke down a bit. Then we got laughing about something and a long ride shortened.

Becca went to her boyfriend's shortly after I got home at 8:30. I was glad to be able to cry without her hearing me. I don't want her to know my thoughts about moving yet.

Thursday, June 28th

"The more faithfully you listen to the voice within you, the better you

hear what is sounding outside you."
- Dag Hammarskjöld

It was a rough night. I woke at three, and I found out later that was the same time you were struggling with pain in your legs. Finally, by 4:30, I decided to give up on sleep and go downstairs. I worked on the computer for a while, answering emails and looking for houses for sale. Not much. Then I looked for support groups for accident victims. The one that kept coming up wouldn't load. Damn! Nothing seemed to be going well. I had several crying jags thinking about all we created here and how much I would miss our gardens if we moved. The thought of leaving our patch of asparagus, the Arbor Society trees that Devin and I planted from seedlings, the clouds I painted on his ceiling, and the starry night I want to paint on the inside of the front door was unbearable. I tried to contact a psychic that Clare recommended, but she was busy and didn't call back before I had to start my day. Becca got a notice that she has to start paying on her college loan. Money! Then Jane emailed saying the Pittsfield police have no record of the accident. Since I mailed her a copy of the newspaper article, and the police report that your dad filled in, and even the phone number of the Williamstown Police, I was not feeling much confidence in our lawyer. What if she's just been bragging over the years and is really a jerk? Oh God! What a shitty mood I'm in. Jane is *the best*! And she will do a great job. All these depressing thoughts…I must need sleep.

By the time I got to you at 11:00, I was more settled down. Driving does that for me. You were asleep, so I sat quietly for half an hour. When you woke, you were so happy to see me. You were in a lot of pain and afraid of them taking out the breathing tubes. You really had me hopping! You looked sleepy by 1:30 so I took a lunch/walk break till 2:30. They came in to extubate you at 3:30. When they said you could have two sips of water, you were ecstatic.

Friday, June 29th
"Success is a state of mind."

- Joyce Brothers

I didn't get to write in this journal for you today. Now that you are out of the coma and down a bit on your pain meds, you have more needs. I'm sure I won't be keeping up with this much longer, but that's okay. The trade off is totally worth it. And you'll remember a lot from here on in, I'm sure. Why does this quote come out of the bag so much?

Saturday, June 30th

"Success is a state of mind."

- Joyce Brothers

Wonder why I picked the same saying two days in a row? It's come up two or three times before, as well. So, love, what are you trying to tell me? Are you in a good state of mind? I hope so, but I'm not sure I am. I'll try to relax a little more.

Today was my day off and it truly turned sour. I should have taken in the message. I couldn't sleep and was up on the computer till four. I slept from four till eight, but it wasn't enough. I was exhausted and, after painting the second coat on the front door, I decided to do as little as possible. But at 11:30 AM someone from work called. I had told Prudence (the other Tarot reader) months ago that I would fill in for her, but I was so tired, I never thought to look at the appointment book. Lots of confusion as to what to do. Waited until about four and still the three guests hadn't called back to rebook. Someone finally decided I was off the hook and didn't have to go in. Ryan and Marrisa[4] came for a sleepover. We had subs for supper and then I went to bed. Can you believe it? It wasn't even seven and I went to right to sleep. An hour later the phone woke me and I couldn't get back to sleep. At two in the morning I caved in and took a sleeping pill. I called your folks around nine that morning and they said you were doing well. You had

---

[4] Rebecca's step-brother and step-sister.

been moved from the ICU to 513C.

Sunday, July 1st
Forgot to pick one.

    I left at nine without coffee, anxious to be with you. Assuming you were still doing well, I didn't bring my overnight bag. *Big mistake!* You were quite agitated when I arrived. Apparently a surgical resident said you would be going home later in the day and you'd be weaned off all drugs in a week. What an unbelievable *ass*! By late afternoon you were in a full-blown panic attack. Turns out they stopped giving you Ativan, but nobody bothered to mention it to you or me. And they wouldn't give you any when you asked. By nine that night you had a migraine and it took the nurse half an hour to find and bring you the Imitrex that had already been ordered. I will bring some from home so that doesn't happen again. By ten the chief resident ordered 1.0 mg. of Ativan. This is *not* the ICU. The care is so different. I'm at a loss. I've tried not to yell at anyone, but believe me, it's a struggle. I called our primary, but because you're in New York, he can't prescribe or help in any way. You fell asleep only twice that I could tell. I dozed off a little each time. What a night.

Monday, July 2nd
"I was the strongest when I laughed at my weakness."
- Elmer Diktononius

    It's three in the morning and I can't sleep, so I'm writing in this journal to blow off steam. You're finally resting, hopefully sleeping. What a horror to have to fight to get what was given in the ICU. We are both exhausted. I haven't decided if I'm staying another night or returning home to do the lecture at 8:30 tonight. We'll see. The room is cold. I spent $4 yesterday on a suit jacket at the thrift shop that is serving me well. I'll have to snag a toothbrush from the linen closet. Sweetheart, if I'm ever in the hospital, find the linen closet right away!

After talking with you and the nurses, Larry and Shauna, I decided it was safe to leave. I was so drained, physically and emotionally. Even though leaving was terrible, I realized on the way home that it was the right thing to do. I got home at six to a depressed and scared little girl. She's so shaken by having "lost" you, her best friend, and by you almost dying. She's not saying anything, but I know she's not convinced that you are going to live. Apparently she started crying Saturday at work and couldn't stop, so she left. She's afraid she'll be fired for it. I think she's nuts. They love her too much to do that, but even if they did, she wants to quit anyway. She's still upset with her friends for being so unsupportive. I've been encouraging her to move on, to find a new set of friends with better values. All the while I'm with her, I'm trying to ask myself, "What would Gayle say?" And another part of me, the mega-tired part, is complaining, "Holy shit! I come home to recharge my batteries and there's yet another drama that I have to deal with." It's impressive how mature and immature I can be, all at the same time!

Becca had a meeting at seven, so I got to shower and lie down for half an hour before going in for the lecture. I did indeed revive a bit, though the lecture was not my best. When I got home at ten, Ginger and I went for our walk. Bed felt *so* good, afterwards. And my new sleeping pill worked like a charm. You know I don't like to take anything more than Motrin, but I'm desperate for sleep. I have to do everything within my power to be there for you.

Tuesday, July 3rd

"How a person masters his fate is more important than what his fate is."
- Wilhelm von Humboldt

I slept till eight and called your mom to have them pick up some stuff for you, the new orange Cape Cod shirt that I altered for you, the picture of me that you like and I hate, more Imitrex in case you get another migraine. I wish I'd had the time to slip an "I Love You" card into the bag before your parents came to take it to you.

I was sad this morning. You told me later that when I called, you couldn't reach the phone and that you cried for three hours because you missed me so much. I had let the phone ring a long time but finally hung up afraid you might be sleeping. I know how hard it is to move your left arm with the ex-fixator on it. Honey, I'm so sorry all this has happened to you.

Becca got home early and we were going out to breakfast, but a call to our legal eagle, Jane, slowed us down. It was a good conversation. She may be able to get you and Devin each $20,000. The money is not to be applied toward medical expenses, so I am hoping Larry will agree we can put some of Devin's toward a down payment on a new one-story house. We'll have to talk more about this.

Breakfast was good. After, we went to Purple Plume and I found another pair of slacks for me to wear to work. I have so few good summer pants. Now if I can just get around to hemming them! I know, I know! Sucks to be short! And you know how much I *love* to sew. I'll tell you later about the shirts I've been altering and how many times I have put a snap in backward or sewn my own shirt into yours. If you were here, you'd be in tears laughing, probably snorting.

I had seven half-hour sessions, a good day. I bumped into Cheryl Ann, who just lost her mom, and Joanne in the halls. Big hugs all around. Both asked about you and reminded me to call if there was anything they could do.

You sounded pretty good when I finally got hold of you. Some idiot had unplugged your phone. I'm heading home now and will call again tonight. I love you so!

Wednesday, July 4th
Didn't pick one.

I'm not going to be able to continue this journal. I'm discouraged and tired, and way too busy with all the commuting to the hospital over the past month, plus work, the kids, the house. I'm only *one* woman! And I'm so blown away by what happened early this morning. At three in the morning, you said, you were awakened by some strange man staring down at you and trying to fondle you.

You told me you yelled, "What the hell are you doing?" and he bolted. I'm still trying to figure out how to feel about this. Normally I believe everything you tell me, but is it possible it was a nightmare, or a reaction to drugs? When I asked you how you felt about it, you said, "Well, in the scheme of things, I suppose it's kind of small." I know you've had the ultimate, almost dying in a car wreck, and I know you're pretty drugged up, but it's awful. Why are you sounding so matter-of-fact? I'm trying to stay emotionally even with you. It's hard! I've asked the nurses and they say that no one reported anything strange. If this did happen, which I'm leaning towards, shouldn't there be more of a response to my questions? As the day progressed, it became clear to me that the event was real. You confused me with your ho-hum attitude, but the more we talked, the more I understood what transpired. I think you also felt proud of yourself for being able to scare him off so handily. Given your extreme limitations physically, I'm impressed, too.

Your father made a formal complaint with security before leaving. He called to tell me that the head guy said someone would be posted outside your door tonight. By eleven, there was no sign of security anywhere. I went down to find out what the problem was, and the guy at the desk knew nothing about the incident or your father having been told that someone would be posted. I told him to please send whoever was in charge up to your room. Three guys showed up twenty minutes later while you were sleeping and did little to reassure us that you would be safe. After complaining and dropping the hint that there could be a lawsuit, one of them said he'd have someone check your room every hour. It was apparent that they were not taking this seriously. Forgive me, but I my anger slipped out as I told them, "Wonderful. So that leaves fifty-five minutes every hour that a patient could be molested again." They had nothing to say. Disgusted, I told him that the family would provide the needed security. Knowing that I was your only line of defense, I slept on and off for a few minutes at a time.

This was the last entry in the journal.

Chapter 3: Medical Notes

Report of Operation 06/04/2001

Preoperative Diagnoses:

1. Open right supracondylar femur fracture with inter condylar extension.

2. Comminuted right patella fracture.

3. Open left supracondylar humerus fracture.

4. Status post dislocation of left hip and acetabular fracture.

Postoperative Diagnoses:

1. Open right supracondylar femur fracture with intercondylar extension.

2. Comminuted right patella fracture.

3. Open left supracondylar humerus fracture.

4. Status post dislocation of left hip and acetabular fracture.

Time of Operation: 12:30 AM to 3:30 AM

Operation:

1. Open reduction internal fixation of right supracondylar/intercondylar femur fracture with retrograde Ace nail (10 mm x 34 mm).

2. Partial patellectomy with open reduction internal fixation patella.

3. Irrigation and debridement of open fractures, right supracondylar femur, left supracondylar humerus.

4. Placement of left distal femoral traction pin.

Estimated Blood Loss: 500 CC.

Anesthesia: General.

Indications: The patient is a 45-year-old female who was transferred from the

Berkshire hospital for treatment of severe orthopedic injuries sustained in a motor vehicle accident on 6/3/01. Her injuries included a left proximal humerus fracture, bilateral wrist fractures, an open left supracondylar humerus fracture, an open right supracondylar femur fracture with intercondylar extension, bilateral patellar fractures and service and had a workup including aortic arteriogram and was cleared for surgery. The material risks, benefits and severity of the injuries were discussed in detail with her friend, who was with her in attendance. The patient arrived at Albany intubated.

Procedure: The patient was brought to the operating room, and she was already intubated, and general anesthesia was continued. Her right chest tube was kept to suction throughout the case. She was placed on the Jackson table, and the right leg and left arm were sterilely prepped and draped in standard fashion. Pulsatile lavage was utilized to irrigate open fractures of the supracondylar femur and supracondylar humerus, using 12 liters of irrigant. Devitalized tissues were sharply debrided with a knife. The areas were then reprepped and redraped, and attention was first turned to the supracondylar femur fracture. It was elected to treat this with a retrograde femoral nail, and an anterior incision was made and carried down through the patellar fracture.

There was evidence odintracondylar extension of the fracture, and the medial femoral condyle had an oblique fracture through it that was mildly displaced. This was reduced and fixated with a single Ace 6.5 cannulated screw. Good compression was obtained. The guide wire was ten placed on A-P and lateral projections with good alignment, and the initiating drill bit was utilized, and the guide wire was then passed across the fracture site. Sequential reaming to 11.5 mm was performed, and 10-mm x 34-mm rod was passed across the fracture site in a retrograde fashion. There was severe comminution at the fracture site that was accepted. The rod was then statically locked with two distal screws with good purchase in the distal fragment and a single proximal screw for locking.

Attention was then turned to treatment for the patella fracture. The distal half of the patella was exceedingly comminuted with significant devitalized bone and fragmentation of articular surfaces, and these fragments were discarded, and a partial patellectomy performed. The most proximal pieces were treated with open reduction internal fixation with a lag screw x2 in a transverse fashion. The patellar tendon was then sutured to the distal portion of the patella, and a cerclage wire was utilized to reinforce this by passing this through the quadriceps mechanism and down through a drill hole through the tibial tubercle. Care was taken not to over-tighten this unloading type wire. The wound was then once again copiously irrigated and closed in layers. The open fracture site, which measured approximately 3 cm in size, was loosely closed as well. At this point in the case, it was elected to treat the supracondylar humerous fracture with a splint at the present time as per trauma's request that the time in the operating room be limited. The remaining fractures were splinted as well, including the left tibial plateau and bilateral wrist fractures. A Steinmann pin was the placed in standard fashion after sterile prep in the distal femur on the left side to use for traction for treatment of the posterior hip dislocation and associated acetabular fracture that had been previously reduced in the emergency room. The patient was then transferred to the surgical intensive care unit in stable condition.

Report of Operation 06/04/2001

Preoperative Diagnoses: Lisfranc dislocation, right foot.

Postoperative Diagnoses: Lisfranc dislocation, right foot.

Operation: Open reduction and internal fixation Lisfranc dislocation, right foot with 4.0 cannulated screws.

Anesthesia:
Tourniquet time 46 minutes.

Indications: The patient is status post multiple fractures from motor vehicle accident, is returning to the operating room for team approach to open reduction and internal fixation of her multiple fractures. This dictation is the care of her foot injury.

Procedure: After the patient's right foot was sterilely prepped and draped in normal fashion a well padded calf tourniquet was applied and inflated to 250 mmHg after exsanguinations using the Esmarch.

A longitudinal incision was made at the base of the first interspace and carried down to the point capsule. Care was taken to avoid injury to neurovascular structures. There was significant displacement of the second metatarsal in relation to the cuneiform first metatarsal. The first metatarsal itself was quite stable. Soft tissue debris fracture fragment was excised and fracture was reduced and held with a clamp. A4.0 cannulated screw was passed from the medial cuneiform into the second metatarsal and a 4.0 cannulated screw was passed with excellent purchase. Position was checked on AP and lateral projections using fluoroscopy.

The percutaneous approach to the fifth metatarsal was performed and again a 4.0 cannulated screw was placed. There was good stability of the forefoot. Tourniquet was then released and wounds were copiously irrigated and closed with interrupted nylon sutures. Sterile compressive dressings were applied.

The patient tolerated the procedure well. During this portion of the case Doctor JL and Doctor Paul Hospodar were performing an upper extremity work and separate dictation of these procedures will follow.

Report of Operation 06/04/2001

Preoperative Diagnoses:

1. Open left supracondylar fracture of the left elbow.

2. Fracture of left distal radius.

3. Fracture of right distal radius.

4. Lisfranc fracture dislocation of right foot and left proximal tibia fracture, comminuted.

Postoperative Diagnoses:

1. Open left supracondylar fracture of the left elbow.

2. Fracture of left distal radius.

3. Fracture of right distal radius.

4. Lisfranc fracture dislocation of right foot and left proximal tibia fracture, comminuted.

Operation: Open reduction and internal fixation of left elbow; closed reduction and external fixation of left wrist; closed reduction and percutaneous pinning of the right wrist; open reduction and internal fixation of the right Lisfranc joint fracture dislocation, right foot; closed reduction and external fixation of right proximal tibia.

Anesthesia: General

Procedure: The patient was placed under general anesthesia and after this was performed, the left elbow and right foot were prepped and draped in usual sterile fashion. After this was performed, simultaneously with two teams, the left elbow and right foot were approached.

The foot was approached through a dorsal incision in the first web space. This was carried down through the subcutaneous tissue to the fascia. The fascia was split in the direction of its fibers. The Lisfranc joint was identified and under direct vision was reduced with a tenaculum. Two percutaneous screws were then placed. A second screw was placed in the lateral forefoot to hold the reduction. The wound was irrigated and closed in layers. Nylon sutures were used to close the wound.

Simultaneously, the left elbow with another team was approached and this was approached through a midline incision avoiding the traumatic wound which was irrigated previously and sutured closed. The midline incision was carried down through the subcutaneous tissues to the fascia, the fascia was split in the direction of its fibers. The olecranon was identified and olecranon osteotomy was performed with Micro-Aire saw. After this was performed the triceps was reflected back and the fracture was identified and irrigation and debridement was performed. After this was performed a reduction was performed using a tenaculum. At this point, provisional K-wire fixation was also performed. This held the fracture until two plates were fashioned and placed on the bone dorsally, one on the radial and one on the ulnar column. After this was performed, screw fixation was performed and this gave excellent fixation and under C-arm good reduction of the fracture. It was felt that this was sound fixation and therefore no bone grafting was necessary due to the risk of infection with the open injury.

At this point the wound was thoroughly irrigated and the olecranon was reattached using a 6.5 cancellous screw and tension band wire. At this point after the olecranon was brought together, the wound was once again irrigated. The ulnar nerve was transposed into the anterior subcutaneous tissues of the medial aspect of the elbow to keep it away from all hardware. It was placed in this subcutaneous sling and several sutures were used to close the interval. At this point the subcutaneous tissues were closed with 2-0 and the skin was closed with surgical clips.

Our attention was turned to the left wrist which was found to be unstable with a distal radius and ulnar fracture. An incision was made directly over the lateral aspect of the radius, carried down through the subcutaneous tissues to the fascia.

The fascia was split in the direction of the fibers, the periosteum was identified and the guide was used to place two external fixator pins. External fixator pins were placed under C-arm direction. At this point the second metacarpal was identified and an incision was also made here, carried down to the subcutaneous tissues and presidium was identified, two pins were placed in the second metacarpal. At this point wounds were sutured closed with nylon sutures and the external fixator was applied. Distraction was applied to the fracture and this gave good reduction and good stability to the fracture. At this point it was felt that the fracture was stable and the sterile dressings were applied. Once this was applied, attention was turned to the right wrist. This was prepped and draped in sterile fashion. Under C-arm guidance a closed reduction was obtained and several pins were placed percutaneously in through the lateral aspect of the radius and into the ulnar aspect of the more proximal cortex. At this point it was felt to be stable and placed in a splint.

Next the left tibia was prepped and draped in usual sterile fashion. At this point it was felt that the tibia was unstable and needed external fixation, stabilization. This was performed by placing two tibial half pins into mid region of the tibia and applying Howmedica clamp to the existing femoral traction pin and making a Delta frame with the external fixator and also a brace to keep the heel off the bed. Once this was completed, sterile dressings were applied.

The patient was then placed in her bed and put in traction to keep the left acetabular fracture reduced and at this point it was felt that all fractures that could be stabilized were and the patient was transferred from the operating room to the SICU in good condition without incident.

Report of Operation 06/27/2001

Preoperative Diagnoses: Left tibial plateau fracture, comminuted; comminuted stellate patellar fracture, left knee.

Postoperative Diagnoses: Left tibial plateau fracture, comminuted; comminuted stellate patellar fracture, left knee.

Operation: Closed reduction and hybrid ring fixator application of left tibial plateau fracture; open reduction and internal fixation of left patellar fracture.

Anesthesia: General

Procedure: The patient was taken to the operating room and placed in supine position. General anesthesia was induced. The left lower extremity was prepped and draped in usual sterile fashion.

After this was performed a midline incision was made over the patella. Once this was performed the inferior pole of the patella was found to be avulsed off with middle third of the patellar tendon. This was reduced and fixed with a pull-out #2 Tyron suture. The tendon was also over sewn with #0 Vicryl suture. At this point the subcutaneous tissues were also closed with 2-0 and the skin was closed with surgical clips.

The patient's tibia was next reduced. It was found that the two wounds over the anterior part of the tibia communicated with the tibia itself. Therefore, it was washed out with pulse lavage irrigation. At this point the wire fixator was applied by placing three wires approximately 1.5 to 1 cm below the tibial plateau. These were then fastened to the ring and sequentially tightened to 100 Newtons. At this point the reduction was maintained under C-arm and the bars were attached to the distal pins with a cluster pin clamp.

At this point the fixation was felt to be quite stable and the pins were in good position. Several joints were evaluated using the C-arm under anesthesia. The left hip as well as the right and left wrist as well as the left elbow and left proximal humerus, all fractures were felt to be stable. However, the right radius did have what appears to be a depressed Barton segment which may need further evaluation and possible open reduction and internal fixation.

The patient was then transferred from the operating room to the recovery room in good condition without incident.

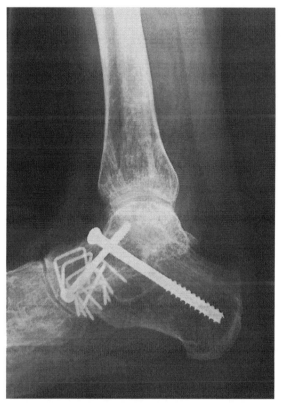

Gayle's right foot.

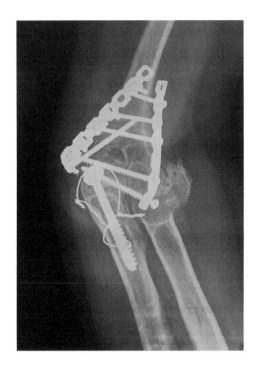

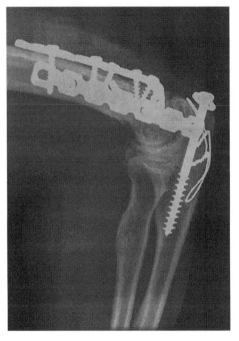

Two views of Gayle's left elbow.

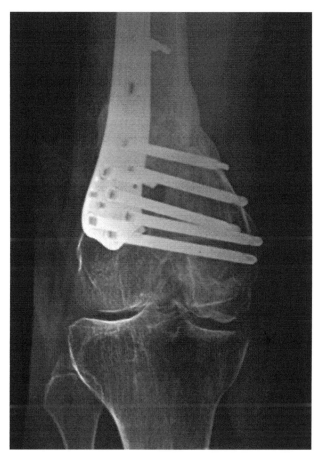

Gayle's right knee.

Chapter 4: A Little Comic Relief

A woman calls a local hospital. "Hello. Could you connect me to the person who gives information about patients? I'd like to find out how a patient is doing."

The voice on the other end says, "What is the patient's name and room number?"

"Sarah Finkel, room 302."

"I'll connect you with the nursing station."

"3-A Nursing Station. How can I help you?"

"I'd like to know the condition of Sarah Finkel in room 302."

"Just a moment. Let me look at her records." A moment passes. "Mrs. Finkel is doing very well. In fact, she's had two full meals, her blood pressure is fine, to be taken off the heart monitor in a couple of hours and, if she continues this improvement, Dr. Cohen is going to send her home Tuesday at noon."

The caller says, "What a relief! Oh, that's fantastic... that's wonderful news!"

The nurse says, "From your enthusiasm, I take it you are a family member or a very close friend!"

"Neither! I'm Sarah Finkel in 302! Nobody here tells me anything."

(An email joke from a friend, obviously a joke before the HIPAA laws.)

Chapter 5: Gayle's Story

The Beginning

The tragic events of 2001, for most people, evoke a terrorist attack on New York and Washington. For our family, it is something more personal.
What I have to say is not just my story; it is my family's story as well. We have all been through our own bit of hell, have had our separate life experiences after the events of June 3, 2001.

Sometimes I hope that I will remember the truck coming at us, what was happening to Devin, the rescue efforts and all; but at other times I'm glad I don't. When I mention my lack of memory to nurses or therapists, the usual response is, "Maybe it's better that you don't remember." Pain medications are often engineered to help you forget. I was in a drug-induced coma for most of the first three weeks.

I remember nothing about the accident itself, except occasionally I get flashes that are activated when I'm trying to take a deep breath, when the car stops suddenly, and when I am startled by loud noises. As you can imagine, this happens several times in the course of a normal day. Thus, the nightmare of June 3, 2001 never ends.

At this point, years later, I remember what a quiet day it was. Devin and I were at home alone. I was helping him prepare for finals, trying to keep him focused. It had been one of his hardest years, emotionally and academically, because of all the turmoil in the house. I had been a year out of radiation and two surgeries for a cancerous tumor in my right hand. His sister had had a difficult time in her junior year at college and was back now, living at home. Then Larry, Devin's dad, announced that he had prostate cancer and had to have surgery. I couldn't imagine a worse year. Little did I know!

Anyway, all of us were trying to help Devin in any way we could. He had left his French book at school, and I thought we should drive up to Williamstown to get it. At the time, it seemed like a good idea. It had rained earlier but had turned into a beautiful day. I thought the ride would be a good distraction.

Even now, every full breath I try to take brings a physical memory of the pressure of the crushed car trapping me, the steering wheel pushing me against the seat. I've been told that that was indeed the case, but I can't say I really remember. I recall feeling squished. As I think about it now, my back gets tense and my throat and chest feel all out of whack. Breathing is definitely the strongest trigger for remembering the event that changed all our lives. But can I stop breathing?

I have a memory of reaching my hand out to touch Devin, but I don't think I could have managed it with the injuries to my arm. He was too far away, even though he was in the seat beside me. My wrists were broken, and the ribs on my right side, nearer him, were more broken than on the left. That might have kept me from reaching very far. Six of my ribs were broken as was my collarbone, so it's still hard to stretch the intercostals muscles to allow a full breath. My ribs feel stuck all the time. It's possible that this "memory" is something I wished strongly that I could have been able to do.

I have no recollection of the rescue. I don't remember any pain from the metal piercing my left leg, but I do remember how cold and hard it felt, as well as the stuckness of it. It was warm that afternoon, but the metal was colder than my body.

When an accident leaves you with amnesia, often you don't remember much from the period of time just before the accident as well. The last clear memory I have of life before then is of Devin's soccer tournament in Nashua, New Hampshire the weekend before. The team and their parents stayed together in a motel, and what a wonderful time we all had! I remember the playoff game at the end against a team from Maine. There was a blizzard going on, and those hardy "Mainiacs" were wearing shorts. Our kids had sweats on under their shirts and shorts, and we were scrounging around for hats and mittens for them. I remember the parents huddling together sipping coffee and hot chocolate. This was at the end of May!

The ER and the Helicopter

I have a distinct memory of a white wall in our local emergency room before they took me by helicopter to Albany. I assume it was really just a curtain, but it felt like a wall separating Devin from me. I remember blood everywhere. I also remember a feeling of calm. It wasn't a feeling of being steely, but of my brain trying to stay lucid enough to help my helpers. There was a fog that kept trying to take over, a wonderful abyss, and a blackness that promised to bring me relief. I don't remember much else except the wanting, the yearning to see Devin, to make sure they were taking good care of him. I wanted to hear everything they were doing to him. I had to force myself to think hard, to stay clear. I was upset with that white wall separating us. If I could have forced it open with my brain, I would have done it. I needed to say goodbye to Jess and tell her my real fears. It was such a relief to tell someone what I was really thinking and feeling. The fear that I wasn't going to make it. I remember feeling the bustling all around me. I remember knowing that I was going to be taken away by a helicopter, taken from Devin and my family. I don't remember the helicopter itself, just the pounding thump, thump, thump. It is a sound that even today brings back haunting memories: the sense of slipping away, the loneliness of the fight, the struggle to stay alive.

My Drug-induced Coma and Surgeries in Albany

By the fifth or sixth week after the accident I started having memories that I can be sure of. Before then I remember drug-related nightmares that were more real than reality. One of the first memories I had was a funny one and a yet horrible experience. A nurse rigged up a morphine pump, a special device made to allow patients control of their own dosage of pain meds, but I couldn't manage it at all. Both my arms were broken, and she was in too much of a rush to notice that I couldn't use the controls. By the time Jess got there, I was frantic and way beyond any semblance of manageable pain. The rooms had big posters with facial expressions to help you rate your pain from one to ten. When the nurse returned quite a bit later and asked me what my pain level was, I yelled, "A twelve!"

That happened more than once with food as well. They'd leave my tray without realizing I couldn't open any of the containers, let alone feed myself. On a good day, some visitor would feed me. I could barely lift a fork, let alone a cup of tea. I couldn't sit up; often I couldn't find or press the button to raise my bed. Many times the cleaning lady would notice that I couldn't open things and took the time to help. But I was too embarrassed to say that I couldn't feed myself either. Once I was so hungry I considered dropping my face into my plate to eat like a dog. The food, when I could get at it, was surprisingly good, especially the fresh fruit platter. The same cleaning lady, a woman with a thick Jamaican accent and lovely singing voice, would call down to the cafeteria and have another one sent up to me.

I can still bring back the feeling of that first intake of air, after they took the tubes out. It seared the back of my throat. Even though I was grateful to have "real" air again, to be off the machine and breathing on my own, the pain was something fierce. It hurt like the dickens. Sometimes Larry would go to the cafeteria to buy me a frozen fruit bar. They felt so good after having tubes down my throat.

I have a vague recollection of only one nurse when I was in the ICU. At first I didn't know if she was real or not, but I described her to Jess later, and she said she was indeed real. The nurse, Monica, was very attentive. When my monitors started going off, she would come rescue me by suctioning the fluid out of my lungs. I felt as though I was drowning. When she did this, it seemed like my insides were coming out. But soon I would be able to catch a breath again. Jess learned to watch my blood pressure monitor. If it climbed into the 140s, she would call for a nurse. That meant that I would soon be frantic. She nearly lost it the day she saw it hit 184. Normal for me was 110.

Once they put me into a regular room, I began wondering who my doctor was. There were so many white coats in and out, and I couldn't figure out who was in charge. I wanted someone to come forward and say, "I'm your doctor. I'm in charge of all these other people and I'm going to take good care of you. If you have questions, I will answer them." They always came en masse at an ungodly hour of the morning, and they were more interested in what the other doctors said about me than what I might have to say. To any doctor reading this book, take your patients' hands and say, "Hi. I'm your doctor. And I'm not too busy to answer your questions." It's so damned scary in that bed.

Then there was a terrible decision made by a surgical resident. We referred to him as "Dr. Ponytail." He took me off Ativan when I transferred out of ICU to a room on the orthopedic wing. Oh, my Lord. I was a mess, and I didn't know why. Since then we've read that coming off high doses of Ativan abruptly can be quite dangerous. To top it off, he came in and said I'd be going home later in the day. "We've done all we can do for you," he informed me. I had one leg in an external fixator pointed toward the ceiling and in traction, another external fixator on my arm, plastic boots on both feet, and this barely post-adolescent white coat says, "You're going home." I was so upset that I started to cry, at which point he immediately exited the room.

By the time Jess got there a few hours later, I was in a tailspin. A nurse came in to assure me I wasn't going anywhere, but that they weren't sure they would be able to offer me more Ativan. It was then I realized that my tolerance for physical pain was greater than my tolerance for anxiety. Now that it was being withheld from me, it was clear that the Ativan was keeping me from going crazy.

Jess was livid. She pleaded with everyone who would listen and a few more who wouldn't. She called my primary physician, who was incredulous. Unfortunately, being out of state, he was unable to do anything. Finally an intern who remembered me from the ER peeked in to see how I was doing. I wasn't even his patient. It was about three in the morning. My stomach was rolling, and I knew I was working on a migraine headache. After much difficulty, he managed to get one milligram of Ativan for me, but explained the differences in departments. Apparently it was important to keep patients' anxiety down in the ICU, but not so crucial on a regular floor. Regulations required that I be seen by a psychiatrist in order to have Ativan prescribed. I could tell he was truly concerned about my discomfort. And I believe I detected some embarrassment over the whole procedural problem.

Little did I know at the time that transferring to a different wing or a different hospital can raise problems. It happened again two years later in Boston. I will tell you about that later. Suffice it to say that patients and caregivers need to write things down, because mistakes are made all the time. Maybe conversations, instructions, and information could be recorded. So many things can go wrong, so if you can't write things down, as I could not, get someone else to take notes or push a record button for you.

Jess rubbed my head, brushed my hair, and sang to me, everything she could think of to hold back the mountain of fear through that horrific night. It wasn't until late morning that a psychiatrist arrived with one of his interns in tow. He interviewed me at length, and finally agreed to prescribe Ativan. I asked him as he was preparing to leave if he would come back to help me with the trauma of the accident. He said that regulations only allowed him to work with me if I was, well, "crazy". I don't know where I mustered up the humor, but I replied, "Give me a couple more days of this nonsense and I will be." He left without even a chuckle. Jess laughed and suggested that perhaps he was self-medicating. Despite the laughter, we were still angry.

Outside of Dr. Ponytail telling me I was going home and the problem getting Ativan, my experience of that wing was fairly positive. A few nurses and aides seemed to like me and went out of their way to be compassionate and helpful. Some of the names I remember are Carol, Kevin, Demaris, and Jamie. My favorite I called "Angel Hair" because of her very fine, beautiful blonde hair. She had such a warm smile. She was in nursing school and only worked on the night shift. She brought me cookies, and we talked about our children. She made me feel less like a patient in a hospital and more like a person she would love to get to know. That went a long way to making me feel human. I believe there are people who become doctors, nurses, technicians, and CNAs because of a genuine, deep desire to help people. I have been fortunate to come in contact with many such professionals. Fortunately, they seem to outweigh those who are just there to do a job and go home.

Transition

Where to go after the hospital is such an important decision for trauma patients and their families to consider. Jess made a lot of phone calls and so did my parents. Mom and Dad looked at two places close to home. They were shown their rehab rooms and therapists, but we didn't know enough to ask the most important questions. Things like, "How many trauma patients have you had in the last six months?" "What is the ratio of patients to nurses, aides, and physical therapists?" "How do you handle emergencies when they arise for a patient?" "What are your rules around family staying overnight, should a patient need more support than you can give?" "Can the family dog come to visit?" "Do you have psychotherapists who do trauma work?" These are all questions we thought of after the fact. I was in such a bad way that maybe we should have gone to the rehab center in Boston straight from the Albany hospital. It would have been hell on Jess and my family to travel that far, but it might have been the thing to do. I was so betwixt and between at that point. With hindsight being so insightful, perhaps I was too afraid to leave the "safety" that I had come to experience in Albany. Transitions can be hard.

I was too injured to go to the hospital rehab unit near home. They required patients to be able to do at least three hours of PT each day. There was no way I could have qualified. Tearing Kleenex was the most I could manage to do in therapy. Actually the Boston rehab place might not have taken me at that point, either. I wish that we had asked these kinds of questions before exploring different facilities, but I was too drugged up and my family had no prior experience to draw on.

In the end, however, it was all moot. When the hospital is ready for you to leave, they send you to whatever facility has a bed. Even if you had done the research and found your ideal place, it's entirely possible they wouldn't have a bed available for you when the hospital was ready to discharge you. I suppose you could raise a ruckus and perhaps get an extra day or two in the hospital until a bed becomes available, but there are no guarantees. And I suppose if your last name is Rockefeller or Kennedy, it might be a different story. Sadly, our health care system leaves much to be desired.

The Challenges of Institutional Living

It was hard leaving the safety of Albany for the unknown of a nursing home. And as horrible as the nursing home was much of the time, it was hard to leave there months later to go home to my hospital bed in the living room.

My best memories of the nursing home were of the barbecue that Jess and Larry did. It was so good to be outside in the inner courtyard. They opened the big double doors of the physical therapy room and pushed my bed to a shady spot. I remember Joan, one of the Huntington's patients. She was easy to be around and so happy to be out with us, but I worried that she would hurt me with her sudden movements or maybe fall onto the bed with me. I remember how Jess and Larry hovered over me when Joan came close to my bed. And I remember how hard it was to stay awake. That was the time they goofed with my meds and had started me on Klonopin while I was still on Ativan. I remember falling asleep with steak on my fork. I remember Jess and Larry drinking what was probably their first beer since the accident, smiling and talking together while Larry tended the steaks. It made me feel like my family was still intact.

Oh, and I remember the day in PT with my parents when a huge turkey flew into that same courtyard. I had been so discouraged with what I couldn't do. I think I was just trying to catch my breath when there was a huge flapping sound. My dad was shocked! This was a huge bird, and he was worried that he didn't have enough room for take off when he wanted to leave. But sure enough, he got into the furthest corner and got off to a jerky trot, then lumbered into the air. What a sight! That old bird must have known I needed some comic relief.

I remember, too, the birdfeeder and the whirly gig that Jess put outside my window. It was nice to have something to watch when I was fed up with waiting. There was so much waiting, waiting for meds, waiting to be put on the bed pan, waiting to come off the bed pan, waiting for company, waiting for food, waiting for good food. The birds, primarily chickadees, were so sweet a distraction. Then my eyes would travel further and see the brightly colored pinwheel spinning in the breeze. And when our garden was in full bloom, Jess brought pictures and filled one whole wall with my flowers.

Then there was the chilly day in early November when Ginger locked Jess out of her car outside my window. Even though we all got a little stressed, it was also funny. She had stopped outside my window to fill the birdfeeder. While she was doing that, Ginger stepped on the power lock. My sweet woman tried everything to get her to put her paw on it a second time to unlock it, but to no avail. She was hopping up and down in the cold, waving to me, shouting commands to the dog, and finally giving up to call a locksmith.

Then there was Doug, one of the night nurses. He always took extra time to ask "How's Jess? When's Ginger coming in?" He'd tell me funny stories about his dog. And I always knew that if I had questions from the day that went unanswered I could ask him. And if I was hurting extra, he found ways to make me feel better. He was the only one who could get my bandages off without ripping skin. He used what he called a lollipop. It had a liquid on it that he kept brushing between my skin and the bandages while he slowly pulled. He was always excited when Jess was going to sleep over in a bed next to me. She was exhausted and he'd come in and sit at the bottom of her bed, bouncing up and down to wake her saying, "Jess! So good to see you! Tell me something about astrology!" Once in a while, she would join us in a few minutes of conversation before he would be called to another patient, but mostly she'd groan back at him, "Oh, Doug, get a life!" and go back to sleep if she could. Doug and I would laugh and talk softly at length if things were quiet that night.

Marlene, my primary CNA, was wildly busy and yet she was the only one who touched me in non-clinical ways. She would put her hand on me just to touch or emphasize something she was telling me. She would talk about her projects at home, wash my hair, sing to me. She was such a mother to me. Washing my hair was BIG! Oh, my God! It was awful not getting my hair washed as often as I would have liked. I know that Jess and Rebecca often washed my hair in the hospital, but I have no recollection of it. I'm sure it made me feel GREAT! But Marlene tried to wash my hair twice a week but wasn't always successful. She knew how important it was to me. She truly cared!

It was hard to have my hair cut short while in the nursing home, but nice of our friend Jamie, one of the stylists at Jess's workplace, to come in and do it. I didn't get it cut short because I wanted it short, but because it made it easier to tend. She snipped and chatted, rested her hand on my shoulder, then snipped and chatted some more. A year later when things were less wild, Jess took the time to nominate her for the employee recognition program.

Then there was the kitten that Colleen, the head nurse, brought to me. It must have felt the warmth of the heating pad on my chest. I remember it plunking down and staying for what seemed hours. It was a good idea, and it was nice of Coleen to think of it. She was often an advocate for me with the kitchen staff. She would go talk to them and they would bring nutritious food for a few days, then they would go back to the geriatric diet until she went down and had another chat with them.

I enjoyed the Monday family suppers. Jess would bring Devin and Becca. She brought dishes and napkins and silverware from home along with a great meal. It helped give me hope that I would go home some day. Larry brought Devin often and even if he was on his computer or doing homework in the library down the hall, I still felt a part of his life. Larry never stayed long, but his visits were much more frequent than I had expected. And the biggest surprise was my brother-in-law. He called from work every Friday without fail. Sometimes it's the little things that can make such a difference.

Probably the best AND the scariest event was what Jess and I now call our "first date." I was given permission for an outing, so Jess made reservations at the restaurant across the highway. I had to get my hair washed. Marlene, my favorite CNA, was so excited for me I thought we were going to have to take her with us. Jess bought me a pretty top from my favorite clothing store, The Purple Plume, and had to cut the shoulders and put in snaps so that I could get it on. Everyone at the nursing home was so excited for me. And my parents were acting like it was my first date EVER! I remember them walking out with us and standing in the parking lot watching Jess push the wheelchair across the busy state highway. My mother had her arms crossed and was biting her lip. My father kept trying to leave. "Come on, Peg. Let's go." She didn't want to go. I thought they might even sneak in and take a table on the other side of the dining area just to make sure I was okay. And I was extremely frightened about leaving my room. That's something most people don't realize. As much as you hate being institutionalized, as much as you hate the room you're in, it becomes your whole world. With all it's faults, it becomes SAFE. The outside world is where you got hurt. It's where bad things can happen again. I was afraid of crossing the highway. I was worried that I wouldn't have the stamina to sit up for as long as it would take to have an entire meal. I wasn't really sitting up straight yet, so they put the wheel chair in a partially sitting up position while my legs were out straight. The doorways of the restaurant were a little tight, and the thresholds were rough to get over. Every bump hurt something. But it was wonderful. It got me out. It gave me confidence. We watched the sunset over the lake. The meal was delicious. The wait staff was more than accommodating. Neither Jess nor I remember what we ate, but we remember it was delicious.

I like to think about the good memories first, because when I think of what was difficult, so many things flood to mind. Ah, let me count the ways. And as I recount the problems, know that I do so not to complain but to inform. If even one reader can avoid even one of the pitfalls, then writing this will be worth the effort of recalling the pain.

First of all, the nursing home was a disappointment; it really wasn't the rehabilitation center they promised my family it would be. Had they ever had a patient as damaged as me? It would have been smart to ask how many accident victims they had housed in the last few months, but then we weren't really given the freedom to choose. It turned out only one accident victim had been in their care in a whole year prior to my becoming a patient. Their specialty was caring for Huntington's patients not multi-trauma accident victims. In short, they were not qualified to care for me. I have heard that many improvements have been made since my stay.

Granted, there were many older people there as well, but they and I were not a good mix. I was constantly worried that one of the Huntington's patients would crash into my already broken body. I had nightmares about it. My neighbor across the hall spent most of the day and night wailing and crying. She sounded like a caged cat. It was very scary and brought difficult memories of visiting my brother in Belchertown State Hospital when I was a youngster. My brother had Down syndrome and had been institutionalized at Belchertown State Hospital. I was very young, but I remember feeling frightened by so many of the people there, even my own brother at times. He was so tall and hard to understand, but as I got older, I understood him better, so much so that I often was asked, "What did he say?" Because of that, I often could understand what the speech-challenged Huntington's people were saying and crying. It was painful to know what they were experiencing.

At the nursing home I was not a person but a number. I can still hear the cry ring out, "Number three is calling!" It didn't seem as though I was ever a priority. Minutes seemed like hours. Drugs were not always on time, which was difficult because you can't catch up on the pain. If the meds were an hour or two late, as they often were in the afternoon and evenings, it seemed forever before the pain became manageable once again. It was hard to say, "I have a need! And it's as important as everyone else's!" I felt like I'd been put away in an institution like my brother had been so long ago. I would have enjoyed more visits.

Nighttime was a challenge. There was so much crying, screaming, and yelling. The food was horrible. Many of the nurses and CNAs, were afraid of me. A head nurse confessed that few of them responded to my calls because so many were afraid to work with me. I was so broken that they feared they'd do more harm than good. Also, they were horribly understaffed. Many times when I needed help, two or three were needed at a time to help turn me or move me or get me on and off a bedpan. There was one CNA whose son had been in an accident. She lived at the hospital while he was recuperating, doing everything for him. She was a relief to have around because she was experienced and not afraid to touch me.

The simplest things were incredibly difficult. Going to the bathroom required two or three people to roll me and another person to put the bedpan in place; the same procedure had to be reversed when I was through. Constipation only complicated matters because they had to reassemble a crowd of aides to help when I finally needed to come off the bedpan.

Eventually it became a little less painful to be moved and I could help a little. And Jess eventually figured out how to engineer the whole ordeal by herself. This is embarrassing to talk about, but could be helpful to someone some day. One night Jess said, "I've got an idea, if you're willing to try." Because it was such an ordeal and took so long every time I had to pee, and because my healing body needed tons of water, she suggested using menstrual pads. She would get a bunch of them together on the bed, then put one in place. I'd have to stop the stream when she told me to, which was a challenge, but we managed. She'd quickly drop the soaked one in a bedpan and position another one under me. Sometimes I'd need as many as six, other times only three. It worked well, and took a lot less time, but the biggest advantage was that we didn't need to ask for help. And best of all, I didn't have to be rolled over, saving me from a lot of pain. Jess thought of it because she was so concerned that the bones that were trying to mend might get jostled and re-broken. I don't know if that would have happened, but I was grateful for her inventiveness and her willingness to take it on herself.

Every doctor visit necessitated an hour-long ambulance ride to Albany. I can't emphasize enough how important it is to be prepared. Jess said it was like going on an outing with an infant. She needed to pack the bedpan, wipes, a plastic bag to put them in when she was done because you're not always near a trashcan, extra johnnies, sheets, drinking water, and reading material for long waits. I know now that Jess got frustrated at times because she had to be so focused in order to remember everything, and even then she wasn't always successful. But she didn't complain much. I know she just got "steely" and did what she had to do. And I felt guilty because I was causing all this extra work. Somehow we got through it. I know it was a wonderful day for Jess when I had someone else to take care of me for a day or even half a day and she could relax. I loved when she told me about the first night in Albany that she and my mom actually sat down at a restaurant and had a glass of wine with the meal. Jess told me it tasted unbelievably delicious!

Sometimes just finding a space that was private enough to toilet me on doctor visits was a challenge. It was a challenge for the ambulance staff to find a place, but it was equally hard to speak up and say that I needed to go. There was no way the stretcher was going to fit in the bathroom. Once Jess was given a storage room to help toilet me with some privacy.

We had to remember to bring snacks, because the EMTs driving the ambulance were rarely able to stop for food. Fortunately, my doctor's building had a deli on the ground floor. We might not have felt comfortable asking to take time to get something to eat, but sometimes they wanted something to eat too.

Overall it was quite an ordeal. Sometimes we left at nine in the morning and got back well after supper. It was a good twenty minutes to get from my bed onto the stretcher, and then into the truck. They had to take my vitals before leaving, then there were all sorts of straps and ties to fasten. When we got to the doctor's complex, there were always a series of x-rays because I had so many breaks and fractures. Often it took nearly an hour to do them all. Then there was the waiting, the visit itself, and back to the truck. Once back inside, they had to take my vitals, strap me down, and lock the gurney in for the trip back to the nursing home. Wow! All that, just to be checked out by the doctor.

Back at the nursing home, few of the nurses had knowledge of the "pin care" that I required. Every place where the metal of the ex-fixator went through my skin to the bones needed particular care so as not to get infected. I had to do a lot of the training in order to get them to do it the way they did in the hospital, gently pushing my skin down from the metal. There should be some way for state or federal monitors to make sure that nursing homes and rehab centers qualify to care for certain types of patients. I would have appreciated the protection.

Certainly the kitchen staff had little knowledge of nutrition, or they wouldn't have been sending the food they were sending. I was trying to mend bones. I needed lots of protein. I was on high doses of pain meds and not ambulatory, so I needed fruits and vegetables to deal with the constipation. One of the CNAs would go to the kitchen and swipe things for me. Jess often brought food from home, or she stopped for groceries before visiting. I had food allergies to deal with, but somehow they never could remember. One of my male nurses stomped down to the kitchen with yet another carton of milk. It was his fifth trip, and he threw it at them, yelling, "What part of lactose intolerant do you not understand?"

They sent their psychotherapist to work with me, but he made me feel worse. Pat, pat, pat on my shoulder. "Oh, that's too bad, dear." I finally asked him not to come back. After that, Jess hired a trauma counselor from work. Eileen was awesome. Unfortunately, it was an out-of-pocket expense. Somehow we afforded several sessions, but I could have used many more.

Eileen gave me a variety of ways to express myself. One day she would just let me talk, another day she would lead me through a short creative visualization experience, while another day she offered me art therapy. When I could finally hold a crayon, she had me draw my anger and my fears. Most of my drawings had peaks like mountains that no fool would ever attempt to climb.

One of the hardest things to deal with was how difficult it was to tell my family how afraid I felt. I didn't want to disappoint my parents, or make Jess feel like she had to do even more. I remember crying for a month and all the while wondering if I could cry myself to death. I asked Eileen if she knew anyone who never stopped crying. I felt so out of control. And as drugged as I was, I worried that if I cried too much, they would give me more drugs to get my emotions "under control" so that caring for me would be easier. Much of the time, I felt like a throwaway.

One day some friends came from Marshfield and stayed across the street in a bed and breakfast. That night they asked if we could go to dinner across the street. I could only sit up for short periods of time, so I told Jess to go with them. She didn't want to go but I knew it would do her a world of good to get away for a bit. And they had come from so far away to visit me. After they left, I felt sick with jealousy that Jess could leave, that she could just walk out of that horrid place. She could forget for an hour, but I couldn't. I was trapped by my own body, by that single regrettable experience of being hit by a truck.

As difficult as all this was, there was one thing worse. The nursing home allowed a physical therapy assistant to work with me. He had unrealistic expectations, and ultimately this did not serve me well. He talked a good game and came across as knowing what he was talking about, and so I went along. He was the expert, after all, and I needed to trust him, to believe in him.

We now know that his incompetence, perhaps his arrogance, was endangering me. At the time, the gap between what he expected and what I could barely manage was hugely depressing. I felt like, "Oh, my God! I'm worse off than I thought!" I couldn't even sit upright when he tried to get me to stand at the parallel bars. He wasn't working on strengthening the muscles that would hold me up as he should have.

Months later a Visiting Nurse PT came to my home and determined with simple tests that I still wasn't strong enough to stand. But the physical therapy folks at the nursing home thought I was. Their PT assistant seemed angry that I wasn't standing well. He seemed to ignore the fact that both arms were broken, as were both knees, my hip had been smashed as well as my left shoulder, and I still had a heavy ex-fixator on my left leg, while my right ankle continued to be a mess. And he only once worked on me in front of Jess, choosing instead to work while my parents were visiting. Perhaps he knew that she would question him. My parents had little experience in the medical arena as they have been very healthy. And unlike Jess, they had never had to undergo physical therapy. They also are from the generation that sometimes sees doctors as infallible, and my parents were so proud of what I tried to do. And I so wanted to take away the worry on their faces; I so wanted to please them. Little did I know that I should not have tried to stand at all. The subsequent re-broken right wrist and left elbow may well have been because of inappropriate physical therapy.

We also discovered that he wasn't honest with how many sessions, exercises, and repetitions he did with me. When I moved on, my new physical therapists were upset that I was not further along, considering how many hours their predecessor claimed to have spent with me. The paper work just didn't fit with the reality of my body. When this was discovered, I felt cheated. At times he wrote in my files that I refused PT, but I never told him that I didn't want to work. I was trying my hardest, but there were some things he was asking me to do which were impossible at the time. Now I know how that looks to insurance companies, and may explain why they didn't want to pay for my later out-patient PT. One insurance woman even brought my outside therapist to tears, saying, "We're not going to put any more money out. That person is a black hole and will never walk again." This false impression was the result of one greedy, poorly trained so-called professional.

I don't know why this PTA walked away when I said I couldn't do what he wanted me to. I know now that he could have suggested so many other things. I've had many compassionate, creative PTs and PTAs since him, and I can't help but feel as though he wasted my precious time. I'm angrier with him than I am with any of my other caregivers. I'm angrier with him than I am with the young man who caused the accident. Lionel made a mistake. He was young. He didn't intend to hurt me. This was an adult. He had to get up in the morning and choose to be the way he was, choose to not know more, choose to treat me callously, and choose to not ask for help from more experienced therapists. And I'm angry with the nursing home for letting a PTA have so much responsibility. I don't remember ever being seen by a PT. I know now that there was a PT overseeing the assistant, but I don't remember ever seeing that person. Didn't they think that someone who lived through five long bone breaks and a total of 123 breaks and fractures deserved better than an assistant? It brought me little relief to be told that he left shortly after I went home.

Visiting My Home

I was still on a lot of narcotics when I went for my home visit, so my memory of that day is foggy. In order to be discharged, your home needs to be inspected. I think that's an excellent idea. The home visit is an attempt to create a smooth transition. Everyone was nervous, especially my parents. I required so much attention, and things were still going wrong. They wanted me to be safe and were afraid that I might slip backwards in my recovery. I think they were also worried that it would be just too much for Jess, Devin, Becca, and themselves. The nursing home administrators kept saying, "Yeah, sure! No problem!" whenever they asked if it made sense for me to stay longer. Of course, they may have wanted to keep a bed occupied for financial reasons. So it was a hard decision. Jess wanted me home a month sooner, but we'll never know if that would have been good or not. And by the time they considered sending me home, Jess and my mom were doing so much of my care that I had become quite the easy patient for them, not to mention the fact that they liked the coffee that Jess made the mornings she had slept over. I had also become close to a couple of the nurses and CNAs. It was hard to think of leaving. For good or bad, they had become my family for nearly five months.

When I was told that I was going to go home for a visit, I was so scared. I couldn't imagine leaving my room. As wonderful as our dinner out across the street was, it was a challenge to even cross the street. You get used to the same four walls. After a trauma, any odd noise is noticed. It seemed so important to maintain the status quo in my life. The pain and the constant effort to keep fighting off the rage at having my whole life changed were all I could deal with. I was overwhelmed, and now it was time for me to go home. I was worried that my parents were right, that it was too much for Jess to handle. I struggled with the very idea of going home. I was still barely feeding myself. I couldn't open a can of soda. I couldn't walk. I had to shower in a basin placed in bed with me. Some days, a bed wrinkle would send me over the edge. I worried that it would be too hard on Jess's back. She was doing a better job than the nursing home, but would it be too much of a burden for her? And would it be too stressful for Devin? Would he be uncomfortable having me around? Would he feel responsible for meeting my needs, making him feel like the parent instead of a soon-to-be thirteen-year-old?

Even the thought of getting into a car for the twenty-minute drive home was something I couldn't imagine. In my trips to Albany, I rode the entire trip lying on a stretcher. This ride would be shorter but it scared the socks off me. Would I be able to sit upright for the drive home and back, not to mention the length of time I would be home for the visit? It seemed physically impossible. I didn't know if I had the courage to get in the car. There would be no EMT hovering over me, taking my blood pressure. What if I wet myself? What if they didn't think my home was good enough? I stressed over how much it was going to cost to make the needed changes to our home. Maybe I should have gone along with the idea of moving to a one-story that Jess had brought up earlier. Would she be disappointed in not getting a new house? Would she know how important it was for me to have the familiar smells, sights, and sounds that had been my home before the accident? It seemed I was worried about everything.

My mother took of a picture of Devin and me sitting at our dining room table that day. It's probably the best picture anyone's taken of me in my whole life. I was so happy to be home! It certainly didn't look like I had been filled with anxiety. And when I saw the work that Jess had put into the ramp and the newly painted living room, saw the hospital bed waiting for me, I had no doubt that this was the right decision. The familiar smells of home struck me immediately, and I was in awe. Even the lighting! It was much warmer light than in a nursing home or hospital. And Ginger was there prancing and dancing and wagging her tail. It was a beautiful, sunny day. Weeds and all, the yard looked wonderful. Jess had hired a contractor to make the downstairs bathroom handicapped-accessible. It was perfect. And even though I was exhausted from the effort, I started looking forward to coming home for good.

The folks at the nursing home were very pleased with all the efforts to make the home safe for me. The ramp especially pleased me. Jess explained that it was less of a slope than code required. She thought code was too steep. It was great to have a little landing before the turn. I could imagine spending time there in the sun watching her work in the yard, and at some point, mayber I would be able to go down the ramp myself. The thought of coming up, well, time would tell.

Coming home was a go!

A Hospital Bed in My Living Room

The week before coming home seemed so short. Everything that happened to me in the nursing home made me wonder, how could we do this at home? How could I adapt to home life? Would we be able to get this or that done? And how would we afford to make the adaptations?

My biggest concern was logistics. Would I be able to get to the bathroom in the wheelchair? Would the transfer board be enough to get me from the wheelchair to the car seat? The wood looked thin. Would it hold my weight? Would it slip and drop me to the ground? I remember the first time my dad used the transfer board with me. He didn't know that Jess had bought me a pair of nylon pants because they would be slippery and would help me slide across the board. Dad got in on the driver's side and pulled hard on my pant leg. My body slid so fast, it scared us both. He had to catch me before I ended up in the driver's seat. As soon as he knew he hadn't hurt me, we laughed about the slippery pants. What a great idea they were!

I still needed help with everything. A simple bath took me an hour. I came home in November so I guess the house could have been warmer. The thought of having to have Jess sleep next to me in the living room on a rickety fold-up bed worried me. Would she get enough sleep? Could her back take the flimsy mattress? I worried about not getting enough help from my family or from the visiting nurses. I needed 24-hour coverage. My parents were already doing so much, and I always seemed to need more. There was literally nothing I could get for myself. Even a glass of water was too heavy hold. I could feed myself. I was strong enough to cut tender foods but I still had so many spasms and nerve twitches that things went flying or just plain fell on my chest or lap and made a mess. It was frustrating. All my fears subsided when we arrived in our driveway. Larry was there when we pulled up, and he'd put balloons on the fence. After the long ride from the nursing home, the hospital bed beckoned. Jess had painted the blue walls orange and yellow. I noticed the new furniture that she had made and couldn't wait to get settled into my new bed and pull up the covers.

As it turned out, everything was much easier at home. Jess was bringing me my meds on time. That had been an issue so often, both in the hospital and the nursing home. Jess and my family were always within voice range. Devin seemed more relaxed now that I was home. There were no screaming or yelling patients in the middle of the night, and I felt safe and loved.

Home cooking—I'd almost forgotten how good it could be! I must have gained thirty pounds in the first few months back home. I had gotten skinny on institutional food. Food was again something to look forward to as opposed to, "Oh, well. Here comes my soggy beans and breaded fish." What a luxury to think about and request a meal I might enjoy. And my friend Lil kept bringing the best cookies! Weekly! We started calling her the Cookie Lady!

On Tuesdays when Jess was at work, Gail would come and cook for me, Devin and Larry. It was nice eating together. When supper was done, Larry would help Devin with his homework, then take him back to his house for bed. Jess would get home from work by ten and often found Gail and me chatting. It was on those nights that Gail clued me in on what Devin had gone through while I was in the hospital and the nursing home. It was good to talk with her. It had been strange when Larry told me he was dating, especially when he told me her name. I remember thinking, "How convenient for him!" then chided myself for being catty. Well, at least it was spelled differently, I thought. When I met her, however, we like each other immediately. I think Larry was surprised and even a little anxious at first that we so quickly became family.

Jess built a bookcase and put it to the left of my bed for much of what I needed. Everything else like my hairbrush, TV clicker, and bed control, she duct-taped into a pouch on the bed frame or the lamp beside the bed. She had taken a dresser and put it on what looked like skis. It was very clever because wheels would have gotten stuck in the deep plush of the carpet and padding. Then she put a big tabletop on the dresser with skis and had Larry put vinyl flooring on the top so it would be easy to wash. It was her version of the hospital table on wheels. It didn't go up and down, but it was just right. So that's where I had my meals and my sponge baths. A year later, Larry took out all the carpet and put in hardwood. It was too hard to move myself around in the wheelchair on carpet with padding.

Until then it was quite a struggle for both Jess and me. I wish he could have gotten to it sooner, but he had his own life to contend with. I was thankful that he had gotten to it at all. We could not have afforded the labor that he didn't charge.

Taking a bath in bed is awful. I came home in mid-November and even turning the heat up isn't enough because there's always a wet place on your body that makes you cold. It was torture! We couldn't think of any way to make that easier. It was so cold. I would wash one part and then I would need to rest before starting again. It was exhausting! We didn't think of it then, but a heated towel bar would have helped. I was cold to begin with because I wasn't moving. And no matter how often Jess went to get more hot water, it was never enough. It was hard, but it was important for me to do as much of the bathing on my own as I could. It meant gripping and bending and twisting. It was good physical therapy. Even moving enough to redistribute my weight was good exercise. At the nursing home they'd scrubbed and scrubbed so I didn't get bedsores. I even managed to get a few short massages which seem to help prevent bedsores. At home, I couldn't scrub as much or as hard, but I was confident that we would notice if a bedsore started.

The rented bed was very comfortable. Because it was adjustable, I could change my position as often as I needed to. It wasn't the Hill-Rom airbed that I was used to, but it was an air mattress and not bad at all. Jess told me the rental guy did a lot of searching before he found me an air mattress. What a difference it makes. Sometimes I needed to shift my weight to another part of my body, or lift my legs up, or sit up more. When I finally moved back upstairs into my own bed five months later, I found myself yearning at times for the adjustable airbed.

I was surprised I didn't miss the upstairs. It felt good to be confined a bit; it was already so much more than I had become used to at the hospital and the nursing home. And the other thing that was good about being downstairs was that someone was always within earshot. Jess or Gail or my mom could be cooking, doing the laundry, or talking on the phone and I would be comforted just knowing that they were there. For the last several months in the hospital and the nursing home, I'd had a call button to press when I needed something. Of course, sometimes it could be a very long time before anyone would come to see what I needed, but it was still reassuring to know that it was there. So Jess gave me a bell to ring in case she was distracted and couldn't hear my voice; when she went upstairs to get something, she would leave me with a phone. If the house had been bigger and I couldn't see or hear her, I think I would have been frightened. I was still so helpless. There was a sense of security knowing that Jess or someone was always there.

I loved when Devin was home. I loved hearing his voice. It was a constant reminder of why I wanted to get strong again. But I was also afraid that I would be a constant "downer" for him. I didn't want to be a reason for him to not come home. The accident was still relatively fresh in my memory, and I was still dealing with the emotional fallout of what I had lost. I wanted to spare him the reality of all my daily struggles. I could put on a smile for a while. But now that I was home, he would see so much more: my anger, my sadness, my frustration. I didn't want him to permanently replace his memories of who I was before the accident with these new images of me, so helpless and needy. I had given that a lot of thought before coming home. I was afraid of how hard it would be for him to come home from school to his broken mother. I worried that he wouldn't bring home friends because life and home were different now. He was still so young, and yet, in the end, he seemed to take it all in stride.

Even years later, Devin still has a hard time talking about the accident. I'm sure some buried emotions still fester there. I have doubts about some of the decisions we made along the way, but it seems as though he is a well-adapted, happy teenager now. I feel we did a lot to make him laugh. Getting two kittens right away, that was pure genius. He so loves cats, and it was something that we could share as a family. The kittens, Champagne and Caviar, made us laugh and lightened much of the heaviness. And I was relieved when Devin would go to his dad's. I missed him terribly, but I thought it would be better for him to have breaks from me. I liked his sensitivity to my needs, but it also made me sad.

Sometimes he would crawl into bed with me. There wasn't a lot of room in the twin-sized hospital bed, but we still managed to cuddle. We would play with the kittens together. And he would fetch me so many things. I'd ask him, "Can you get this, do that?" Mostly it was picking up things I dropped. It reminded me of the drop and fetch game babies like to play. We watched a lot of TV together, taking both our minds off much of the hard stuff.

Being home turned out to be the best thing, in spite of all my worries. I had my family, my friends, and my wonderful pets. I was healing quicker than in the nursing home. I didn't have to wait, cry out, or plead for what I needed. I could even ask for things I wanted. What a joy.

Yet there was the pain of Becca not being home when I returned after the accident. It was confusing and a bit hurtful that she had moved out while I was in the nursing home. I worried that Becca couldn't be around me that much because I was too disfigured, too different, too wrong, or too painful a reminder for her of all that she had lost. I know she had a boyfriend, school, her job, and a lot of other things that kept her busy, but I still wanted more of her time. These things are painful to say, but they are my truth; and I am certain that someone else out there has had a similar disappointment in what a loved one has done or not done. I understood that she was old enough to be on her own, but I couldn't help thinking she might still be home with us if it weren't for the accident.

I got so angry with Lionel for smashing into me and causing all of this pain and all of the changes for my family. So it became essential to move away from this pain. What helped most was concentrating on small pleasures like playing with Devin's hair, scratching Jess's back, even though it hurt. I liked listening to Becca tell me about her day or her troubles, even though I was tired. I found these everyday activities to be calming, grounding, satisfying. I needed to take care of others rather than always being the one to be taken care of. That made me feel less angry, also more like the true me.

Visiting Nurses

The nurses from the local VNA were awesome. The PTs, OTs and nurses became friends quickly. They were people I trusted, people I felt I could call at any time for any reason. They came up with many helpful suggestions, the best of which was how to get blood. Every visit meant a blood draw for various tests. My veins were shot by then. After a trauma and especially after so much time in bed, circulation is challenged. After the innumerable blood draws, IVs and all, I felt like a dartboard at a popular neighborhood bar. A compilation of information from two of their nurses and one PT taught us some tricks. At their suggestions, I was always drinking lots of water, but I would drink even more for two hours before they came. Hydrating helps to plump up veins. Then for about ten minutes before they came, Jess would bring me hot towels to put on my arm. The heat helped bring even more circulation to the area. I would relax and hang my arm down at my side, well below my heart. All of this helped tremendously. Nobody at the hospital or the nursing home had ever tried any these techniques. Of course it also could have been an issue of time.

Joe Jackson, their social worker, was amazing. He came to the house and went over everything we were entitled to, then helped us fill in the application forms. It was Joe who told us that we should have been getting Social Security Disability already. We missed six months because the social workers at the hospital and the nursing home never mentioned it. A lot of paperwork and doctor visits were needed to get me approved. Then there was another month delay because they denied me, claiming that I was an alien. That would have been funny had we gotten more money from our insurance or from Lionel, but since we were struggling to make ends meet, we were pretty disgusted. Did they think I was from Mars? Or Mexico? Jess made several phone calls and had to mail them another copy of my birth certificate before they relieved me of my alien status. I wonder if these antics are stall tactics to save them from paying. What do people do without a Joe or a Jess in their lives? I couldn't do all that was needed to get the benefits I was due. At that point I couldn't even talk for ten minutes without my throat hurting, often my voice failing completely. Sometimes Jess would be on the phone for forty minutes at a clip. I swear, it was a third job for her.

Joe also suggested contacting Ad Lib, a non-profit organization that helps people with disabilities by paying someone to give care. I qualified to have a paid aide helping with the things I couldn't do for myself. That was a godsend! Having

Jess take so much time off from work set us back. Because Lionel's family had few assets, a lawsuit would have been fruitless. I got $20,000 as did Devin. We got $8,000 for the car. Our lawyer got everything she could as quickly as she could, and for that we were most grateful. Lionel's minimal car insurance as well as mine gave him the same amount of money as me. I wrestled for some time with that fact. I am handicapped for life and didn't cause the accident, and yet we both get the same amount of money. It seemed skewed.

Finances are a constant worry. How do I continue to ask my family to cover all the changes we need around the house? How do I justify spending money that should be going to daily necessities that we now need to put into making home modifications? It's very upsetting, and I often end up feeling guilty that I cannot work. I don't know what I would do if I were alone. The money from Social Security just about covers the mortgage and my share of the groceries. I could not make it on my own. I would have had to move in with my elderly parents. What do people do?

It was so expensive just to spring me from the nursing home. Then there were other modifications that we made to the house that were not required but were needed because of the wheelchair. All these things were expensive. In writing about finances, I feel as though I'm whining. But it's a fact of my new life and a consideration for many who will read this.

I wish everyone would spend a day in a wheelchair. Think how much compassion people would feel if they could know what it's like! My fingers would bang into the doorways because they weren't wide enough. No one understands that until they try to do it. I remember Jess making the ramp with less of an incline than the building code required, because she thought it would be too much for me. As it is, with two broken wrists and a dislocated shoulder, I cannot muscle myself up the ramp or along the carpet. It hurts too much. Jess actually put a landing halfway along so that we could rest. What a great idea!

Of all the wonderful inventions of Jess's, my favorite thing of all was the toilet paper holder for my commode. It may sound silly, but at the time seemed fabulous—she taped a pencil to my commode as a toilet paper holder. She was afraid that I might drop the roll while she was upstairs, and it would roll away somewhere where I couldn't, or shouldn't, reach for it. I thought that was so clever! Thank God for duct tape! Speaking of commodes, nothing involved in toileting is covered by insurance. That meant the handicapped-accessible shower wasn't covered either, nor were the handicap bars that Jess put here and there for stability as I began to walk. It's impressive to think of all the things that insurance doesn't cover. And even though my health insurance covers most medical expenses, co-pays added up quickly and can be daunting.

Trauma therapy at home was not covered by insurance, and so Jess asked Eileen, our friend and psychotherapist, to come to the house. She had already done several sessions with me at the nursing home. She very generously lowered her rate and we paid for the sessions on our own. I had made a better transition from the nursing home to our home, but it was becoming increasingly clear to me how much had changed in my life, how much I had lost as a result of the accident. I had so much more trauma to work through with her now that I was home because it was truly in my face.

Saving My Leg

My right knee was having trouble healing. It just wasn't getting stronger. We went to Dr. Hospodar for more x-rays and tests, and finally discovered I had an infection in my right femur. The infectious disease doctor here in Pittsfield, had me on constant antibiotics to keep the infection at bay. Every time I tried to go off the medicine, my knee would swell and start burning up. I ran a fever and felt like I had the flu. Putting even the slightest weight on it was excruciating.

I remember the time Jess forgot to replenish the antibiotics in my weekly pillbox. She had a system that worked well, but the one time she messed up was with the antibiotics. After four days without, I ended up in the emergency room with a raging fever. They started talking about removing my leg. The local doctors had always thought it might be the only way to rectify the situation, but now they were convinced. The possibility of my body becoming septic and killing me was strong.

I was right on the edge of agreeing with them when Dr. Hospodar told me to delay. He wanted to send me to Boston for a second opinion. The physician who had trained him for orthopedic trauma surgery was the man he wanted me to see. So off we went, PICC[5] line and all, to consult with Dr. V. at a Boston hospital. Apparently he was using a new procedure with a decent chance of success.

On our second visit we decided to stay in a motel because the three-hour trip was so tiring. On the Internet, Jess found us a Priceline.com hotel for less than we expected. When we got into the room, my "MacGyver" once again sprang into action. After looking around the room and taking a coat hanger from the closet, she hung the bag of antibiotics and saline on something in the ceiling. We settled in, turned on the TV, and immediately fell asleep. An hour later, Jess woke shocked that we had both fallen asleep so quickly. The IV bag she'd hung from the ceiling was filling with blood. She was still feeling bad about leaving my antibiotics out of the pillbox, when this new episode of "Kill Gayle" occurred. She calmed down remembering that the nurses from the VNA had told us this might happen, but seeing it was frightening. I woke to her standing on the bed taking down the bag of blood. It was a hell of a thing to wake up to, but soon I understood what she was doing. When gravity returned my vital fluids, Jess disconnected the bag. Oh, my!

The next day with the Boston doctor we learned all about the new procedure. He would take out all the metal in my right leg and place antibiotic "seeds" in every nook and cranny. Then he would debride, or scrape away, the tissue that was damaged, leaving my knee in pieces for a week while antibiotic seeds fought off the infection. Then they would remove the seeds, put everything back together, and secure a big plate on my femur. The plan was to send me to a nearby rehab center for a time while they pumped four different antibiotics into me. From a clinical perspective, it was wonderful. But from my perspective, that of a patient, it was "Oh, my God, they're going to do what?" I was scared witless.

As always, however, I mustered up the strength to do the inevitable with

---

[5] A peripherally inserted central catheter (*PICC* or PIC *line*) is a form of intravenous access that can be used for a prolonged period of time.

fabulous results. This amazing two-surgery procedure went well, although the spot where they harvested bone from my hip hurts to this day. Dr. V. said that the staph infection infiltrated the bone closest to the metal more than the bone further away, which was very good news.

The first surgery took two and a half hours. The wait for my family was difficult, being in a new hospital. All of the other surgeries were done in Albany and they had become familiar with the routines there. Now they were in a strange place hoping that I would not lose my leg. The tension was palpable. I don't remember much because I was on high dosages of drugs. In order to keep my leg from moving between surgeries, I was restrained and my metabolism slowed almost into a coma. This was to keep me from moving my disassembled leg. The second surgery was more painful. They took a bone graft from my right hip and bone from a cadaver, made a pulp of the two, then inserted it into my right femur in order to extend the length of my leg. The nurses had warned that the bone graft would hurt more than the knee operation, which is fairly common. It seemed hard to fathom, but they were correct.

The antibiotics were a powerful experience. The infectious disease docs told me how long I'd be on each of the four medicines. I'm pretty good at remembering those kinds of things even while on pain meds, but I would recommend that you write these things down, even if the doctors think they've got it covered. I say this because, in transferring down the block from the hospital to the rehab center after the surgeries, they lost some of my paperwork. Perhaps a gust of wind off the Tobin Bridge—my view from the rehab center for a long, long month—blew it into the Charles River. In the middle of my stay, my infectious disease doctor went on vacation. I remembered how long I was supposed to be on each one, but they seemed to be guessing. I ended up being on the strongest of the antibiotics for an extra week, which was rough on my body. Thank God for my sporty life prior to the accident and all the PT after it. My muscle tone started out in good shape, but after a month in bed again, I was pretty weak. It seemed like every time I saw a lab coat go by, they were after me for more blood. They had to keep a watchful eye on my potassium levels as well as this, that, and the other thing, because the antibiotics were so powerful. But I can hardly complain; it was a successful procedure. Harrowing as the month was, they saved my leg, and that was all that mattered.

Rehabilitation was a difficult experience for me. They didn't warn me I might be there for a month. It might have been easier if they had told me so I could have prepared for that long a stay. It was a year since the accident had altered my life so completely. I had been home for such a short time and now I was in two more strange environments during that month.

As I recovered, there was still no guarantee that the surgery had been successful. And to make matters more stressful, they had to place me on an amputee ward, because the other floors were full. It was frightening to see the patients in the other beds. Every day I saw people facing a life with only one leg. I knew that I might be one of them someday. Even now, no one can say that the infection won't reappear. It's never gone, only dormant, the experts all agree.

Because of the schedule of infusions, and possibly due to the antibiotics themselves, I wasn't sleeping much. I spent a lot of time crying. I felt as though I had been abandoned *again*. Jess spent three days at home working and three or four days on the road and in hotels. And no matter how often I was with her or my parents or Devin and his dad, I felt alone and scared, away from everything familiar. And once again I was taking backward steps in order to move forward. The few hard-won forms of independence I had gotten back since the accident were temporarily gone, and for all I knew, gone forever. My body was hurting, and once again I worried about how my life would turn out.

Jess was doing all that was humanly possible to work and be with me. Larry brought Devin a few times. My sister and my parents also came to visit after the two surgeries, but it seemed that everyone but me had gone back to their "normal" life.

It was exhausting for everyone, but especially for Jess. She tried so hard to keep my spirits up and convince me that I was in the best place doing the right thing. She kept reminding me that home would still be there when this was over and if we could get through this, we could get through anything. But I wasn't convinced. I was still mourning all that I had lost. I had survived the accident and the nursing home and had been in my own home for so few months, and now this! It seemed like an outrageous setback. I was sad and angry. I was starting to realize in physical therapy just how dependent I was going to be for the rest of my life, that I would never get back to the life that I'd had before the accident. No matter how much physical therapy and pain I endured, my body had been forever crippled and the threat of infection would always haunt me. Life could turn on me and, after all my efforts, I might still lose my leg.

The reality, it has turned out, is both better and worse. There is wear and tear on joints that are not "normal" and arthritis eats away at much of the progress that I may make. I try not to think about more surgeries to replace the replacement parts and what happens when parts can't be replaced. What do I lose next? It just feels as though I am facing a never-ending battle, a never-ending worry. This is the biggest change in my life since the accident. I used to be a strong and independent woman, confident about my ability to forge my own future; but now I understand the fragility of life, how you can be one thing one day and something completely different the next.

The rehab center in Boston was amazing as a rehabilitation center. In the beginning they worked only on my leg, but they quickly realized there was more that they could help me with. They assessed my left arm and shoulder that had a minimal amount of movement; I could only move it about an inch in any direction. If they could manipulate it to a certain point, they said eventually I would be able to move it on my own to the same extent. They made me realize that if I wanted to put the time, effort and pain into it, I could have more use out of both. And of course I did.

One of the ways I was able to build myself up was to count the steps I took and push myself to go one more step the next day. If I kept pushing, I believed I would be able to walk someday. If I pushed myself even harder than the PT staff pushed, I would succeed. I actually counted the floor tiles to measure my progress–four floor tiles today, five tomorrow.

This was not a place to rest. There was constant noise and bustle around me for other patients; constant attention for my IVs, meds, Heparin shots, blood work, all kinds of bells and whistles going on and off. I learned my machines so that my roommate wasn't disturbed by the constant beep, beep, beeping when the antibiotics were finished being pumped into me. I learned to press the Pause button and wait for a nurse. If one didn't come, I would press Pause, hear it beep a few times, then pause it again until a nurse came. So I was constantly monitoring my own machines in order to be as considerate of others as I could be, especially my roommate. She was having a rough time, too.

The lack of sleep didn't help. I wept my way through many a therapy session. They tried a few sleep aids, but I was allergic to one of them, Trazodone. It made my right eye get very blurry to the point that I couldn't read. I was immediately taken off it. Ambien ended up giving me about an hour of sleep, and that was better than the fifteen minutes I had been getting.

Some of the things that helped me get through each day of that long month:
1. Trying to be present in the moment instead of thinking about what tomorrow might bring.
2. Reading.
3. Playing games I played as a child—I would see shapes and interesting patterns on the ceiling and floor tiles. Then I would study my huge wooden door. There were interesting images in the grain. Sometimes I looked out the window to see things in the clouds.
4. Watching the cars go by on the Tobin Bridge—the bridge itself was beautiful and very different from day to night and night to day.
5. Focusing on the next time someone was coming for a visit—that didn't always work well because the visit seemed so far off, even if it was only an hour away.
6. Trying to relax my body as much as I could—I brought back all I had learned about progressive relaxation. First I focused on my breathing, inhaling and expanding my belly, then exhaling and squeezing all the air out. Once I got into a good rhythm, I would start to count the breaths, inhaling to a count of six and exhaling to the same count. Then I

concentrated on my left big toe, asking the little muscles to relax. With every breath, I would try to let go of more tightness and pain. Once my left toe was as relaxed as I could get it, I would continue releasing the pain and restlessness in all my other toes one by one. Slowly I would work my way up to the top of my head.

7. Imagining I was at the ocean, my favorite place—in this process of creative visualization, I would experience the sounds of the waves and the seagulls, then let the smell of the salt air wash over me. It certainly smelled nicer than my hospital room. I wasn't always successful because of nurses coming and going or machines beeping, but when I could escape for a while, it helped a lot.

My rehab doctor, Hilary Siebens, was wonderful. She loaned me a book about staying in hospitals and asked me to critique it. I remember reading and then writing about each chapter. Because of my extensive experience in hospitals, I felt as though my written words were important to her. She seemed open to my perspective. We often discussed the book during her visits. She encouraged me to keep a notebook beside my bed to write down questions, thoughts, and concerns that I might want to share with her. One thing I wrote down that stays with me to this day: I feel like I've been crushed in a compactor into the shape of a truck.

The Heparin shots, which were needed daily to keep my blood from clotting, felt horrible. My entire belly hurt, with huge bruises, which for me is unusual because I don't bruise easily. My nurses were careful not to push the plunger in too fast. Years before the accident I learned to relax my muscles as much as I could before any needle went in, and to keep it relaxed while any fluid was being administered. Your body's normal instinct is to tighten with any pain, so this was quite a trick. The nurses were diligent about shifting from side to side so as not to overstress one area of my belly. I am grateful to them for being so caring and knowledgeable. You can be sure that a celebratory hoot and a holler arose when I was told there would be no more Heparin shots. Yippee!

Showers were amazing. I so looked forward to them, but they were a tremendous amount of work. My first shower at the Boston rehab center was actually my first real shower since the accident. It was the best thing ever! What a relief knowing they could use tape to keep dry what shouldn't get wet. It took them at least a half hour to bandage and tape my wounds. After I was protected, they put me on a plastic chair that looked a little like a commode on wheels. I wasn't able to reach all the places that needed washing, so I needed still more assistance. It was difficult to bare myself to strangers, because I am a modest person. But the feeling of a continuous flow of clean water on my skin was so wonderful that I was willing to put up with the tedious preparations and embarrassing lack of privacy.

While in the shower I remember being terrified to shave my legs. What if I should nick myself? I couldn't imagine bleeding. I was afraid to see my own blood again; I was afraid of getting an infection beyond what I was being treated for. Eventually I was able to relax about shaving myself. As I did, I remembered Jess's cousin Nancy and the way she spent hours shaving my legs with the utmost of care.

Jess brought music for me, even though my attention span rarely lasted as long as a whole song. Some might find it comforting to have a player of some sort, but for me it became too emotional. The songs brought up too many feelings, and I preferred to remain numb at that time. I wanted just to do what I needed to do and be done with it. That well of emotion was something I couldn't face while I was rehabilitating in Boston. I didn't have my trauma therapist to help me cope. Because I cried so much and couldn't sleep, they sent in a psychiatrist who performed a two-hour battery of psychological tests; we discussed my childhood and home life, but in the end, he decided I was simply homesick.

The turning point during this month-long ordeal, which became a major turning point in my new life, was the use of the rehab center's adaptive sports program. I was lucky enough to catch the last week and a half before the program ended for the season. On one of my long hallway walks I read a notice on the bulletin board that I could sign up to go outdoors with a physical therapist, be hoisted by a Hoyer lift and lowered carefully into a canoe fitted with pontoons into the Charles River. I was giddy with excitement. It was a delightful break from things like learning to use the bathroom, something more enticing than trying to walk another three tiles, stretching of my recalcitrant left arm, the grueling three-hour long sessions in the handicapped kitchen baking brownies. I was going to do something from my past that I loved. I used to be a canoe racer.

The program consists of canoeing, kayaking, and windsurfing. People of all abilities were encouraged to give it a try. I recruited Jess to come with her camera to document the experience. She got in the canoe with me and we went off with two PTs. As a former canoe racer with trophies, I was more experienced than anyone in the boat. So during the first trip out and back, I whipped them into shape. When I was asked if I wanted to go for another spin, I was ecstatic. The people on the dock timed us and were in shock when we returned. We had done almost as well as the all-male staff team. What a rush!

For the next two days, I paid a handsome price for my efforts, but it was worth it. Four days later I tried kayaking, which I still do today with a lot of Jess's help. She unloads the boats off the top of the car. Then at the water, she steadies the boat and helps me maneuver into it. Often when I get tired or hurt, she is there with a tow rope. I don't know how long my shoulder will allow me to do this, but until that bitter end, I'm going to enjoy every second of my freedom on the water.

As challenging as it was for me on many levels, I remain amazed at the quality of care and the compassion of the entire staff, from doctors to housekeeping.

Post Traumatic Stress

We were watching the TV show *Third Watch*, the episode in which the character of Bobby is shot by his best friend from childhood. Jess and I were crying an ocean of tears as the EMTs did their work and he was taken to the emergency room. It was too close to home for us: the surgery, his flashbacks, the reactions of his mother and friends to the surgeon telling them he was gone. Watching it on TV brought my own experience back so strongly, especially watching someone lying there helpless, with tubes in him. The scenes in the chapel were so real. I know my parents spent a lot of time there. The confusion played out by actors on a TV show gave me a glimpse of what everyone went through, as well as what the ER activity must have looked like. I remember everything moving fast and yet in slow motion at the same time. Someone creating the show had clearly had first-hand knowledge.

My Post-Traumatic Stress, or PTSD, is triggered often by TV shows, but also when I'm a passenger in a car. If we stop suddenly, I flash back to it all. Sometimes lying in bed at home, I'll hear squealing brakes and it makes my heart race. There are many reminders every day.

Even after all the surgeries I had to go through, each one left me feeling utterly helpless, knowing they would set me back. I knew I needed the two Boston surgeries to save my right leg, but they still made me feel like I was going backwards. I had to start all over again re-learning to walk. I had been walking a bit in PT, doing stairs and all, when a hip replacement interrupted my progress. After recovery and being given weight-bearing status once again, I was a week into attempting to walk when my hip dislocated. It was excruciating. And it meant weeks of healing and months before I'd be walking again. When my hip was good to go, I needed to have a huge surgery on my right foot to make it stable. I was in two hard casts for ten weeks and then a walking cast. So once again I had to build the muscles back and learn to walk. I was always thankful, but my frustration level was ever increasing. I have asked doctors about the reason for the continuous need for surgeries. The first answer is the most common: Few people survive as many breaks and fractures as you have. The next answer is quite logical to me: When you have that many breaks, it's like putting Humpty Dumpty together again. Few bones are where they are meant to be, and because of the many misalignments, you are left with opportunities for future breaks and wear.

Each and every time, the helplessness was overwhelming. It took so much out of me. Everything was frustrating. A part of me just wanted to lie there in bed and want nothing! I didn't want to bother all of my already stressed-out family and friends. I didn't want to try to walk again. I didn't want to take up space. There was a little girl inside of me that was stamping her feet. "Stop! Pay attention to only me! I'm scared and I'm hurting. Can't you see I need someone to tell me that everything will be okay?" My inner child wanted someone to magically roll back time and erase that horrible car accident.

There was so much energy I had to put out, always having to strive, to push, to be charming and entertaining, and on top of all that, to be brave, too! Just waking up in the middle of the night to go to the bathroom seemed like a mountain that I would have to climb. Every single morning was excruciating. Everything felt swollen and tight. There were times I could almost ignore all of this when I was doing something like beading a necklace which involves my body as well as my mind, however, sometimes a simple conversation would be a challenge, and I was still struggling to read. After one chapter, the pain was often too distracting to continue. I could only read for short periods of time.

One night, just as I was falling asleep, I was startled by the sound of glass breaking. I thought perhaps it was the cat knocking something over, so I listened intently for a few moments. When I heard the same sharp sound of shattering glass a second time, I began struggling to get out of bed, not wanting to wake Jess. As I slipped my feet into my sandals, I distinctly heard Devin crying and calling to me in a frightened baby voice, "Mommy, Mommy, Mommy!" Quickly I slid into my wheelchair. As I rolled down the hall, I heard it again. "Mommy. Mommy. Help me!" I moved toward his bedroom thinking he was having a nightmare of the accident or worse, and I was still curious about the breaking glass. "Oh, well," I thought. "I'll figure out what broke later. He needs me."

But when I opened his door, he was sleeping soundly. I realized that I was having a flashback just before going into deep sleep. This flashback, however, was more real than any other I'd had. The sound of the glass shattering, twice, was so real. Devin's voice was as clear as could be, crying out for me. When I realized there was no present danger, I felt shaken and sick to my stomach. My adrenalin was pumping and my heart was racing. I was shocked to the core that something from so long ago could come to the present as a new experience. My body was ready to take on the world for my child. It took me some time to get back to sleep. I couldn't stop thinking how completely my brain and body had been tricked by this flashback. It was frightening that it could take me so far from reality.

That flashback remains a part of me years later. I am blown away by the vividness of it. It remains one of the few memories I have of the actual moment of impact. I have had many flashbacks featuring smell, sensations, and sounds that are brief and pass like an ugly dream that you can't quite shake. The memory of the cold metal piercing my body also remains vivid to this day. But all these have taken place in a matter of seconds. This one of the shattering glass and my son crying out lasted for many minutes. It is one of the reasons that this book has taken so long to write. When Jess reads chapters to me for editing, we both end up in tears; so many passages bring the reality flooding back as if it were again that Sunday afternoon in June.

Sometimes it's the difficulty breathing that gets my attention. Breathing is still work. The scar tissue from my collapsed lungs and broken ribs restricts my breath. And ribs don't get set like arms and legs, so they don't necessarily heal straight. They feel crammed and are out of place. I get pains that feel like a heart attack, but I now know it's just my crazy new ribs. Yet I am doing pretty well despite the constant pain. And yesterday, Jess took down the ramp that she built for me. A friend built new stairs that are like a curving waterfall. Each stair is wide enough to rest the wheelchair and the steps have a shallow rise to make bumping up the wheelchair easy. It's scary without the ramp, but it's exciting to see a part of the house looking less like the house that I returned to after the accident. I may need a ramp again in the future, but for now I am going enjoy the look of my new stairs.

Photo Journal

Gayle one year before the accident.

When the fire chief of Hancock, MA, Dave Rash, approached the scene, he thought that no one could possibly have survived such an accident.

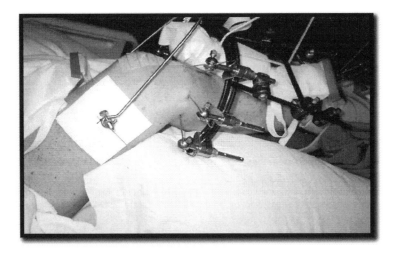

The force of the impact combined with Gayle's determination to stop the car exploded 6" off her right femur and crushed her right foot. Her left leg suffered multiple breaks and was secured by this ex-fixator. It was in traction for several months.

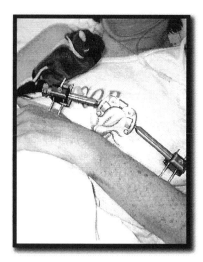

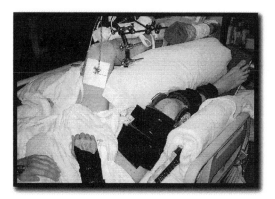

Her left shoulder was and remains dislocated. She lost 2" from her left arm
and it also was secured with an ex-fixator. Both wrists were broken,
and very little was left of her right knee.

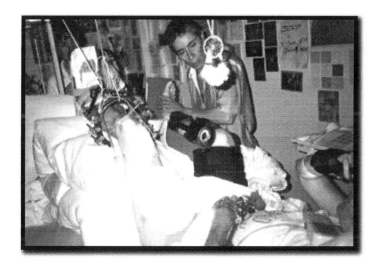

Gayle's first occupational therapist, Jan, was most creative. She gave her Kleenex to tear.
She struggled to make 10 rips in one-ply tissue by the time Jan returned the next day.

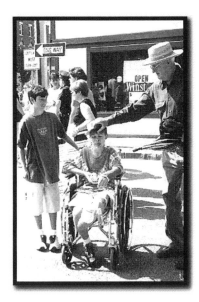

Gayle's son Devin was twelve when the accident happened. He sustained twelve breaks and fractures including his nose, toes, left arm, and wrist, and his left ankle just above the growth plate. Here he is at the Pittsfield, MA 4th of July parade. Behind him is his grandfather and on his lap is his niece. (Left) His friend Tim helps with the wheelchair.

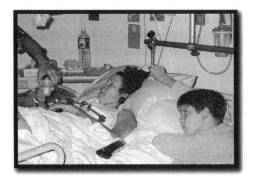

Visits from Devin were the highlight of this mom's painful days.

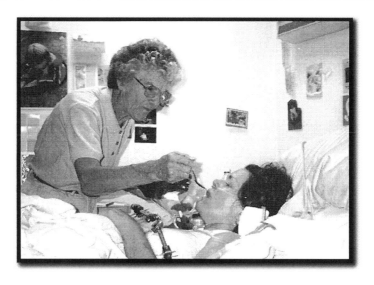

Gayle's mom feeding her in the nursing home.

An "outing" with her dad to the parking lot of the nursing home was exhausting.

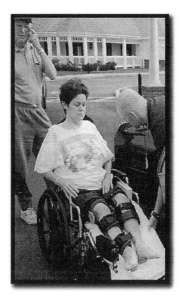

Physical therapy at the nursing home was grueling. Later we discovered that
trying to hold up her weight with two broken wrist, a broken elbow, and a
dislocated shoulder was certainly ill advised. And getting into the car
for a home visit was frightening for many reasons.

Leaving the nursing home for our own home was euphoric.

"Grandma" Lil was there to welcome Gayle home. For over a year, she came for a weekly visit, each time bringing bakery treats. Now she's called "the cookie lady". The living room became Gayle's bedroom. When it was party time, it all happened there. Before she got a stair lift to return to her upstairs bedroom, she hosted her father's birthday in November, her mother's in March and her own in April. And yes, the Christmas tree was in her bedroom that year too.

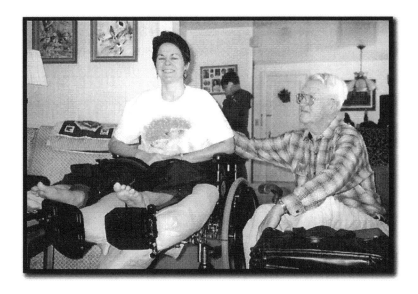

Gayle's first visit to her parent's house.

With a little imagination, Gayle was able to participate in the annual
selection of the Christmas tree. Jess takes her turn as the horse for the sleigh.

The summer after the accident, Gayle's doctors discovered an infection in her right leg. She underwent two surgeries a week apart in Boston. There was an unexpected month-long stay at a nearby rehab center right after the surgeries. Devin was back playing soccer and visited before going to a tryout for an Olympic summer camp in the area.

Well into her rehab stay, Gayle was told that she could get in a canoe and paddle the Charles. After getting outfitted, the PTs hooked her up to a Hoyer lift which took her up, swung her out and over the canoe, then slowly lowered her into the waiting boat. It was a stellar day!

When her daughter, Rebecca, graduated from college, Gayle was there. And when Jess threw a surprise birthday party for her, three Lanesborough Fire & Rescue chiefs came.

Gayle and Jess missed both their June vacations with the kids and their own in November, but the following November they were able to go. Jess, a/k/a "MacGyver", rigged her Canadian crutches with discs for added stability. And Jess was at the ready with the wheelchair.

Devin continued to work through his injuries and over the years his soccer skills got him on the Taconic High School varsity team. In his senior year, he was co-captain.

Gayle can only stand and walk for short periods of time and spends most of her days in a wheelchair, but still she goes to some pretty fabulous places. Here she is at the Epona Center in Sonoita, AZ where she experienced communicating with a horse named Kairos.

Gayle enjoyed a windy night in Boston watching the Red Sox.

Gayle looks forward to her annual "walks" along the beach. If it weren't for her equus therapy, she wouldn't have been able to build the strength and stamina it takes to stand and walk on occasion. Here she is showing her gratitude to one of the horses.

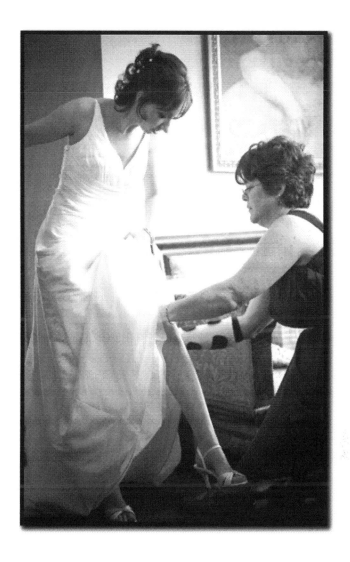

After the accident, Gayle promised Rebecca that she would walk down the aisle at her wedding. Fortunately for Gayle, Rebecca married in 2008 giving her time to make enough improvements in her gait and build the necessary strength. Despite an arm surgery the week before, Gayle steadied herself on Devin's arm and made it gracefully down the aisle. The inn that Rebecca and Glenn chose was beautiful and the aisle was blessedly short. It was a gorgeous wedding and a memorably happy day for all.

Chapter 6: Interviews

Dave Rash, Fire Chief of Hancock, MA

Dave Rash joined the Hancock Fire Department when he was eighteen. For the past twelve years, he has been their Chief, persevering despite a dramatic increase in government regulations, paperwork, and training. Dave and his team of volunteers were at the scene.

Gayle: Dave, do you have a memory of the accident?

Dave: Yes, I do.

Jess: Were you at the station when the call came in regarding the accident?

Dave: No. We're very seldom at the station when a call goes out. I can't remember where I was that day, probably home when the call came in for mutual aid for a motor vehicle accident.

Jess: When they say "mutual aid," is that a tip off that it's a really bad accident?

Dave: Well, for us...maybe I need to give a little background before answering that question. Quite a few years ago there was a very bad accident in Williamstown, and there were no Jaws of Life or vehicle extrication tools available, so Village Ambulance started a grass roots fundraiser and purchased a set of jaws. So Williamstown ran the jaws from the Village Ambulance for many years, then as they got busier and busier, often with the rig going out of town, they'd take the jaws out of the ambulance. That way the jaws would be in the bay and available if a call came in. There was some political wrangling for a while, and the Williamstown chief at that time decided he didn't want the jaws on any of his trucks. I'm not sure why, but perhaps he didn't want the responsibility. At any rate, Village offered the jaws up to us at the Hancock Fire Department if we would agree to include Williamstown and New Ashford in our charter. We, of course, agreed, so we took the jaws and have been carrying them ever since. When it comes to Williamstown, we respond mostly to the southern corridor, which is where your accident happened. So to answer the question, it's not always because of the severity of the accident.

Gayle: Was Hancock the first on the scene?

Dave: No. Lanesborough was. There was a little confusion as to who should respond, so we both did.

Gayle: I really was lucky then!

Dave: Yes, you were! As it turned out, it took two sets of jaws to get you out.

Gayle: Where were the jaws placed?

Dave: By the time we got there, Lanesborough had the roof off of your car, and they were trying to do what we call a "dash push."

Gayle: Pushing the dashboard away from me?

Dave: You actually push the dash up to create more room in the leg area of the vehicle. We were trying to get you out without creating more damage.

Gayle: That makes sense.

Dave: Your car was so crumpled up that there was no solid place to push from. When we tried to push the dash up, the floor was going down instead of the dash going up. So we put our set of jaws on the other side of their unit and between the two sets, we were able to get you out.

Gayle: So I was in the middle of both Jaws of Life?

Dave: Yes.

Jess: Wow! That's impressive!

Gayle: That is amazing! Now, Dave, when that was happening, where were you?

Dave: I was in the middle of it.

Gayle: I have no memory of any of this. I have flashbacks, but I don't remember it, fortunately or unfortunately.

Jess: So if you didn't have the two sets of jaws, you might not have gotten Gayle out?

Dave: Oh, we would have gotten her out. There's no question about that, but the speed of the extrication would have been diminished and the injuries may have increased.

Gayle: I know that minutes in the ER were crucial. Minutes were important in where they chose to send the helicopter. Apparently, Albany is a minute or two closer than Springfield. So minutes must also be crucial on your end.

Dave: Yes, very much so.

Gayle: When you first came on the scene, do you remember what you thought?

Dave: I thought that the person in that car couldn't be alive! (Short pause) Lanesborough was doing everything they could, so when we arrived, we just jumped in to help. They were making the calls since they were first on the scene and already knew what needed to be done. They just hollered to us to get our jaws set up and running and we did.

Gayle: Was I conscious?

Dave: Yes.

Gayle: Was I talking?

Dave: (Long pause and no answer)

Jess: Was Devin still in the car at that point?

Dave: No. He was out of the car by the time I got there.

Gayle: So your first impression was that no one could have survived, but they were working probably at a fast pace.

Dave: Yup! So we knew we were needed.

Gayle: Do you ever hear what happens to the people that you help?

Dave: Not often…a lot of people that we go and treat, you never hear anything more about them.

Gayle: How does that make you feel?

Dave: It's very difficult. You have to let it go, even more so now with the patient privacy act. That has made it very hard to find out how a patient is doing. The way we have to look at it is, we did our best and we just have to let it go at that. You pray for the people, and hope for the best.

Gayle: There must be a lot more than just the privacy act that has changed your job over the years. How do you keep working as a firefighter with things like the privacy act? I'm sure there's more red tape.

Dave: It's ongoing with no end in sight. I think if I tried to become a firefighter now with all that you have to do, I probably wouldn't. Because I started at such an early time in my life when all you did was run in and put out fires, I eased into the EMS side of it. And because Hancock has no ambulance, we rely on

Williamstown for the EMS expertise.

Gayle: But you're often there first?

Dave: Yes. We roll on all medical calls as first responders. Our job is to stabilize the patients until more qualified personnel get there. So it's a challenge to do what I do. I think to do what I do, you just got to have it in your blood. The frame of mind that you have to have is simply to go out and help other people and expect nothing in return. That's just the way it is. You're either that kind of person or you're not.

Gayle: That certainly does make you a special person.

Dave: (Shrugs his shoulders.) It's just in my blood.

Jess: I threw a big party for Gayle on her 49th birthday to celebrate her courage. I invited as many healers and helpers as I could think of at the time, and three chiefs from Lanesborough came in full dress. They were in tears when they saw Gayle come in on her walking sticks. Then she went up to hug them and thank them. They all agreed that you don't usually get to connect later with the people that you help. They said that it was such a treat!

Dave: For sure!

Gayle: One of the responders from Lanesborough recognized me from twenty years before when I worked at the Olde Forge (a local restaurant). It's such a small community. You must often recognize the people who are in trouble.

Dave: Yes. And you certainly see a lot of people at their worst.

Gayle: So how do you separate your feelings from the work you have to do?

Dave: I think a lot of it is in the training. You're trained to react a certain way. Whether it's a fire or an accident, you're trained to do whatever it takes to make the situation better. Our main training is to stabilize the person. When it's all over, then the emotions hit us.

Jess: So you've been trained, in a way, to stuff your feelings until your work is done?

Dave: We're not so much trained to hold back our feelings. We're trained to just do our work. We spend many hours practicing. We practice going out to put out fires. We practice CPR and oxygen, and the whole nine yards. So when you go out on a call, your training kicks in. You're working on what you've been practicing. After the situation is stable and the EMTs have taken over, that's when the thought process kicks in and you feel the emotion.

Gayle: How do you cope with that emotion?

Dave: (Long pause.) I don't know. I just do.

Gayle: Do you take a deep breath? Go home to your wife? Do you go for a walk?

Dave: (Another long pause) Carry on. I think to some degree, routine is important. For me, it is. You can't keep dwelling on what's in the past.

Jess: Returning to routine was what helped us cope.

Gayle: Sometimes it was getting back to old routines. Other times we had to create new routines, like in the nursing home, Jess would bring in a dinner from home for the kids and us. That was something I could set my clock by and was so helpful as a coping mechanism. It was something that helped me get through the rough moments. I could say to myself, "Well, tomorrow, or in a couple hours, we're having our family meal together. That will be wonderful!"

Dave: Routine is good.

Gayle: When you respond to an accident, is there someone that is usually in charge?

Dave: Yes, usually a police officer is in charge at the scene, and we just do what we're told.

Jess: We're having trouble getting pictures of the accident because the one in the paper wasn't by one of their photographers, and the front cover is going to be a picture of the wreck while the back cover is going to be a picture of Gayle on horseback.

Dave: (Pulls out a packet of photos and looks at and talks to Gayle while he hands them to Jess.) I don't know if you're going to want to look at these.

Gayle: (Tearing up and speaking softly as she takes Dave's hands.) Thank you for saving my life.

Dave: (Also tearing up.) We do what we can do.

Gayle: It certainly has been a journey, and I've met so many wonderful caring people. (Laughter) It's a heck of a way to meet people!

Dave: If you're interviewing people from fire departments and ambulance squads, those are the kind of people you're going to meet. People who don't have that attitude towards others and life, aren't in that profession. They may start it thinking it's a job with prestige, but when the rubber meets the road, so to speak, that's when you can tell the ones that are truly in it for helping. They're not there for the show. It's truly a mindset you have to have to be in this profession, to be willing to continually go out and help people. That's not just what you do, it's who you are.

Gayle: It's what you were meant to do.

Dave: Exactly.

Gayle: But the stress and the burnout must be tremendous.

Dave: Yes. There's an organization now called Critical Incident Stress Debriefing that's available to emergency squad people, and it's highly recommended by anybody who's been through anything like your accident to have a session two or three days after. They found that in paid departments where people would go to traumatic incidents or house fires where it was particularly difficult…firefighters especially…that day after day after day…they'd just keep plowing through this stuff. Even though it may not show immediately, there is mental stress that builds up. There was one story of a firefighter who had a traumatic experience, and it was four or five years later that he just went off the deep end. Well, they dove into it and found it was related to what had happened four or five years earlier. He had carried that stress around for so long, and one small incident brought it all back.

Gayle: My ex-husband was in Viet Nam and is working on what they call Post-Traumatic Stress Disorder.

Dave: So they've set up these teams to help.

Jess: We'd like to take part of the proceeds from this book and make a donation, but we haven't decided where. This organization sounds perfect.

Dave: That would be great. They have meetings where trained people come in and help you talk about what happened. And there's a hard and fast rule: What's said in the meeting, stays in the meeting. There's no point of blame. It's just a time to try and get everything out in the open. The trainers are very keen on saying, "You didn't cause the situation that happened. You went to make the situation better."

Gayle: Right.

Dave: So through discussion, venting, whatever it takes, people go away better able to cope.

Jess: We were appalled that on Gayle's end there was no trauma counseling available. Insurance paid for the trauma to her body, but we had to hire someone out of pocket to help Gayle deal with the trauma done to her heart, her life.

Dave: It's an important part of the healing.

Gayle: Dave, how do you help someone who is new to the job and comes on to an accident like mine?

Dave: I guess reassurance, but you never throw a rookie into a situation where he's the only one there. That's where training is so important. If a rookie is performing to the level of his training, the only thing you can do is reassure him, "You did the right thing." (Long pause) I don't know if you're religious or not, but I think to a certain degree that all things aren't in our hands. Sometimes it's just not meant to be, and you lose someone. In your case, it wasn't your time.

Gayle: I agree!

Jess: Gayle got a card in the hospital that said, "Did you ever think that maybe your guardian angel went out for a smoke? Hope you're getting better."

(Laughter)

Gayle: Yeah. She must have blinked.

Jess: But then she must have called in all her favors, because everything happened perfectly. All the right people showed up at the right time and did more than their best. If you look at the pictures, you know that she shouldn't have survived. But as you say…

Dave: You look at those pictures…(Choking up a bit)…I think you're right.

Gayle: Dave, what other memories would you like to share?

Dave: I guess that after the whole thing was over, I was just hoping you'd make it. I prayed for a miracle. It's great to see how far you've come. You're getting your life back together. For me, it's answered prayers.

Gayle: Thank you.

Dave: It's amazing that people like you, who have gone through the trauma and heartbreak that you've gone through, are the people who want to give something in return. The people that never have this happen to them, never get into the frame of mind that they need to give anything back. It's a shame.

Gayle: But even before the accident, I've always wanted to reach out. That didn't go away just because helping is more difficult now.

Dave: It's in your blood.

Gayle: Was it the worst day of my life? Or the best? I think everything fell into place for it to be my best.

Dave: That's a gutsy way of looking at it.

Jess: (Laughter) She's one gutsy lady!

Dave: For sure. How is your son doing?

Gayle: Great! He played soccer six months later. He pushed hard. He's just a nice person to be around, very helpful, very funny.

Dave: That's good.

Gayle: Is there something you would like to say to drivers?

Dave: Yes. When people get behind the wheel they need to realize that it's a huge responsibility. It's getting worse with cell phones, MP3 players, and all the other distractions that are available to drivers today. Driving's a full time job, and to do it safely, you can't be distracted. Many people don't look at it that way.

Jess: It's just a means to an end.

Dave: You're right. Many people are just looking at getting where they want to go. Maybe they don't teach that it's a responsibility any more. Seat belts are important, and fortunately, it's a law in Massachusetts and New York. Handheld cell phones are still allowed in Massachusetts. I hope that changes soon.

Gayle: I do, too. Well, thank you for your time, Dave. You were very generous.

Dave: You're more than welcome. It's good to see you upright and doing so well.

Elise, X-Ray Technician

In all the years since the accident, from coming in to Dr. Hospodar's office on a gurney to walking in on my sticks, this particular x-ray technician has always been there. She is empathetic, and loves to make us laugh.

Gayle: What do you remember when I first started coming here?

Elise: No matter what we did, we hurt you.

Gayle: That must have been difficult.

Elise: Well, we do our best to make the patient comfortable, despite the pain they are in and the additional pain we cause in moving them this way and that in order to get the necessary pictures. That's the downside of the job. The upside is that day in and day out, we see people improving.

Gayle: Oh, that's so true.

Elise: So many patients come in terribly injured, and they're thinking, "Oh, my life is over!" So we have to think of creative ways to move them because they are already in so much pain. I mean…you were a wreck. Didn't you break every bone in your poor body?

Gayle: (Laughter) Almost!

Elise: (Pokes Jess's arm) Hey, aren't you glad her face wasn't trashed? (All laughing!) "Hey, honey, I love you, but…"

Jess: I love your sick sense of humor.

Elise: You've got to have a sense of humor. I've been doing this for twenty-two years. There's so much change, and many techs burn out quickly.

Gayle: I've seen a good number in this department come and go.

Elise: This office is so busy. We can see 300 patients in one day!

Jess: Holy smokes!

Elise: Well now, there's a good side to that. If you don't like a patient, they're gone soon and you're on to the next. (Laughter) But don't get me wrong; you have to work with compassion. Some of the people you see are so injured.

Jess: Do you remember in the beginning when Gayle came in on a gurney with the EMTs?

Elise: Yes. And there was no place to touch you that didn't hurt.

Gayle: You know, one time I got a tech that was a little rough with me and the EMT got very protective. She gave him "what for" and wouldn't leave the room.

Elise: She probably glows in the dark because of you! (Laughter) Is that tech still here?

Gayle: No.

Elise: You see, he just wasn't cut out for this work.

Jess: Were you surprised that Gayle improved the way she did?

Elise: Not surprised at all! Gayle's got a good head on her shoulders, and she's a mom. You have to get better. People who are upbeat like you, Gayle, heal faster. It was a hell of a ride, but I knew you'd make it. You were always updating me about your son, and asking about my kids.

Gayle: How do you keep from thinking about all the pain you see at work when you go home?

Elise: That's easy. I have adopted special needs children. I can't bring this job home with me. I've got too much to do once I get home.

Gayle: My goodness, you're amazing!

Elise: They're great kids.

Jess: Did you know that Gayle's been riding horses for PT?

Elise: Oh, that's wonderful. You know, there was an article in the Times Union about some people rescuing horses. I think there's a copy of it in the deli downstairs.

Gayle: Well, that's where we're headed next. We'll be sure to read it. And thank you for taking a few minutes out of your busy day to talk with us.

Elise: My pleasure. And good luck with the book. It sounds like it's going to be very helpful to a lot of people.

Jess: That's our hope.

Elise: All right then. I'll see you guys in a few months.

Gayle: I hope you're still here.

Elise: I will be. You guys take care, and don't forget to read that article.

Jess: For sure!

Tootie (Cynthia) Boudreau,

Gayle's First Out-Patient Physical Therapist

Tootie did her undergraduate study at Hamilton College in Clinton, NY and got her Masters of Science in Physical Therapy from Widener College in Chester, PA. At the time of the interview she was working as a PT in the Catskills area and is considering creating an Equus Center with her husband. She has two horses and three dogs. Gayle worked with her while she was at Family & Sports PT in Lanesborough, MA. She is an insightful healer who quickly became a friend. It was apparent from the first session with her that she possessed a strength of character that inspired immediate trust.

Jess: What were your thoughts when you first saw Gayle as a physical therapy client?

Tootie: The first thing I remember is the amount of information that Gayle gave me. There were packets upon packets upon packets of medical history. Still to this day, I have never spent so much time combing through records to understand a client. I feel a lot of people will flip through and skirt the issues, but I feel it's important to read through every little cotton-picking detail. In your case, nothing was silly. Everything I read was integral to your therapy. I had to understand what had happened to you. It took me two to three hours just to get through the history. Working in private practice, you don't get paid for a lot of the things you do. I remember taking it home and reading and reading and reading and thinking, "Oh, my goodness! What are we going to do? Where do we start?"

Gayle: I was still such a mess.

Tootie: When I knew you were coming to interview me, I thought of what some of the questions might be, like how would I know you would succeed? And how would I assure you? And what could I say that would make you think you were going to come out okay?

Jess: That's a great couple of questions.

Tootie: One of the things that I noticed about you immediately was that you are a healer, and healers heal fast and heal well.

Jess: You mean a healer that heals others?

Tootie: Yes, and likes to help people and is good at that. It's not so much what your line of work is, because I know that you both do forms of alternative medicine, it's the kind of person who enjoys doing things for other people and has success doing that, especially the kind of person who helps other people feel good about themselves in some way. That's what I mean by a healer, and you obviously have healed so many people. So I knew that no matter what, if I could instill confidence in you, you would get better.

Gayle: That's what I felt about you the first time you worked on me, total trust. I knew that I could just relax and follow your lead and listen to what you had to say. I knew that you could help me communicate to this new body of mine. I trusted you so much. You were the first to help me maneuver outside of the house. When I began working with you, I was afraid of everything.

Jess: Gayle has had many wonderful PTs, but we knew we needed to interview you for this book.

Tootie: Well, thank you. That is a compliment that I will hold with me forever. When people asked me what I was going to do today, because of the HIPAA laws I didn't mention your name. I said, "My most complicated patient ever is coming to interview me for a book that she and her partner are writing." I would never have said that you were my most difficult patient, because you weren't. You were easy to work with, a delight and a pleasure. But you had, my God, 123 breaks and fractures! That number still sticks in my head! And it's been over three years! A hundred and twenty-three breaks and fractures! It was easy to get you to trust and go along with my ideas.

Jess: How did you know what to work on first? Was it intuitive? Schooled?

Tootie: I would say, even to this day, I didn't learn jack in school. (Much laughter!) The truth is, I went to a fabulous school, and I learned a lot. It's one of the top in the nation in all the reviews. But you really don't know squat until you're out in the field, until you experience some of this stuff yourself. I think for me, what makes me a decent therapist is that a lot of injuries that people come in with, I can say, "I've been there! I've had that!" Now, have I had 123 breaks and fractures? No! But did I have a few of the things that Gayle had? Yes! One of the times was when I herniated three discs in my back and experienced paralysis in my left leg. To me it seemed life-threatening. Was it life-threatening at the time? No! But I was a high-level athlete. When I sustained this injury, I was playing college basketball. And I was reduced to a completely dependent person. I could not walk. I could not get to my classes. I had to get the security people to pick me up at my door and drive me to class.

Jess: So you understood what Gayle had lost.

Tootie: Yes! Lots of times I couldn't even make it through class. I remember talking to my professors and saying, "I don't know if I'm going to make it through the class so if you see me getting up and lying down or standing against the wall, it's because I can't sit in those chairs." Had I experienced anything remotely like what Gayle had experienced? No, but most therapists are healthy human beings who haven't had injuries or limitations. Maybe they were in a cast for a few weeks, but that's not the same.

Gayle: That makes perfect sense! That explains so much of why I trusted you so quickly. You'd been there.

Jess: In Yoga teacher training, I came in with a cast on my arm and one of the teachers actually said, "Oh, thank God!" I said, "Thanks for the sympathy." My feelings were hurt until she said, "You're going to be a better Yoga teacher now. You had no limitations. You weren't going to understand people who do." It was such a small injury, but there were things I couldn't do.

Tootie: I think those things make you more human. And, yes, I had a lot of little injuries growing up, but that back injury changed my life. It made me know that PT was going to be a good career for me. Prior to that, I was hemming and hawing between PT and going on to medical school. That injury plus a PT internship that I did at Burke Rehab Center. You may have heard of it. It's very famous and just outside of New York City in White Plains. At the time that I interned, it was rated the third in the nation. It was an incredible place. I had two units. One was respiratory and the other was amputees. My work was comparable to what is now a CNA. Once your shift was over, you had to remain there, you know me. I had to be busy in some way, so I would just hang with the PT people. And wow! They were amazing! They were the ones who were talking to patients and helping and fixing. And every time I'd work with a doctor, we'd zoom in and out of all these rooms, and he would sign papers and prescriptions. Sometimes he'd say a quick, "Hey, how ya doin'?" "I feel terrible." "Okay, here's a prescription," and walk out of the patient's room. I thought, "I don't want to do this! This is terrible!"

Gayle: How discouraging!

Tootie: These doctors weren't taking any time with their patients, and things only got worse with the balanced budget act and the invention of HMOs. I spend my days talking to nurses and secretaries instead of doctors. I could be calling with a question about a client at death's door and still get a secretary or a nurse. "I need to speak to the doctor now!" And still sometimes they will give me a hard time. So sometimes I'm embarrassed with the medical system that I am a part of, but on the other hand, I know I can do a good job doing what I'm supposed to do. But I digress.

Jess: It's a good and relevant digression. The book isn't just Gayle's story. She wants it to be helpful in many ways.

Gayle: And we certainly have had our share of difficulties with doctors and certainly with "the system" and with insurance. We write about that in the book because we hope others can avoid some of the problems we encountered if we address the issues.

Tootie: Well, nonetheless, I think the reason you trusted me, Gayle, was because I had been through something similar. And that experience of being dependent made me more human. The doctors in the ER said to me at that time, "You're never playing basketball again. And you're certainly never going to run again. And you might not walk again." My response to that was, "You know what! Forget about you! I'm going to do what I want to do! And I am going to play basketball." And I did. And you had that same spirit in you. I knew you'd be walking again. And I knew you'd be on a horse someday.

Jess: So you weren't surprised today to see her get out of the car and walk with her sticks today?

Tootie: Of course not. I knew you'd be walking. It didn't even cross my mind. There was never a thought that you wouldn't.

Gayle: Obviously I have dismissed a lot of what some doctors have said, but there's still a certain amount of trusting my own body that comes in to play. In the winter and in mud season, walking outdoors is a little scary. But there's a part of me that isn't going to accept these limitations.

Tootie: I think a lot of physical therapy can be equated with athletics in that it's 80% heart and 10% physical ability and the last 10% conditioning. Same thing is true of PT. You may say to yourself, "Am I going to run that marathon? No." But if you see that big expanse of ice or big bog of mud, you'll say, "I AM going to walk through that." And damn it, you do it! I knew that if I firmly and gently pushed you to do things, that you would do what I asked. And you have.

Jess: To this day, I remember leaving Gayle off with you at PT to do some errands. It was a beautiful sunny day in spring, and when I came back, you had Gayle walking outside and doing the three stairs at the end of the sidewalk.

Gayle: My first stairs! And I remember the look on my parents' faces.

Tootie: Yup! I remember your father the first time you walked, with him following with the wheelchair. It was the most incredible thing!

Gayle: It was that level of trust that you weren't going to ask me to do something before my body was ready. And more important, that you weren't going to hold me back either.

Jess: I had faith in you, too. I would't leave to do errands with anyone but you.

Tootie: The thing to recognize here is that it's good to push a patient a little bit beyond their mental limits, but not beyond their physical limits. Also, in recognizing that you might put not only the patient in danger, but put yourself in danger as well.

Gayle: Oh, yes! Remember when I stumbled a little on the rug because I didn't lift my foot high enough? I remember starting to fall, and you were like a cat. I don't know if your back hurt after that or not, but you moved so fast. You were under me before I had a chance to hit the floor.

Tootie: Right. And you have to be able to know that…

Gayle: Did you get hurt? I don't remember.

Tootie: No, because I was ready for it. We always give what we call "contact guard". It's when you're touching the patient but not really helping them. I always give a little more than that. Had I not been there and simply walking beside you, you would have been down. I prefer to be extra safe rather than sorry. And had I been walking next to you, I would have had to jump across and probably would have hurt myself in trying to save you.

Gayle: I didn't get hurt at all.

Tootie: That's because I put my hands in such a way that I knew that if you did stumble, I wouldn't be holding on to something that had been broken.

Gayle: That's true.

Tootie: You see, all that reading of your packets paid off. I knew which shoulder was broken, which wrist, which elbow, which ribs had the problems. There were so many things. I'm amazed that I remember all these things! (Laughter) It's been three and a half years, and most of that stuff is still in my head. There were very few patients in my entire history as a PT that I would have thought, or come right out and said, "I don't want anyone else to touch that patient." You were one of them. I just didn't trust that anyone else had taken the time to review those records and would really know what was okay and what wasn't. Was I comfortable with others doing certain things with you? Sure. But learning transfers from your wheelchair and the more difficult things like walking and stairs, I wasn't comfortable with that. They could do some joint mobilization, some massage and that kind of thing, because it didn't put you in jeopardy. Yeah, you were one of the ones I said, "Mine!"

Jess: How did meeting Gayle and working with her for the length of time that you did change you? Did it change your life as a person? As a therapist?

Tootie: Well, her case is imprinted in me forever. I will never forget all those little things that I read about. It's been so long and I still remember so much. I've probably had hundreds, even thousands of cases, but there's only those few patients that you remember each and every baby step with. And remember for a lifetime! Then there's the gratitude, thinking how grateful you are with the things that you have, and the lifestyle that you have and can maintain. Somebody else, like Gayle, wasn't so lucky. My sister-in-law's husband died very young. It was tragic. She was left alone with a son who is now sixteen, and Susan struggled for years and years and years. She suffered horrible depression, horrible anxiety. And every once in a while she would open up to me and say that the only thing that kept her alive was her son. And I heard that from you, Gayle. A lot! On days when you would question, "Is life worth this struggle?" I'd see you say, "But I have this son." I'd see you fight mentally, "But my son, my son. He deserves my best!"

Gayle: (In tears) You do remember a lot.

Tootie: Yes, and I knew that given a couple of years, you'd have that vibrancy back.

Gayle: I really had to hold on to the needs of my children.

Tootie: That will forever be imprinted in me as well!

Jess: What was the hardest part? Was it the day the insurance lady said Gayle was a black hole and they didn't want to put any more money into someone who wasn't going to walk again?

Tootie: Oh, God! That was just a royal pain in the butt! The real struggle for me was the daily task of getting myself up in order to convey that to Gayle. I had to have the enthusiasm that I wanted Gayle to have.

Jess: And as I recall, those weren't the best of times for you in your life.

Tootie: No. I was wrestling with a lot of things. There were a couple times, maybe you don't remember, but I had gotten into a pretty bad accident myself and was very injured for several weeks. I had been trampled by a horse, but I never missed a day of work.

Gayle: And horses are so important to you.

Tootie: Yes! It was a place in my life where I had always had control. So this one day the horse steps in a bee hive and goes berserk. I was a mess with bruises and a concussion. Now I'm at work with one of my greatest challenges, and I have to be on my game for you. The minute I walked into the room to work with you, you said, "You don't look good. Let me help you!" There were a couple days that you and Jess worked your magic. I remember thinking, "This is backwards!" (All laughing!) So this is somebody who basically died and came back and is trying to make me feel good. I thought that was not only a special moment, but a special bond that a lot of therapists don't get with their patients. You were such a caring person. It took me aback. How could someone that broken want to help me?

Jess: Well, it was a little self-serving. We want you to be at the top of your game, so we'll do what we have to do to help get you there! (Laughter) You know, Gayle actually did that in the ER.

Tootie: Why am I not surprised?

Gayle: One of the nurses or techs was visibly shaken and overwhelmed with my injuries. I was told that I was making little jokes and lots of eye contact to help him settle down so that he could do his job.

Tootie: I wouldn't call that selfish. It's just something that happens when you care for others. And I see a lot of people getting into PT for the wrong reasons. If you don't have a heart, you can't help. You can be technically the most knowledgeable PT in the world, but how much of a difference are you going to make in your patient's lives if you don't care? Sometimes it's hard to maintain your "heart" with all the junk with insurance and doctors and red tape, but it's worth it.

Gayle: I've had many who were technically impressive, but none that made me feel, "Okay! I can do this! If I can just get to Tootie today, I'll be able to get through this." Those simple little phrases were so helpful. Once we were working, it was, "Just one more step. I can take one more step." I would blank everything else out and focus on you and the work and how much I wanted you to help me get better. There's an energy between us that helped me to get out of the house, transfer into and out of the car. It was a painful process.

Tootie: Sure.

Gayle: It's hard to go do something that you know is going to hurt.

Jess: You were the one who told us about Equus Therapy. We knew nothing about it at the time. Why is it such an important part of Gayle's recovery?

Tootie: My whole life, I have known what horses can give me. They are a tremendous gift. They help keep me sane as well as happy. Currently, riding is one of two exercises that I can do that doesn't make me hurt. The other is swimming. When I am going through difficult times, the horses help me escape for a while. Those animals understand unconditional love. They not only understand it, but they practice it. Those animals love you no matter what. They're perceptive. They're receptive. The horse is the only creature alive whose gait mimics the human gait. What you haven't gotten from traditional physical therapy, you will get from riding horses. It's gait imposes components of the normal human gait on to you. It helps you get stronger. It helps your balance. Then there's what it does to the nervous system. Impulses go to the brain which then spread throughout the body telling it, "Hey, this is how I'm really supposed to walk." With repetition, you can eventually get a 'normal' walk.

Jess: It was amazing to see the improvements when Gayle first started to ride, last March. It was so much, so fast. It was a wonderful thing to witness.

Gayle: And then when I stopped riding because I had a lump on my right arm and had to have surgery, my walking quickly deteriorated. My legs felt like they were locking up. I was walking like a tin soldier again. When I'm riding, it seems that everything widens somehow, and both legs start to trust each other. I don't know if that made sense.

Tootie: Absolutely! And as you advance, you start to understand how a well-trained horse is sensitive to the smallest cue or command. As that happens, the cues that you give your own body are going to sharpen, too. Not only are you going to become a better rider, but your posture is going to get better, your balance is going to get better, not to mention, it's just dang fun!

Gayle: It is fun!

Jess: When Gayle comes home from riding, she always tells me how the ride was and how her instructor's doing, but then her mood changes and she starts talking about her horse. Whether it's Saint, or Mirage, or Sweet Pea, she talks so sweetly about them. I love it!

Tootie: The bond that you can form with that animal, who also knows that he needs to take care of you, is amazing.

Jess: Oh, Monday!

Tootie: What happened Monday?

Gayle: Mirage is a strong-minded horse and tends to fight back. He's fairly dominant in the herd there at Oak Hollow. Charm was feeling crabby, and she has her limitations. She's got great gaits, but she's a little temperamental and has been known to kick. Well, on Monday, the person riding Charm in the group lesson in the indoor ring was having a bad day and let Charm get away with a bit too much. Charm came over quickly to kick Mirage. Now normally, Mirage would have kicked right back. It all happened so fast. Linda, the instructor, shouts, "Get Charm away from Mirage!" She's so protective of me. Mirage settled down, almost clutching the earth. He knew there was no way I could have helped him. I was boxed in. So instead of kicking, he settled in and was going to take whatever Charm had in store for him. That was a first for me. He reacted in a way that protected me.

Tootie: And that's the most important characteristic you look for in a therapy horse. Now that bond is going to grow even more. You will be able to do more amazing things because of that trust.

Jess: Gayle's first instructor said something that really allowed me to understand what a horse is like, emotionally. He said that a horse is like a big dog. They'll do anything for you. If you tell them to go over the cliff, they'll go over the cliff.

Tootie: If they trust you, and if they are confident in your skills, and if you have that kind of relationship where they want to work for you. My two horses out in the coral are very young. The bigger one is not quite four. I've had her since birth, so I've done everything with her by myself. The other one just turned three and he is a rescue horse. He had basically been abandoned and abused, left out in a field to die. When he was not quite one year old, a rescue facility picked him up. He was one of five left in a field in western New York in the middle of winter.

Gayle: I just can't believe people can be like that!

Tootie: This particular rescue organization is in Claverack, New York, and is a wonderful place to get a horse. I can't say enough good things about them. So this poor guy, Logan, was one of the most difficult animals that this place ever had. He kicked the owner of this rescue place and his primary caregiver. And he hadn't kicked them just once! He wouldn't stand for the Ferrier, and he wouldn't stand for the vet. Horses will run if they are afraid, and if they can't run, they're going to kick and scream and jump around. So when we adopted him, he was pretty angry and he almost nailed me a couple of times. I'll never forget the one hot day I tried to shower him with the hose. He tried to beat me up!

Gayle: Thank God you have catlike reflexes!

Tootie: I've trained horses most of my life, so within two months time he became a kitten. Now what's interesting to watch is that he's young, he's full of himself, and he's very strong. When it's very cold, he tries to run whether there is a person on him or not. Now my husband Ken has never ever ridden, and he's taking care of Logan. He's become my husband's horse. We got him originally as a companion to my four-year-old, Sadie, but eventually I wanted to turn him into a riding horse for Ken. When I "broke" Logan, and I hate using that word because I only use kindness, it took me seven rides to do with Logan what I did with Sadie on the first ride. Because of his mistrust it took longer. I rode him twice a week for about two months, breaking him in slowly. Well, one day I came back from a ride and there's Ken standing there telling me to get off that horse. I'm saying, "What do you mean, get off that horse?" He says it again and I ask again, then he says, "I'm going to ride him." I'm starting to freak. My God! He's going to die! He doesn't know how to ride. This horse is barely trained. And Ken is wearing shorts, sneakers and doesn't have a helmet. I spent ten minutes trying to convince him not to do this, that it was very unsafe. He said, "You can't stop me. So you can either make it easy for me or hard. So I hand led Logan around the park where I'd been riding and that horse didn't flinch. He went around like a twenty-year-old therapy horse, and he was two and barely trained!

Jess: So I guess he likes Ken.

Tootie: Well, Ken is his primary caregiver and he loves him. Ken oohs and aahs over him and brushes him, and Logan just eats it right up! Once when we rode together, Ken accidentally went into a canter and I could hear him go, "Oooow whoa!" And I was ready to cut them off at the pass, but Logan hears Ken's fear and slows down. Logan is taking care of him. Now with me, he'll buck, he'll spook, he'll try to kick. Not Ken. He loves Ken. And he knows that Ken doesn't know jack about riding a horse. So basically, Logan is training Ken. They have a trusting relationship. And that's what a therapy horse will do. They will protect you. So my hope for you is that you continue to ride. It's your best therapy.

Devin Andrew Shea, Gayle's Son

Devin was seventeen when we interviewed him, finishing his senior year in high school. He's very active in school. Soccer has proven to be the love of his life, and this year he was chosen to be co-captain of the varsity team. Last year, friends asked him to join the Business Professionals of America and create a short film. He did, winning first prize in Massachusetts, then went on to Orlando, Florida to win third prize in the nationals. Devin has a wonderful sense of humor and is a loyal friend. His family is very important to him.

Gayle: I knew that you would be the most difficult person for me to interview. That's why I've waited so long. I'd like to show you the photo journal that Jess put together for the book. When I look at it, I'm amazed that we're still alive. Do you ever think about the accident?

Devin: I try not to.

Gayle: Does it pop up and you avoid it like the plague? Or do the thoughts never pop for you?

Devin: They don't pop up much anymore.

Gayle: I wish they didn't for me. I keep wondering if I had more memory of it, if it would go away. I wonder if my brain keeps searching for what isn't there. It's kind of weird to have a black hole in your memory. Anyway, the questions that I have for you, I have formulated over a long period of time, hoping they can help someone else that is in these circumstances. What do you remember of the day before the accident? Do you remember anything? Let's see, it was a Sunday. We were studying for finals. It was raining that morning. I think we were sitting at the kitchen table before we left. The weekend before, we had that soccer tournament up in New Hampshire.

Devin: I think the accident wiped out most of the detail.

Gayle: Okay. You don't have to have any memory of it. Do you remember anything of the car ride before the accident?

Devin: I just remember reading something before we left.

Gayle: So, you were reading a book? Cool. Can you tell me what you remember of the accident?

Devin: I was reading and I heard tires screech. I looked up and saw the truck coming.

Gayle: So you remember the sound. Do you remember metal or glass?

Devin: No.

Gayle: Do you remember the air bag coming out?

Devin: No.

Gayle: Or the powder from the bags?

Devin: The smoke after…

Gayle: The smoke from the airbags. Do you remember the sound of the police and fire trucks?

Devin: No.

Gayle: Do you remember the people around?

Devin: I remember someone looking in through the driver's side window… maybe talking.

Gayle: Did you feel like they were talking to you? Did you understand them?

Devin: No.

Gayle: You must have told them Dad's name and number or something.

Devin: I don't remember saying anything… just them asking questions.

Gayle: Oh, maybe they were trying to keep you focused by asking you things. Do you remember the man from your school coming on the scene?

Devin: No, I can't remember him specifically.

Gayle: Obviously it's been a long time since the accident and some memories have faded. But do you feel like your memory has faded?

Devin: The sensations are clear. Everything else is foggy.

Gayle: So you can kind of see what's going on? Do you remember seeing blood? Your nose was broken. It must have been bleeding.

Devin: It was all dust. I don't remember blood.

Gayle: Something I talked to my neurologist about recently because of my headaches was that sometimes our brain doesn't always "make" a memory. He said I might not have made any memories of that time because it was too traumatic. So I literally didn't make memory. So you may not have made memories either.

Devin: *Hmmm...I remember seeing my ankle...I don't remember blood...but it's hard to imagine not making a memory from something like that.*

Gayle: The doctor said they aren't sure how or why the brain does that. Do you remember pain?

Devin: *No.*

Gayle: Do you think it's possible that you didn't feel any pain because your body was kind of over and above it?

Devin: *Probably... it felt kind of dream-like.*

Gayle: Was it all in slow motion? Or did it feel all sped up?

Devin: *No. Not really. Just spacey...*

Gayle: What do you remember?

Devin: *I remember waking up and seeing my foot dangling from my ankle and thinking it couldn't be real. I also remember climbing over the middle to take the key out.*

Gayle: You had to have gotten out of your seat belt somehow and crawled around to the back where the EMTs found you.

Devin: *I guess.*

Gayle: Do you remember any specific people?

Devin: *I remember the EMT in the ambulance ride. She kept asking me what I do, my name, and my birthday.*

Gayle: Maybe to make sure you kept conscious?

Devin: *It was hard to concentrate.*

Gayle: Did they hook you up to any IVs or anything?

Devin: *Not that I can remember.*

Gayle: That's all right. What do you remember about the ER?

Devin: *A lot of bright lights and people all around me...lots of lights...getting pushed around...some weird neck brace thing...I couldn't move, and some doctor was making jokes about it. They told me I had to keep the neck brace on in case my neck was hurt, or whatever. Then they had me count back from ten.*

Gayle: So they were trying to sedate you, you think?

Devin: I'm not sure.

Gayle: Were you able to count like they asked? Or were you confused or hurting?

Devin: No. I could pretty much do whatever they asked. I think it's when the doctors are going to put you under, they have you count.

Gayle: Do you remember family in the ER?

Devin: No.

Gayle: Do you remember me being next to you in the ER?

Devin: Yeah...it seemed really quick and then you were in a different hallway...

Gayle: Interesting. Obviously I mostly only remember what people have told me, but I do remember a curtain between us, and Dr. L. has told me that we were talking to one another. My strongest memory is of them telling me that you had no internal injuries and would be staying there. Do you remember Dad in the ER?

Devin: No.

Gayle: Were you told that I was being airlifted to Albany?

Devin: Not that I can remember.

Gayle: When you found out that I wasn't in the hospital, do you remember how you felt?

Devin: I remember not understanding why you would have to leave.

Gayle: Do you remember anything after the ER? Do you remember the week you spent in the hospital?

Devin: I remember people coming to visit. The soccer team came one day. I also remember they wheeled in a TV so Jacob and Daniel and Scott and I could play video games.

Gayle: Were you in a room by yourself?

Devin: Yes.

Gayle: Nice. Was it lonely? Or were you just sleeping a lot and didn't care?

Devin: It was fine.

Gayle: Gail told me Dad never left your side. Where did you sleep when you went home?

Devin: I was in a bed downstairs.

Gayle: Yeah, he didn't want you near the stairs. Do you remember what was broken?

Devin: Yes.

Gayle: Tell me, because this is all about you.

Devin: My ankle, three of my toes, my wrist, and my nose.

Gayle: Do you remember any bruises? I didn't get to see you during that time.

Devin: Just on my chest.

Gayle: Why do you think your chest got bruised?

Devin: From the seatbelt.

Gayle: What about your tummy?

Devin: No.

Gayle: Did you like your doctors?

Devin: I didn't dislike them. I guess they were okay.

Gayle: What about your orthopedic doctor?

Devin: Yeah, I liked him, but I don't remember any of the hospital doctors.

Gayle: I imagine you were pretty focused on your discomfort.

Devin: Probably.

Gayle: Was the food good at the hospital?

Devin: It was okay. I kind of felt sick so I didn't eat a lot.

Gayle: That makes sense. Was your pain manageable?

Devin: I don't remember a lot of pain.

Gayle: You were much younger than you are now. Did you cry much?

Devin: No. I'm sure I was on a lot of meds.

Gayle: Do you remember crying at all?

Devin: No.

Gayle: Did they start PT in the hospital?

Devin: Yeah.

Gayle: Did they do that thing where you have to walk up a couple of steps before you could go home?

Devin: I don't remember.

Gayle: Were you in the hospital a whole week?

Devin: I think so.

Gayle: How'd you feel when you could go home?

Devin: Happy and relieved.

Gayle: When you got home, did you sleep in the guest bedroom?

Devin: No. I slept in the dining room.

Gayle: And Dad slept in there with you?

Devin: Yeah.

Gayle: Did you have nightmares?

Devin: Not that I remember. I probably did, but I never really remember my dreams.

Gayle: How was your home at Dad's changed to make your life easier?

Devin: Just that the bed was downstairs. They moved a table next to the bed so I didn't have to move much. Whatever I wanted was on the table.

Gayle: Were you afraid of being in a car?

Devin: I think so, for a little while.

Gayle: Did you or Dad or Gail find ways of making the ride to PT and to visit me in Albany more comfortable?

Devin: I don't think I ever wouldn't get in the car. It's just that it was weird.

Gayle: Did you have any trauma therapy?

Devin: A couple times, but I didn't like it.

Gayle: Did it help at all?

Devin: I don't know. Probably not. I wasn't really open to it.

Gayle: Was it just talking?

Devin: Just talking. I didn't get very far with it. She made some suggestions, but I don't remember what they were.

Gayle: That's okay. You've known for a long time that we've been working on a book. Have you thought of anything that a parent should know that could help a young person?

Devin: Make sure they have stuff to do and included them in things. Keep them busy to keep their mind occupied.

Gayle: Like going to the Fourth of July parade?

Devin: Yeah.

Gayle: Do you mean, being included in decisions around you?

Devin: Make sure you're given options and have some fun things to do.

Gayle: How long did it take for you to feel as though you were physically back to normal?

Devin: I still don't feel normal.

Gayle: You mean what you might have been if the accident hadn't happened?

Devin: Yeah.

Gayle: How do you feel about that?

Devin: It sucks!

Gayle: Is it mostly your foot and ankle? Like it might be holding you back in soccer?

Devin: I'm probably less aggressive, less physical.

Gayle: How come?

Devin: I just don't want to get hurt again.

Gayle: That's a good insight. So you were afraid to feel that pain, or afraid …

Devin: Yeah. I was afraid to feel the pain.

Gayle: Do you feel like you've worked through some of it or is it still as big in your heart as ever?

Devin: It's still there.

Gayle: I certainly can understand that. How did you feel when you first saw me in the hospital? (Long pause) I was all messed up, and worried that seeing me would scare you again.

Devin: Probably scared.

Gayle: Did anyone, probably Dad, tell you right along how I was doing? I know Jess emailed you from Albany. Did you read any of those emails?

Devin: No. Not till later, but Dad always told me how you were.

Gayle: He told you of my progress?

Devin: Uh-huh.

Gayle: Was there a time when he told you something that scared you?

Devin: I don't remember.

Gayle: Were you aware that for those first three weeks nobody was sure that I would make it?

Devin: Yes.

Gayle: That must have upset you?

Devin: I think it's hard to comprehend something like the uncertainty of life at twelve.

Gayle: You've always been extremely intuitive about me. We've been close forever, and sometimes you can sense how I feel even before I do myself. You might simply have known in your heart. (Long pause) Do you remember any specific visits with me?

Devin: I just remember going to get a hot dog every time.

Gayle: (Laughing) So, the food in the cafeteria was okay?

Devin: Yeah, that was good food for a hospital.

Gayle: I thought it was actually pretty good too. Do you remember your PT with David?

Devin: Kind of.

Gayle: And playing soccer with him?

Devin: Yeah. That was fun.

Gayle: Besides kicking the ball around, do you remember what else you did for your PT?

Devin: I had to stand on my foot and point in all these different directions with my other foot and try to keep my balance.

Gayle: Was that hard?

Devin: Yeah. Pretty hard.

Gayle: Those muscles were messed up. Was it hard to spend so much time away from home, going to the hospital, going to PT, and running over to Albany and then the nursing home?

Devin: I got used to it.

Gayle: Did your friendships suffer?

Devin: Not much.

Gayle: Was it hard to talk to me when I was so drugged?

Devin: Yeah.

Gayle: Was it scary? Frustrating?

Devin: Both.

Gayle: Did you feel compassion at any time? Like wanting to help? Worried?

Devin: Just worried. It's hard to help in a situation like that, especially at twelve. It was overwhelming to try and figure out how to help.

Gayle: Well, there were other people helping.

Devin: I didn't really know what to do.

Gayle: Except your did know to hold my hand a lot. Did you ever feel anger towards me? Or Lionel?

Devin: Not really.

Gayle: Not even when he came to the house to work off his community hours?

Devin: I just tried to avoid him. I guess I was angry.

Gayle: Did you feel sad?

Devin: I just felt like it sucked!

Gayle: Like you felt defeated?

Devin: No.

Gayle: It sucked. I wonder how that feels.

Devin: Like you can't do anything about it, but that it's bad, and, oh well, can't change it.

Gayle: True. What was it like in the nursing home? You were starting to get your life back physically. School got started again about a month into my stay. Let's see, was your cast off by then?

Devin: No.

Gayle: What was it like at the nursing home for you?

Devin: Lots of old people. A lot of yelling and weird sounds from people with mental disabilities.

Gayle: Yes, the Huntington's patients. That was rough. Did you ever worry that you could "catch" their disease?

Devin: No. It just annoyed and scared me.

Gayle: Do you remember going to the library there to do homework?

Devin: Yeah.

Gayle: Was there anything that was helpful like Monday nights when Jess would make dinner and bring it in for you and Becca to feel like a family?

Devin: Yes. I think it was important to have some form of normalcy.

Gayle: Jess was trying to create some sort of routine amidst the chaos. That was something that I looked forward to. Do you remember the bird feeder Jess put up outside my window? Or Ginger coming to visit?

Devin: I don't remember Ginger, but I do remember the bird feeder. And I remember getting my Mac PowerBook.

Gayle: Yup! Your "survivor present," as Jess called it. How was that for you, spending a little bit of the money from the accident on a dream?

Devin: It was cool.

Gayle: What was it like when I came home?

Devin: I remember you being downstairs.

Gayle: I remember you being pretty happy the day I came home. You were jumping up and down and dancing all around. Do have any other memories of me in a hospital bed in the living room? Was it hard to have me there?

Devin: A little bit.

Gayle: Why?

Devin: Things shifted. If I needed something, I had to get it myself instead of other people getting me stuff.

Gayle: So you became less of a focus as the kid?

Devin: Yeah. It forced me to mature quickly.

Gayle: I realized that and tried to think of all the ways it would change your life in a hard way. I didn't want things to be more difficult for you. Was it uncomfortable to bring friends home?

Devin: A little bit. I don't think I really did much.

Gayle: No, I don't think you did in the beginning. Was there any way we could have done that better for you?

Devin: I don't think anything else was possible.

Gayle: Maybe not.

Devin: *I wanted to be away from home when I was with my friends, anyway. Being at home, I couldn't really ignore how my life had changed or how much pain you were in. Wherever I wanted to go in the house, I had to walk through the living room.*

Gayle: So there was never a time at home when you could just relax and forget about the accident; your mom was still a mess. Yeah, that had to be hard. There was no down time except for school or going to your friends' houses. Would it have been different if we'd let you stay at Dad's house till I was better?

Devin: *It was a tough choice. It's still good that I was around you.*

Gayle: Was there anything good that you can see now in retrospect, having gone through what you went through? Do you think you've gained anything? Any perspective?

Devin: *I certainly gained a lot of maturity, and I gained the perspective that life is fragile and you can't be certain of everything.*

Gayle: Can you explain that a little more?

Devin: *I know how easily life can change completely.*

Gayle: Do you think the accident affected your experience at school?

Devin: *Yeah.*

Gayle: Did it make you care less about school because you cared less about the future?

Devin: *It made me care more about what was happening in the moment rather than anything in the future.*

Gayle: Interesting. Do you like that about you? Or do you wish you were different in some way?

Devin: *I like it. I don't worry about a whole lot of things, so it makes life a little easier.*

Gayle: But it makes it harder on parents who are thinking and worrying about the future. Does it make it more difficult to love? (No response) I notice there's a lot of love in you. You're very affectionate with your cats and your friends. So I think you're very bighearted.

Devin: Loving is easy.

Gayle: I'm glad you feel that way. Are you different with your friends in any way? Are you with them more just in the present moment?

Devin: Yeah.

Gayle: Okay. What was it like to go to the pound and get the kittens when I was camped out in the living room? Was that a good idea for you?

Devin: It was tons of fun. Kittens are the best!

Gayle: It was something Jess thought would help return some joy to our lives, and bring innocence back into our days. I agreed, thinking that a couple of kittens might give me something to concentrate on besides my pain and my healing, and we both knew how much you love cats.

Devin: Hmm.

Gayle: She thought it would make us all giggle. So for her it was an idea stimulated by the accident. Was there anything about the house that changed you? Like the ramp?

Devin: No. None of that stuff bothered me.

Gayle: Was it hard to concentrate on your everyday stuff when all of this was happening, like going to school? Was it difficult to concentrate when you knew another operation was coming up?

Devin: Yeah. I'd try to think about other things, but it was hard. It was all just so in my face and it was hard to see you in so much pain.

Gayle: I thought it was. I just wanted to make sure. Was there any way we could have done that better for you? I wanted you to know in case something horrible came up. I didn't want you to be shocked.

Devin: Hmm.. hard to say.

Gayle: What was it like having Lionel around? Were you afraid of him at all?

Devin: It was definitely hard having him around, and I guess I was afraid. I'm not really sure why but I remember being afraid.

Gayle: Yes it was hard having him around at first. I had to work through a lot of feelings. For me it was like being thrown into a sink-or-swim situation, emotionally. It was like an intense therapy session for me, which had its good moments as well as bad ones. I remember being worried about you and Becca. She had very strong emotions. She wanted to go and punch him. But for you, you just wanted to avoid those feelings altogether maybe? There was nothing you could do about it.

Devin: Exactly. I had to accept it and move on. Anger wouldn't have helped.

Gayle: He was helping us by working. You felt helpless instead of angry?

Devin: Yeah.

Gayle: Do you think the accident has changed your awareness of driving?

Devin: I know what the consequences of poor decisions can be.

Gayle: Okay.

Devin: But as a driver, I haven't done anything different than I would have done anyway.

Gayle: Well, we're pretty close to the end of my questions. Here it is five years later, and I'm still not anywhere close to what I would have been like if the accident hadn't happened. And you feel as though you've been affected physically and emotionally. Are you ever frustrated about what you feel was taken away? Are any of your dreams tempered by what happened?

Devin: Just in soccer.

Gayle: Are you ever frustrated with what I can't do with you?

Devin: No. I've come to accept it.

Gayle: Have you ever been?

Devin: I might have been in the beginning.

Gayle: Are you affected in any way by how hard I try to be with you and do things for you?

Devin: Yeah.

Gayle: Cool. I feel I've worked so hard to regain as much perspective and emotional maturity as I have, mostly to be an example to you of not giving up, of not letting it beat me, of showing you how much I love you. Once you mentioned your pride in me when I did the horseback riding demonstration. Is there any way that you'd like to tell me how that all has affected you?

Devin: What do you mean?

Gayle: I'm sorry. Have you felt pride besides that once?

Devin: Yes. I do when you get through surgeries and you try to beat the recovery expectation given to you by the doctors.

Gayle: Do you ever feel proud about what you have accomplished?

Devin: Hard to say. I was accepting of what I had to do and just did it.

Gayle: Were you pleased that you could get back to soccer so soon after being injured? I think it was only about six months.

Devin: Yes.

Gayle: Last question. Do you have any other thoughts that in any way could help someone who might have to go through what you've had to endure? There was so much focus on me and not you during that time while you were growing up. You've already said that it kind of bothered you at times. Does it still bother you?

Devin: No. Not really.

Gayle: Anything you'd like to share? Any last thoughts?

Devin: That's a daunting question. (Long pause) Just that it's important to not let things affect you. You can't change what's already happened to you.

Gayle: Are you saying that you try not to let life changes get you down?

Devin: Basically.

Gayle: Okay. Well, thank you, honey. If you think of anything else, tell me.

Devin: Sure.

Rebecca Dickerson, Gayle's Step-Daughter

Rebecca is Jess's daughter. She met Gayle when she was eleven years old at Devin's third birthday party. Gayle and she were best of friends within half an hour. Gayle was a supportive friend and second mother through the best and worst of times. Rebecca attended Wheelock College and MCLA, where she earned her bachelor's degree in psychology. Interestingly, that was Gayle's degree also. While attending MCLA, she worked at a local spa in the dining room, the medical department, and finally in program advising. During the time of Gayle's initial hospitalization, she was Jess's rock.

Gayle: Do you remember what you were doing before your mother called to tell you that Devin and I had been in an accident?

Rebecca: All too well. I was driving to my father's house with my brother Ryan, and sister Marissa in the car. Thank God for cell phones!

Gayle: Do you remember much of what you were told, and what your initial thoughts and feeling were?

Rebecca: I don't remember the conversation much. I was in shock and had to pull over. I remember Mom telling me not to freak out, just to go to Dad's and wait for her to call me with more info. I remember hanging up the phone and sitting there, not sure what to do, until Ryan said something. I told him what happened and then slowly drove the rest of the way, my mind running a mile a minute. Being the worrywart that I am, I was thinking the worst. The hardest part was the realization that I had to be strong for the kids. My dad and stepmother were out of town and my stepmother's parents were watching the kids, so I didn't have anyone to comfort me. I had to keep my composure so I wouldn't worry the kids.

Gayle: What did you do next?

Rebecca: I sat and waited impatiently for my mom to call back, and held the kids in my lap as much as they would let me. My strength came from their presence and innocence. When mom called to say you were being airlifted to Albany I told her to wait for me and we would go together. Then I called my boyfriend, and told him to meet me at my mom's. I wanted him to drive since I knew neither Mom nor I were in any shape to be behind the wheel, but Mom insisted, so I didn't argue. We drove quietly to Albany where again we had to wait to speak to the doctor.

Gayle: What did you think to do that helped you prepare for what was to come?

Rebecca: I don't remember what I did at that point, except to stay cool and calm so that I could take care of you. Even though I wasn't with you, I knew you needed me. I was right. When the doctor came out to speak to Mom, I was listening. Mom was totally distraught at this point and not thinking clearly. I remember hearing the doctor ask about any medical history he needed to know about, something to that effect, and Mom quickly said no. I thought, wait! This isn't right. So I stepped forward and told the doctor you were highly allergic to Compazine and that you were prone to anxiety attacks and used Ativan.

Gayle: Is there anything you wished later that you had done differently?

Rebecca: I wish I had gone immediately to my mother to comfort her, rather than stay at my dad's. I think Mom was just worried about me driving, but she needed me, and I needed her.

Gayle: When you found out I was being taken to Albany by helicopter, what were your thoughts and feelings?

Rebecca: First, I was totally freaked out by the thought of how serious it must be, and then I was relieved because I knew it was a better equipped hospital than our local one. Then my thoughts shifted to Devin: What about him? Who was going to take care of him? How could I choose? I hated that! It was awful, but the choice was clear: he was going to be okay and his dad was there, you were in serious trouble and I had to be there, and no one better get in my way.

Gayle: What did you notice first when you walked into my ICU room in Albany?

Rebecca: It was really weird. I guess I was expecting a really grotesque sight. But they had a blanket covering you so you could see the bulges of the casts and stuff, but if I just looked at your face, which I did, you looked totally unscathed. It was amazing. You had broken almost every bone in your body, but your face was not even scratched. Only you could make this look good!

Gayle: How did you react when you first saw me?

Rebecca: I looked at all the casts and everything and could only imagine the pain you were going through. That broke my heart. I wanted to cry, scream, and hug you tight. But I felt I had to be strong for you and Mom, and I was afraid to touch you for fear of doing more damage. I didn't know what to do.

Gayle: What was it like, sitting through so many surgeries?

Rebecca: Torture. I need to be doing something, helping somehow, and I couldn't. All I could do was sit and wait. And every time I feared that there would be complications and we would lose you. It was awful. Luckily I'm good at keeping myself busy. One time I brought a project from the restaurant I was working at; I sat there and wrapped 300 sets of plastic utensils in napkins. As long as I had something else to focus on, I was okay. But it had to be a mindless task. My brain was too overloaded to read or watch TV or even talk to family. I had to do something really monotonous so that I would drift off into LaLa Land.

Gayle: When did you get to see Devin?

Rebecca: I don't remember. I think I went home the next day to get some stuff for Mom and me like toothbrushes, clean underwear, etc., and I went to see him then. The days are all a blur.

Gayle: What was it like to see him so injured?

Rebecca: It was hard to see him hurt, but I was grateful that it was minor, compared to you. My main concern was to convince him you were going to be okay. I wanted him to focus on getting better knowing you were in good hands.

Gayle: Were you able to be with Devin as much as you wanted during his healing process?

Rebecca: No, and I feel guilty for that. I wish I could have cloned myself twice: one of me to be with you all the time, one of me to be with him all of the time, and one of me to take care of everything else and work. I was always feeling torn between responsibilities.

Gayle: I know you did a lot to keep our home running. What do you remember about that?

Rebecca: Mostly I did the little things… sort the mail and bring important things to Mom, bring her more clothes and stuff at the hotel, check the messages. That was the biggest thing. Every day there would be a million messages from concerned family and friends. My cell phone bill was astronomical that first month! I just kept calling everyone and their brother, most of whom I didn't know—which was a big feat for me, and explain what happened, then do my best to play down how bad it really was. I felt I had to convince them that you were going to be okay. Every time I said that to someone, I wanted to throw up because I was having such a hard time believing it myself. But I knew I needed to be strong so that others could feel their feelings.

Gayle: What extra things were you responsible for?

Rebecca: All the things you used to do. Laundry, making sure Mom ate, keeping everyone informed, making sure bills were paid.

Gayle: What was the most difficult part of your "duties"?

Rebecca: It wasn't the duties themselves that were hard; it was leaving you each time. I wanted to stay by your side, but I knew it was more important for Mom to be there, and someone had to take care of things at home. So I did what needed to be done.

Gayle: What was the easiest part of all of it?

Rebecca: Nothing was easy during that time.

Gayle: What part of your life suffered because of these added responsibilities?

Rebecca: The responsibilities didn't cause any suffering, but the situation definitely affected my life. My whole world got turned upside-down overnight. It was like one never-ending nightmare. The hardest part was nighttime. I hated coming home to an empty house each night. It was the biggest reminder of what was going on.

Gayle: Do you regret any decisions or actions during that time?

Rebecca: I don't regret anything, but I do wish things could have been different. I wish I could have stopped working and had more time to be with you, Devin, and Mom. Also, as a result of my loneliness at home, I moved in with my boyfriend. I don't regret this, but I wish I had thought it through more. I realize now that it made it easier on me, but it made it harder on Mom when she finally came home. So I guess it was selfish, but at the time it was self-preservation.

Gayle: What ways did you find to get through all the stress?

Rebecca: Just distracting myself as much as possible. As hard as it was to continue working, it was important to keep something stable in my life and be busy. Also, when I was at the hospital, I always brought stuff to do. There was no knowing whether I would be allowed in with you. When you are worried, minutes feel like hours and hours feel like days. If you have something to do—a puzzle, book, craft, knitting, etc.—it makes the time go by faster and it keeps you calmer. Also, talking to people was important. It gave me an outlet. It's okay to need sympathy. And hugs help.

Gayle: What can you remember of the people who helped? What did they say or do to help you get through each day?

Rebecca: God, I don't know. I was so focused on helping everyone else get through it; I didn't have time to think about myself. I guess the best thing was honesty and compassion. I hated it when people said, "Everything will be okay." Everything was not okay and we needed to accept that. So when someone simply said, "That's awful, I'm so sorry," that was what I needed to hear. And hugs. I needed people to let me break down and cry, to just hold me. I needed to know it was okay to stop being everyone's rock for a moment and let myself feel.

Gayle: You lost your mom and me for a long while. We did not know how long or in what ways we would be absent, and you were in a state of shock and mourning. What was that like for you?

Rebecca: Really difficult. I've always hated the unknown and I was forced to accept it indefinitely. There was no way to plan for the future because you didn't know what the future would hold.

Gayle: As I got better and went to the nursing home, how did things change for you?

Rebecca: It made things easier in ways and harder in ways. Now you were closer, which was great. I could see you much more, and I had Mom back home, and it was a huge leap of progress medically, which made me breathe easier and worry less. But it was still hard; you were home, but not really home. And you were in a nursing home, which was weird.

Gayle: How was the Monday night dinner at the nursing home for you? Was it difficult? Helpful? And why?

Rebecca: Both. It was helpful because it brought structure and regularity into a world of irregularity. And it was a time that we all set aside to come together and try to be a family again. But it was hard because it made it seem fake. Here we were, having a family dinner, but it was in this weird place, with weird people. I felt like we were trying to be normal when there was nothing normal about it. But, as hard as it was, I needed it even if I had to pretend sometimes. Sometimes you have to fake it 'til you make it, right?

Gayle: Right. Did you need more ritual around being a family? And what could have made things better for you?

Rebecca: I needed you. I needed everything to go back to the way things were before this happened. But that was impossible and it was important for me to be reminded of that. So, yes, ritual was helpful even if it was hard at the time. The more time we spent together as a family, the easier it was to accept the changes that had come from it, and the more natural it became.

Gayle: What was it like, visiting me in a nursing home?

Rebecca: I have always hated nursing homes. I think they smell like dead people. So it was really hard for me to have you there. It didn't feel right. You weren't old, you had family who wanted to take care of you, and you weren't dying. But it was what you needed, and once I met the people caring for you and realized you were in capable hands, it was easier. Plus I was glad to have you close by.

Gayle: When did you decide to move out of our home?

Rebecca: After enough lonely nights of coming home to a big empty house with all the constant reminders of what used to be.

Gayle: What were the motivations and reasons behind the move?

Rebecca: Looking back, I think the biggest motivation behind moving was avoidance. I couldn't handle the situation the way it was, so I chose to distance myself, physically. I needed a "safe" place to go at night to get away from everything. I needed someone to be there for me, and my boyfriend was willing to do that.

Gayle: In retrospect, did it help?

Rebecca: Yes. Absolutely.

Gayle: What feelings did you have around my not being able to help with your first apartment?

Rebecca: The hardest part was that you couldn't see it. You were my best friend. I wanted your approval. And that was just not possible. It seemed so weird to go shopping and make all these big decisions without you.

Gayle: As your mom created a more handicapped-accessible home for me, how did you feel to see things changing?

Rebecca: It took some getting used to at first. Change is hard for everyone.

Gayle: When did you feel as though you could tell me about some of your stuff, your problems, your day, and your hopes?

Rebecca: It took a long time, and even then it took some prodding. I wanted to talk to you so badly, but I didn't feel like I could. After all, what you were going through was so much worse than anything I had going on; it just didn't feel right. I didn't want to seem selfish and I didn't want to burden you with anything else. It was a slow process, opening up to you again and realizing I didn't have to protect you all the time.

Gayle: What was it like the first time you pushed me in a wheelchair in public?

Rebecca: It felt foreign and awkward. Also I was really scared to hurt you. I was self-conscious at first, but I was just glad to be with you again.

Gayle: What is it like now?

Rebecca: Now it feels totally normal. It's just become routine and part of the deal. I don't even really think about it. In fact, that's been a problem sometimes because I forget that you are in a wheelchair, and that has to be taken into consideration. Otherwise, it's just an outing with my "Gayley-Gayle".

Gayle: How did the accident change your relationship with your mom?

Rebecca: At first it was a role reversal. I became the responsible one and had to take care of her. So I felt a certain level of dependability that had never been there before, but it also showed me a side of her that I hadn't really seen before. It was good to know that she could need me as much as I often needed her. That strengthened our bond. Plus, later, it became our joint goal to take care of you and watch out for you, so that helped.

Gayle: In what ways, good or bad, has the accident changed you?

Rebecca: It changed everything, neither good nor bad, just different.

Gayle: How have you grown?

Rebecca: Not only did I become stronger, but also I realized my own power. It happened, and I handled it. I didn't crumble and fall. Also I learned how to be a better friend. I had to make a lot of adjustments and admit a lot of things in order to get our relationship back to what it was, but I think that made it that much better in the long run. Also I learned that bad things happen. You can't control it, but you can control how you react to it. Acceptance is the key.

Gayle: What can you tell others that might help them?

Rebecca: *If this happens to you, your life is never going to be the same. Don't try to mend it. Instead, work to rebuild it with a different foundation. These things change people. Accept it and move on. If you dwell on what used to be, you will miss what is. Above all, if you love someone, be there for him or her no matter what it takes. You may have to make sacrifices that are hard at the time, but it will be well worth it because you never know what could happen and you will regret it if you miss your chance. And don't hide your feelings. It's okay to cry, it's okay to scream, and it's okay to laugh. Chances are, everyone around you feels the same way and understands. If you keep it inside, it only hurts more.*

Peg & Gene Andrew, Gayle's Parents

Peg and Gene had already lost a son and nearly lost their elder daughter over forty years ago to a brain tumor. Their loss of Gayle, if that had occurred, would have been unimaginable. They are devout Catholics, hard working, hard playing individuals. Peg is an avid athlete, volunteers at a local hospital, plays bridge, as well as tournament golf. Gene bowls, hunts, fishes, and is an organic gardener. They raised Gayle on home grown vegetables, fruits, nuts, as well as venison, wild turkey, and fresh fish. At the time of the accident they were seventy-nine and eighty-one and were ever-present after the accident, giving all that they could and more.

Gayle: What were you two doing when you found out that Devin and I had been in an accident?

Peg: I think we had just come back from golf.

Gene: Yes. We'd just come home and the telephone rang. The police said that there had been a serious accident.

Gayle: Do you remember if they said Devin was also in it?

Peg: He didn't give too much information. We only had a few minutes to get to Pittsfield before–

Gene: He just told us to come right down.

Peg: It was a very bad accident. We knew that from what he said. If we wanted to see you off before you were taken by helicopter, we'd have to get there in a hurry. We didn't know how long they'd been trying to contact us.

Gene: He didn't say anything about a helicopter. He just said you better get there in a hurry.

Peg: Yes, he did.

Gene: I was surprised to see a helicopter when we got there!

Peg: Well, I knew that helicopter was for Gayle.

Gene: We saw it circling the hospital getting ready to come down into Wahconah Park. I remember saying to you, "This is serious." But then we went into the hospital, and they had you all wrapped up and bandaged up. Nurses and doctors were running in all directions and you were on a gurney. As I remember, we just had enough time to wish you well, and away you went.

Gayle: So it was that quick?

Gene: Oh, yes. We didn't have any visiting time.

Peg: I don't know...maybe five, ten minutes.

Jess: I was there about fifteen or twenty minutes before they made the decision that Devin did not have internal injuries and would be staying there. That meant Gayle was going alone to Albany.

Gayle: Wait. I'm confused. Mom, did you answer the phone?

Peg: Yes.

Gayle: So Dad was listening as you related what was going on?

Peg: Right. Right. I knew we had to get going quickly.

Gene: I remember after they took you away meeting the young boy's mother. She was all alone and talking to the oral surgeon. I knew the doctor from the country club and said, "Busy night?" And he said, "Yup!" She was all alone and she said her son's teeth had been smashed.

Peg: This was the driver of the truck that hit you.

Jess: Did you know at that point that he had caused the accident?

Gene: Well, we didn't know much at that point.

Peg: I think we saw the doctor and he said that.

Gene: "This is the man driving the other vehicle," he'd said. But how it happened, I don't remember hearing that in the hospital. Do you?

Peg: Oh, no.

Gayle: So all you knew was that he was another person involved in the accident?

Peg: I think we knew that he hit you. Devin was in one room and Lionel was in the one next to him.

Gayle: I don't remember Lionel in the ER at all.

Gene: He wasn't anywhere near you. He was down another hall. It was later that he was in a room near Devin.

Gayle: How did you know it was Lionel's mom?

Gene: She mentioned it.

Gayle: Hmm.

Gene: She was all alone and a bit of a wreck. She didn't know what to do or where to turn, so I said, "He's getting the best care we can hope for."

Jess: Did you get to talk to any of Gayle or Devin's doctors or nurses?

Gene: Nope.

Gayle: So then what happened?

Gene: So we talked together. Jess was going to go to Albany.

Peg: Jess was gone so fast.

Jess: Yeah. As soon as they said Gayle's going to Albany, I said goodbye, and I love you, to Devin and then to Gayle, went home, waited for Rebecca, packed a few things and made a bunch of quick phone calls. I remember sitting in the car with her waiting for her boyfriend and seeing the helicopter rise up over our trees. That was the first time I cried.

Peg: Oh, it all went so fast.

Gene: And we stayed a while in the ER with Devin.

Peg: (to Jess) You were gone so quickly.

Jess: I remember you guys were white as ghosts. I could only imagine what you were going through.

Gene: Now Devin was across the hall from the waiting room.

Peg: No. He was right next to her.

Gene: I'm talking after she left, Mother, after she left.

Peg: Oh, okay.

Gene: They had a lock on the door and you couldn't get in. That's when Larry's parents were there. You and I decided we were going to stay with Devin. I had cataracts, and couldn't drive at night. The next day we headed out early for Albany. That was the plan that we made that night.

Gayle: That must have been a little stressful because you guys didn't know if I was going to live the night.

Gene: No. We didn't.

Jess: Were you able to sleep? I know you got to Albany pretty early!

Gene: No. There was no sleeping.

Gayle: So did you stay at the hospital with Devin?

Peg: Oh, no! Everybody left.

Gene: We stayed till we heard that Devin was going to be all right! He was pretty busted up, but he was going to be all right. Larry got that information from the nurse, so we said, "Let's go home, then go to Albany in the morning." In Albany, there was a waiting room. Somebody could go in for five minutes every hour. I'm not sure; something like that.

Jess: We could stay for as long as we wanted, but they often kicked us out because they had to do something to Gayle and didn't want us in the room.

Gene: I remember bells and whistles! One time they kicked us all out. They almost lost you.

Jess: That was probably one of the times when Gayle's lung collapsed.

Peg: Oh, that was awful.

Jess: I remember in the waiting room we'd buzz to get in and no one would answer, but when he [Gene] buzzed, they'd say, "Sure, come on in!"

Gene: Well, they were nice-lookin' nurses! I winked at 'em! (Laughter) No! I'm just kidding, but there was one nurse for every two patients, I remember. That nurse was right outside the two cubicles. That impressed me that such close monitoring was going on.

Gayle: What were your first thoughts when you saw me in Albany?

Peg: You didn't look good!

Gayle: Can you say more? This is going into a book that may help other parents, other family members.

Gene: Our first thought was that we hoped you'd make it. We hoped you'd live. That was the thought for many days, not just the first day but every day! When the telephone would ring at home, we'd think, "Did she die?" And then, well …

Gayle: What helped you get through that part?

Gene: I think your body and mind reaches into a different depth saying, "We gotta get through this. We gotta get through this, we gotta help! We can't break down! If we break down, you'll break down."

Gayle: Do you remember any way you helped each other?

Gene: I remember your mother washing you and putting cool cloths on your head. You couldn't do anything for yourself. And the thing that impressed me—the worst, I guess—was the external fixations. I had never seen them before. I saw these wire cages on your leg and arm and–good God!

Jess: I was lucky. I had seen my first one on my mother's arm a year before. She had broken her arm badly.

Gene: And to think they drilled holes in the bone!

Jess: I know! I was horrified when I first saw it, but then I started to study it, to see how it worked. It was fascinating. So I'm grateful I saw one before I saw them on Gayle.

Peg: They were awful!

Gene: Yeah, but amazing. I wanted to see just how they worked. I looked them over carefully, you know. I'm being nosey; generally they put a cast on. What's this doing? I'm wondering, "Is this some kind of experiment?" Then you find out they've been doing this for years.

Jess: (to Peg) How did you cope?

Peg: I don't know. You felt so helpless, completely helpless. (to Gayle) I couldn't even touch you, really. I was afraid to hurt you.

Gayle: Jess remembered, in writing her part, that you and she were brushing my hair and picking out glass shards.

Peg: Oh, gosh, yeah.

Gene: I can remember that, too.

Peg: For the longest time we just kept finding more glass. And I scratched and tickled your arm. You always liked that, even as a child.

Gayle: So you did find ways of getting through to me, letting me know that you were there?

Peg: Oh, yes. That was important.

Gayle: Since I was in a coma, it must have been hard to know what to do.

Jess: Drug-induced.

Gayle: But it was a coma. And I was not aware of much.

Jess: It's a good thing because I was singing to you a lot! (Laughter)

Gene: And then we stayed over a few nights. Jess stayed over all the time. I'd go over with Mother, and she'd say, "Well, I'm going to stay with Jess." So I'd drive home alone, then come back the next day and pick her up. Sometimes you'd call me at home and say, "Oh, I forgot my such and such." So the next trip, I'd bring your hairbrush or something. Larry would come over, too. Then Devin started making the trip. Ellie and Linda went a couple times. They helped with the driving. So everybody was pulling together.

Jess: Remember finding the parking places in the sun? They'd kick us out for hours at a time and we'd move the car so it was in the sun and then try to nap.

Peg: Yes. I remember that.

Gene: And the people there that you meet in the ICU waiting room were special. You learn fast that you're not the only ones with problems. This one man's mother was in there talking about her son and how he'd been on a motorcycle or something–

Jess: Oh, yeah. I cracked a joke about all the car and motorcycle accidents and that we should go back to the horse and buggy. The daughter of the man said, "Oh, I don't know about that. My father's here because he got kicked in the head by a horse."

Peg: They were such nice people, weren't they?

Jess: Yes. I especially liked the grandmother. She had so many stories. And her granddaughter was studying for the bar exam. She was the one who told me to keep a journal, saying, "I know I won't remember the details that my father will want to hear when he's out of ICU."

Gene: There was someone who ran into a gate. And he didn't come out of it while we were there. They transferred him to another hospital.

Jess: There were so many coming and going. And when they didn't come back, you worried that their loved one hadn't made it.

Gene: You meet people like that and form a friendship. You see them every day.

Peg: How long were you in the hospital? I forget. It seemed so long.

Jess: She was two months in Albany.

Gayle: And wasn't it three weeks that I was in the ICU?

Jess: Yeah. Then you went to that awful room, 5E. It seemed they were trying to kill you.

Peg: Oh! Wasn't that awful?

Jess: Remember the lady that was hired to "babysit" because Gayle was trying to pull her tubes out? She was nice, but you got such poor care. There didn't seem to be much staff for that floor. I don't know why.

Gayle: That's where you and Larry figured out the thing with the oxygen. The cap was loose and I wasn't able to breathe.

Jess: It was Saturday and you were waiting for hip surgery on Monday. And they kept saying, "Oh, she's fine. Just struggling a little with her breathing." Larry and I didn't buy that for a minute. You looked awful.

Gayle: And instead my gall bladder went.

Gene: And the doctor came into surgical waiting room, holding a jar, saying, "That won't bother her anymore."

Jess: Dr. H. He was very nice, except when they were finishing prepping you. He says to me, "Give your daughter a kiss goodbye now." (Laughter) I must have looked pretty bedraggled.

Peg: That was pretty funny!

Gene: You know another thing I remember. I don't know whether Mother does or not, but she was combing your hair or something and I was sitting down, and all of a sudden you started to say the Hail Mary.

Gayle: Oh, yeah.

Gene: Mother said it along with you. And then you said something about saying it again, so you both said it again together. You were in all kinds of pain. You couldn't even feed yourself, but you said the Hail Mary. Another thing that stands out, it's a good thing for your book; after a period of time, I don't remember exactly when, but someone said that you were going to have some physical therapy. You're laying there in traction with those ex-fixations and I'm thinking, "What the hell can they do?" And in comes Jan. I'll never forget her. She says, "I want you to rip tissues." And you couldn't do it. I'm sitting there, dying. God! She can't even rip tissue!

Jess: And it was only one ply!

Gene: But in a week she had you doing it. I never thought therapy would have to start at ground zero.

Peg: It's amazing what they can think of to get you going again.

Gayle: PT and OT people have to come in and start at the very beginning, but how was that for you guys? You had a fully grown infant.

Peg: Yeah. It was odd.

Gene: *That's a good way of putting it.*

Jess: What was it like as parents? There will be other parents reading this book. What do you want to tell them?

Gayle: You had been through losing Tommy and nearly losing Judy, and then along comes this. You do have to kind of go back to the beginning.

Peg: I think any parent is going to do the very same thing that we did.

Gayle: I don't know, Mom.

Peg: Well, if that's what needs to happen, then you baby your baby.

Gayle: I don't know if all parents do know what to do in a crisis.

Gene: I think that the thing that kept me going, the thing that I kept looking for, was a little improvement each day. And each time might be once a week, every two weeks. Maybe one day your color was a little better than the day before. Maybe you wiggled your arms a little more. Maybe they took out one of the ten tubes that were in your body.

Gayle: What happened to that hope when I went backwards?

Gene: We just called it a setback. That's what I did. I just called it a setback, like dropping a rung on the ladder.

Gayle: So you got steely like Jess does.

Peg: Yeah. A little.

Jess: I remember one day where none of us were very steely. We were probably at one of our lowest points, way overtired, and we just kind of fell apart and cried in the hallway. And then you guys went home, and I roamed the halls.

Gene: Wasn't that the time when your lung collapsed again?

Gayle: Probably.

Gene: I can remember it was just pain, pain, and more pain for you. Bells were ringing and doctors were running. That really shook us up.

Gayle: How did you get to sleep? How did you go about your business, your normal day? Do you remember a normal day?

Peg: I can't remember much of what we did while you were in the hospital.

Gene: We went to the hospital. That was a normal day for sixty some-odd days. Back and forth and back and forth. And I remember a phone call from that social worker in Albany. She was a miserable pup! Later in the nursing home, I remember a lot of ambulance trips.

Peg: You never know, looking at nursing homes. They all look the same. There's no way to know until you're in there as a patient.

Jess: Most of the CNAs at the nursing home agreed that it was the best of the worst. So they were saying that they're all bad, all understaffed.

Peg: That's what I hear. Everyone I talk to now has some horror story to tell of one nursing home or the other.

Jess: That's what Marlene, our favorite CNA, thought. Wasn't she something?

Peg: Oh, she was. You belonged to her.

Gayle: She'd scrub me raw! I wasn't getting bedsores on her watch.

Gene: She'd say in her thick Scottish accent, "Now, girly. Don't you cry. You're going to be all right. Come on, girly!" Then she'd always wave, going by your window when she left to go home.

Peg: But I hear more and more bad things about that place than I do about any other place.

Gayle: So you went to each one that they recommended?

Peg: Except the one they sent you to. We didn't get to go inside.

Jess: The social worker in Albany didn't make any recommendations. She didn't know the rehab centers in our area. She only knew of one in Schenectady and somewhere in Connecticut. Imagine that! Maybe she was new to the area. There was a possibility of going back to our local hospital's physical therapy wing, but then we found out you had to be able to do so many hours per day of PT in order to be admitted. Your condition limited where you could go. And in the end there was little choice at all. We had to leave when the hospital administration said to go, and to whatever place had a bed.

Gene: And this was all coming at you because they were going to put you out tomorrow!

Peg: We didn't have time to study the nursing homes. At the time we didn't know anyone in any of them to tell us what each one was like.

Gayle: In retrospect, can you think of what you would have liked to do differently?

Gene: We wished we had more time. That's all I can remember. You're in a car running from here to here to here–

Peg: And you're already tired.

Gene: Then you get a phone call saying that they have a bed for you.

Jess: Well, the time factor is probably because of insurance saying, "Okay, we've spent enough money here, now get out!"

Peg: That woman in charge of finding a place for you was terrible!

Jess: She said, "There's no guarantee that you'll get into the one you like. You'll get into the one that has a bed!"

Gayle: Oh, my!

Peg: She was terrible! I don't really know why she bothered to tell us to look if in the end we didn't have a choice.

Gayle: It must have made you feel helpless.

Jess: You know it was also that woman who should have told us to get started with Social Security Disability.

Gene: Oh, she was miserable!

Gayle: Yes! We missed eight months of benefits because of that person and her counterpart at the nursing home.

Peg: Well, we were busy taking care of you!

Gene: That was our priority.

Jess: For sure. There was still a lot of caregiving that wasn't happening even in Albany, and a lot of monitoring of meds and machines. We kept a pretty close watch on you.

Gayle: So people reading this book should know from our experiences to check into benefits from the very beginning. They need to push the people in charge to help you with it. We got into a terrible financial hole because of what didn't happen that we didn't know anything about.

Peg: That's right!

Gayle: If we had known, we could have asked the right questions. Like, please tell us when the insurance company is pressuring you to get me out of the hospital.

Gene: I think you need to caution your readers that you are very pressed for time, and that you can't do things four weeks ahead of time because you don't know what's going to happen in four weeks. You just can't anticipate these things.

Peg: But once it's all over with, then you hear things. I've heard so many horror stories about that place since you left. You know, you're talking about your own kid's experience and someone says, "Well, this place was this and that place was that." Now it's too late.

Gene: If you listen to everyone, you can find ten people from every place that say, "It wasn't clean. The food was lousy, and so on and so forth." A buddy of mine went up to the nursing home up the hill from you and can't say enough good about it.

Jess: And yet when it was Gayle's time, it was a very different place, run by a different company. It was one of the worst places to go.

Gene: The one on the north end of Pittsfield was nice, but they didn't have any beds when we went there. They put us on a wait list.

Peg: Yes, someone we knew said it was good.

Jess: When did you know that Gayle was going to make it?

Peg: Well, I don't really remember. Certainly before she left the hospital. She was talking and visiting.

Gene: But we knew it was going to be a long road.

Peg: For sure.

Gayle: But was there a time when you stopped worrying that I was going to die?

Peg: Well, you could see each day that there was a little bit more of you alive, talking to us, doing this and doing that. So we knew the worst part of your accident was behind us. We weren't sure you would be able to walk yet, but we were hopeful.

Gayle: From Jess's journal, it seems it was three weeks before the doctors stopped worrying.

Jess: Well, when you started trying to pull out your tubes, I was pretty sure you were going to make it.

Peg: Yeah! Gayle's back! (Laughter)

Gene: You spent a lot of time on the operating table.

Peg: It was touch and go for a long time.

Gene: They would have a four-hour window while you were on life support. I remember a doctor saying, "There's four of us working on her." Or was it six?

Gayle: I think it was six.

Peg: It was always good when the doctor would come out and tell you what they did and how well you responded.

Gene: Then we'd sit and wait for them to bring you back up to your room.

Gayle: Would only one doctor come out after surgery?

Gene: I can't remember which doctor was which.

Jess: It was always Dr. Hospodar.

Peg: I remember the very tall doctor who took out your gall bladder. He was very nice; he took time telling us all about your condition and that you would be so much better now. Then they put you in the room you stayed in for the rest of your two months there.

Jess: The orthopedic wing.

Peg: Yes. We all hated the room you were in before that.

Gayle: You must have given some thought to the fact that I was going to be disabled.

Gene: That didn't bother us. You lived.

Peg: We were so relieved.

Gene: Many times we'd see someone we knew and they'd ask, "How's your daughter doing?"

Peg: Every day! Still!

Gene: And I'd say, "We're thankful she's still alive!" So that wiped out anything about one foot short or one arm short. You're still alive! You're still alive!

Jess: There had to be a part of you that was concerned or disappointed that she probably wouldn't play golf again, or ski.

Peg: Well, we didn't know that early on.

Gene: *That happens more now than it did then.*

Peg: Oh, Gayle. You were always so vivacious. You always had so much going on, so much of the time. Good or bad, you had it going on!

Gayle: Still do!

Gene: You haven't lost that spirit.

Gayle: It's not easy.

Peg: No. It's a lot of work.

Gene: There was one doctor that radiated so much confidence, that doctor in Boston that worked on your knee. He was Hospodar's professor.

Jess: Dr. V.

Gene: We'd never met him and he comes right up to us after surgery and says, "Everything went fine. Very successful operation! See ya later!" We're wanting to know more, and he's already gone. I guess he was that confident in his work.

Jess: Or that busy.

Gene: The waiting rooms were so big and noisy. There was so much more bustle than Albany.

Jess: It was more like a factory there.

Peg: The waiting room in Albany was so friendly.

Gayle: But he saved my leg. That was when they went in and took out all the metal, cleaned out the infection, left my knee apart for a week, then went back in and put everything together again. That was amazing!

Gene: Right!

Peg: Isn't it wonderful what they can do?

Gayle: That infectious disease doctor in Pittsfield told me twice that he was ready to take my leg. I called Dr. Hospodar in tears!

Jess: Yeah, he had his name on her leg! We didn't tell you all this at the time.

Gayle: Dr. Hospodar says, "Whoa! Let's slow down. I'm going to send you down to Boston. We'll see what Dr. V. has to say about it. That was when we had the PICC line and the antibiotics going in several times a day. Remember, I told you how we hung the bag from the ceiling of a motel room and went shopping the next day?

Peg: Oh, jeez!

Gene: You look at all the doctors you had, even when you had the hand cancer, you had top notch doctors, especially that Red Sox doctor who did Schilling's ankle in the series.

Gayle: Bill Morgan. What a sweetie!

Gene: You know, when you were in Albany you got a letter from him and Jess put it on the wall with all the other cards and letters.

Jess: I put it in a prominent place for the doctors and nurses to see. I wanted them to know that they better take good care of you or the Red Sox doctor would raise holy hell if they didn't!

Gene: Dr. Bill! That's how he signed it.

Jess: We just recently got to go to another of Hospodar's teacher's in New York City and he says, "I invented the shoulder replacement I'd be putting in, but I don't think you'd have as much movement as you've got now, and I really don't know how you got that much out of that shoulder."

Gayle: Hospodar's answer to that one day was, "Gayle, you ride a special bus!"

Peg: No kidding! That's funny!

Jess: In all these years since the accident, what was the hardest part?

Gene: The setbacks.

Peg: The worry. How's she going to feel with one arm shorter than the other? What will she be able to do? Then there's another operation and I guess it's the thought, "When is it ever going to be over for her?"

Gene: *Yeah. You don't stop worrying.*

Peg: And that's the toughest part. You're suffering for your child. We didn't want you to hurt.

Gene: It was hard trying not to let you know how much we were worried.

Gayle: Well, I know how I feel watching Devin. I hate to see what he's lost.

Gene: We're the same way with you! We don't want you to see us peeking at you to make sure you're all right.

Peg: One of the things that I was thinking about earlier when I knew you were coming to interview us for the book was the changes in your household. When you came out of the nursing home there was a hospital bed in the living room, this is there and that's here. And someone had to be around you every minute.

Gene: Nurses were going in and out.

Peg: So it was like a nursing home in your house!

Gayle: That's what it was!

Peg: Now your house is beginning to look normal. After that bed was gone and you went upstairs, using the chairlift, everything looks more normal so what is there to worry about?! You're doing fine!

Gayle: You're right about worrying about your child. When I'm watching Devin run, I'm worrying, "Will his ankle that was broken roll on him or will it hold up?" And he doesn't always know I'm looking. His foot has become very thick with scar tissue. He plays soccer and is very tough on his body. But as he's getting older, it seems to be getting better. I feel the need to check it every so often and don't talk about the worry with him.

Jess: What did you think when Gayle announced that she was going horseback riding?

Peg: I said she was the most vivacious kid. So, it wasn't a surprise. That's Gayle!

Gene: I was glad. I knew that the muscles that you'd be using would be muscles you wouldn't be using sitting in the wheelchair. When I saw you on a horse, I was shocked! I couldn't believe how quickly you'd progressed, how well you were sitting and how you were able to go with the rhythm of the horse. That rhythm of the horse isn't easy to pick up. If you've ever ridden, you know. You've got to have power in your legs to do that.

Jess: Well, that's Gayle. I taught her to play racquetball years ago. I won the first game, and that was the last game I ever won. (Laughter)

Peg: I'd like to go back to when you were in our local ER. I remember that Devin was in the bed next to you. And I remember when I went to you, you said to me, "He's okay."

Gayle: I don't remember much about it, but when I went into one of Devin's doctor appointments in my wheelchair, Dr. L. came over and gave me a big hug. He said that he would never forget Devin and me in the ER, and how instead of focusing on ourselves, we were continuously talking to each other, even with the curtain between us, saying, "I love you. How are you doing?" We were talking the whole time. And the EMT said the same thing. He said that we were talking to each other even in the car.

Gene: The Hancock fire chief thought you were dead. He said the car panel had crushed right in on you. He was having a hard time but he'd just completed a training with a new Jaws of Life and he said, "I got a hold of such and such part of the car, and when I hit it, it took that part right off." And he said, "Boy was I glad to see that!" They were all there ripping that car apart as fast as they could.

Gayle: Mark, the first EMT on the scene, said that my lung kept collapsing but Devin and I kept talking, trying to help support each other.

Gene: Devin wouldn't get out of the car!

Gayle: No! He knew I wasn't breathing.

Gene: One of my friends went by just minutes after the rescue people arrived. He sees this wreck and wonders, "How many are dead?"

Gayle: Yes. I've heard about other people who had driven by the scene.

Peg: It must have been a busy time of day, because I've heard that, too.

Jess: Did either of you feel as though you gained anything from all of this? I mean it was a horrible thing, but often something good can come from it all.

Peg: Something good? I guess you think how lucky you are. It could have been worse. Here she is, and maybe you've prayed enough for it to happen.

Jess: You know, for the shape we were all in, we laughed a lot.

Peg: We did.

Gene: I think that's a way to relieve tension.

Jess: I know we (looking at Peg) did a lot of crossword puzzles.

Peg: (Laughs) Well, we tried!

Jess: I don't think we ever finished a one.

Peg: I don't think we did!

Jess: We ate a lot of candy bars!

Peg: Oh, yeah! Nutrageous! I'd never had one of those before. They were good!

Gene: We stopped in Canaan for coffee and Danish fifty or sixty times. They were good people always asking how our daughter was. Then we'd take turns in the cafeteria at the hospital. Get a bite to eat.

Peg: Their chicken sandwich was good.

Jess: There are things that bring up emotions for me to this day, like the sound of a helicopter. Just yesterday I was mowing the lawn and heard that thump, thump, thump. I shut off the mower and it all came back to me. It chokes me up, and I always look up and say, "Thank you!"

Peg: I always look up, too. It means something to me now. Right after it happened, though, I didn't like the sound. You knew someone was in trouble enough to get the helicopter.

Gayle: For a while the sound would bring back such a strong feeling of panic.

Gene: When you ask, "What did you learn? Was there something good?" I think of all the professional people and all of the help that Gayle had from so many people. It was outstanding! I know there were one or two bad ones, but of the total conglomerate, outstanding! It's amazing what doctors can do today, what nurses can do today, what physical therapist can do today. Those things are astounding!

Jess: Even some of the cleaning ladies. Remember the one that would sing more around Gayle because we mentioned how much she liked hearing her sing. So she made a point of singing and also, she noticed lots of times when your food came, you needed help opening things.

Gayle: Oh, that was awful. They'd drop my food off and I couldn't do anything with it. They weren't paying attention, but she was wonderful. She'd open my fruit plate and my juices.

Peg: I think what we were most thankful for was that your mind wasn't hurt.

Gayle: The airbags worked well, and we were wearing our seatbelts. If not, I don't think we could have survived.

Jess: I remember the story you (to Gene) told about the turkey that came into the courtyard while you were out there with Gayle. I remember you saying, "How the hell is that turkey going to have enough room for take off?"

Gene: And it went right up over the building!

Peg: That was funny.

Gene: Remember the other woman with Huntington's? You were in your room. Devin was doing some homework on the other bed and she came in and saw his book and said, "Trig-oh-nom-eh-try!"

Gayle: I was told that she had been a math teacher. We all liked her a lot. Her name was Joan.

Jess: I'll never forget the day when I'm trying to come up with someone's name and out of the blue, Gayle says his name. She couldn't remember a name to save herself before the accident. There was no brain damage, but something shifted around up there. She always remembers names now!

Gene: Shook some dust off that part of her brain. (Laughter)

Gayle: Are there any last things you want to say?

Peg: We're just glad you're alive.

Recently my mom was cleaning out a filing cabinet and found something she wrote five years after the accident. Jess and I were both deeply moved by her words.

Our Vivacious Young Daughter

We were coming in the house from a golf game on June 3rd when we answered a call from the Williamstown police telling us about a car wreck involving our daughter and her son. They told us to head to our local hospital in a hurry, because she would be on her way to Albany's medical center by helicopter. I was absolutely stunned. Gayle always drives so well and carefully. We jumped back into the car and drove as quickly as we could to Pittsfield. On the way, we saw and heard the helicopter above our car. What a sinking feeling for both of us. Her father was driving and I was crying. It was the longest five miles ever!

Gayle was being bound up to a stretcher. We only had time to kiss her and tell her how much we loved her and off to Albany she went. Her father had just had eye surgery and could not drive after dark. And not knowing the way to the hospital in Albany, we were in a quandary. Jess was already on her way, so we finally decided that the next morning we'd be there early.

Our grandson, who was staying overnight at the Pittsfield hospital, was well cared for. His injuries were not as severe. Before she flew off to Albany, his mother realized that her twelve year old son was faring well and had plenty of attention as he had been in the next cubicle to her while she was being readied for her trip. The accident was caused by a young man falling asleep at the wheel.

After months at the hospital and many more months in a nursing home, Gayle went home. The next four years were difficult for Gayle and Jess as they had hopes and dreams that were shattered. Their home became more like a hospital room with the bed, the medications, the bandages, the nursing crew, and the bed pans. The cooking was mostly done by Jess, but family and friends all had a special day to be with Gayle.

Today Gayle is doing well. She has a keen love of living. Devin is proving to be a strong, bright young man and still is there to help his mom with her needs. The house has become a home again. There will be more surgeries to overcome, but our Gayle can do it.

Lionel White, The Other Driver

At the time of the accident, Lionel was near the end of his junior year in high school. After graduating, he attended St. Michael's College in Colchester, VT. During his college years, he ran varsity cross-country, was a member of the varsity ski team, and participated in the track club. In his senior year, he served as captain on both teams and president of the track club. He graduated in '06, and currently works as a manager in Burlington, Vermont. In the one hundred hours appointed by the court, we got to know him as a capable and compassionate young man. We were able to reconnect with Lionel through his college coach. When we explained the purpose of the book, he was happy to answer Gayle's questions. Despite the unfortunate way we got to know him, we have grown to like him and felt proud when we learned he had finished college.

Gayle: What do you remember about your day before the accident?

Lionel: The day before was just another Saturday for me. In the morning I had practice for track. Later in the evening I went out to a graduation party for friends who lived across town. It was a normal Saturday for me.

Gayle: Do you remember anything about the accident itself?

Lionel: The brief memory I have was when I woke up from being unconscious and saw a cracked windshield, blood, emergency vehicles, and I noticed that when I raised my right leg, my ankle was just hanging there with nothing holding it up. The last thing I remember was giving a police officer my Social Security number and information. The next thing I remember was talking to my parents before surgery.

Gayle: Have you had any flashbacks?

Lionel: Everyone drives tired; it's a fact of life. However, anytime I am remotely tired, I get scared behind the wheel and think about the past. I do not like to drive at night much because it brings back memories.

Gayle: What was your experience of the ER?

Lionel: From what I remember, it was excellent. All of the nurses were attentive and the doctors seemed to care.

Gayle: What were your injuries?

Lionel: I suffered from a shattered right ankle; I lost two teeth and suffered from minor head gashes.

Gayle: Can you describe your surgery?

Lionel: I had temporary braces on my leg and ankle. The surgeon put in a plate and five screws to hold it together.

Gayle: What was your recovery like?

Lionel: It was an amazing gift. Since I went into the accident in good physical shape, my ankle healed at a very fast rate. My doctor is an athlete himself, so he got me into an air cast as soon as possible. This allowed me to do my own physical therapy exercises. I also got back on roller skis and began to bike.

Gayle: What did you find most helpful in your recovery?

Lionel: The thing that helped me the most, physically, was probably my previous athleticism. My desire to heal allowed me to endure the pain.

Gayle: What did you find most helpful in your recovery emotionally?

Lionel: Aside from my friends and family, the fastest recovery occurred when I was able to get back outside and begin training again. Although at times, another good healing experience was the community service hours that I performed at your home.

Gayle: Who helped you? And how did they help?

Lionel: My immediate family and extended family were always there to talk. My friends and teachers from school wrote me several cards and posters.

Gayle: In hindsight, is there anything that would have made your trauma more manageable, that could help others in a similar situation?

Lionel: There is only one thing that could have helped me would have been to know the status of you and Devin. For two months I was not sure whether you were even alive. The accident was bad enough, but not knowing made it worse.

Gayle: How did the accident change your life in positive or negative ways?

Lionel: I sincerely believe that it made me a stronger person. The experience as a whole was a positive one. But if such a situation were to arise again I would want to be more prepared. During my healing process, two other tragic events occurred. Two people who I knew well and cared for, died, and we lost our house to a fire. Those two events brought back memories of hurting you, but it also helped me understand some of what you've been through. And I knew that if I made it through before, that I would make it through again.

Gayle: How did you work through your injuries and go on to compete in sports, graduate from college, and get a good job? You could have used the accident as an excuse to fail.

Lionel: Physically, it was easy. I have always loved sports and the month that I could not participate, I was always thinking how I needed to get back out there and train harder, once I could. So when I did got back out there, my motivation was actually stronger then before. Emotions were the part that I had trouble with. College is not an easy four years. I was taking tough courses and balancing that out with all of my sports. Those two I could just barely manage. At times, events would come along and I would not do anything for a couple of days. For example, when my house burnt down, I was worthless; I left my room only to eat for a couple of days. This same thing happened when two of my neighbors died of cancer at close proximity to each other. I would use all of these as an excuse at times, but only for a day or two. Sometimes I needed to take this excuse just to get a break from life, but dwelling too much was dangerous.

Gayle: Lionel, thank you for your willingness to do this interview.

Lionel: I hope it helps the book that you and Jess are writing. Let me know if you need anything else.

Jess Kielman, Gayle's Partner

Jess has been Gayle's life partner for over seventeen years. She makes her living as a humanistic counselor using feng shui, astrology, numerology, handwriting analysis, and tarot. She has been Gayle's primary caregiver from the beginning of this journey. Gayle suggested interviewing her, too, because "Caregivers need to know what you have learned, and I'm sure they can benefit from your experiences."

Gayle: What were you doing when you got the call from the Williamstown Police?

Jess: As you know, I had filled in unexpectedly for a colleague at work that Sunday and afterwards had gone shopping at Ames for a few things. I went to the card section looking for an "I love you" card, but nothing hit me. Then I got very spacey, shopping aimlessly, forgetting what else I had come for at the time the accident was happening. I bought a funny necklace watch with water and a bubble on the face, a burnt orange blouse, and something else but I don't remember.

When I got home, you and Devin weren't there, and there was no note. I got started on supper. As time passed, I got more and more upset when I didn't hear from you. It wasn't like you to not leave a note or call. Finally I called your folks and found that you weren't there. Then a quick call to Larry to see if he knew where you'd gone, but he didn't pick up. So I worried and stewed for another ten or fifteen minutes. It's strange how many people, myself included, have said, "But you're a psychic! Didn't you know?" Many months later, I did indeed begin to question my abilities. Why didn't I know? All I can say is that I had been spacey at the store looking for cards and later, feeling angry and tense. Those feelings match up with what I found out later that you and Devin were going through at the time, but I didn't "know" there had been an accident until the Williamstown police called. When they said you two had been involved in a motor vehicle accident, I replied, "A fender bender?" Their response was chilling. "No! It's serious. Get to the hospital." I'm not sure if I said thank you. I ran for the keys, the car, and drove carefully but quickly the few blocks to the hospital. When I arrived, Larry and Gail were already there and trembling. Gail started to tell me what had happened, but I just needed to see you and Devin. I found the charge nurse, Susan, and she was amazing. I told her who I was, and she said, "Gayle's been asking for you." She took me right in. They were doing something with Devin and had a curtain drawn between the two of you. Your injuries weren't apparent, but your words were clear as I touched your face and hair and got close. "Honey," you whispered, "I'm not sure I'm going to make it."

Even then, I had no doubt that you would, and told you so in a joking manner. "Hey, I get paid the big bucks to know these things!" Then in hushed and tender words I said, "Do what you have to do. I have faith in you." At that point I was told I could see Devin. He looked so little in the hospital bed. I touched him in the same way and said, "Hi, baby. You look terrible, but it looks like they're taking good care of you." All he wanted was to know was how you were. I kept the tears back and told him they were doing a great job on you, too. Then your parents came, and it got confusing as to whether Devin was going in the helicopter to Albany with you or staying put. Your parents were ghosts. Having already lost one of three children and having almost lost a second, I couldn't imagine what they were going through. I called Becca, who was visiting her dad, one town north of the hospital. I told her what happened and that I would be going to Albany. I asked her if she was okay to drive. I knew she was holding back her own hysteria. She said "yes," so I told her to meet me at home. After I hung up and returned to you and Devin, the decision had been made that Devin had no internal injuries and would stay right there. I held back my own hysteria at that point, knowing that I couldn't be with both of you. I felt as though I was being ripped in two.

Gayle: How did they treat you at the local ER?

Jess: My only real contact was with Susan, and she couldn't have been more competent, caring, and available.

Gayle: How did you cope with your feelings?

Jess: Well, you know me. First rescue, and then collapse! I remember getting home before Becca. I ran to the bedroom and packed, if you could call it that. I grabbed some underwear and a clean t-shirt, which I knew, was one of your favorites. Then I put on a pair of earrings that Devin had given me. They're the ones that look like shields. It seemed appropriate at the time. I never thought about a toothbrush or any other essentials. Downstairs, I made several phone calls. I didn't consciously think, "Oh, what a great idea it would be to call people to take care of other people." It was a crisis reflex, I guess. First, I called my mother to tell her what had happened and ask her to check in on Devin and take care of the dog. I called Lisa and Ed to take care of Larry and Gail then Ellie to take care of your folks then my brother to take care of my mother. By then, Becca was there and it seemed I'd done the best I could. I had Becca to take care of me. We sat in the car waiting for her boyfriend to come with us so that there would be someone for her. She asked if I minded, and I said, "Of course not, honey. I'll be useless to you. I'll need him to take care of you!" We hugged and cried and then I heard a sound I will never forget, the sound of a helicopter taking off. Thump. Thump. Thump. From the car I watched as it rose up above the trees, hovered, then took off westward. To this day I am filled with gratitude whenever I hear that distinctive sound. I know that for you it brings up very different feelings. You were frightened and alone for a 16-minute eternity, knowing that death was beckoning. I was watching you fly, hoping you would make it to Albany.

Gayle: What were you told about my condition at the hospital?

Jess: They didn't have to tell me anything. I could tell by the pace that you were not in good shape. It would be a long time before I would know the extent of your injuries. It wasn't until midnight in the ER in Albany that Max, the on-call orthopedic surgeon, sat down with me and talked about all that had been broken. He said that many people die when they break one or two long bones because of the fat globules or something that the body releases and that you had five long-bone breaks. I said, "Gayle's an Aries. If she made it this far, she'll make it the rest of the way." He was very kind and supportive, trying not to get my hopes up or bring me down. At one point I lost it to my tears, remembering what we'd been through with the cancerous tumor in your hand a year before. My chin quivering and my voice breaking, I said, "Bill Morgan is going to be so upset to hear about this!" He said, "Bill Morgan? What did Bill do?" After I gave him the short version about your hand cancer, he said, "I'm Bill Morgan-trained!" I can't tell you how relieved that made me feel. I felt at the time, and still do, that Bill is more than just a compassionate healer. He is angelic. So now I felt watched over by him. And I felt more connected to this Max guy, more confident in his abilities, and I know he felt more connected to you. As he stood up, he said, "We'll do our best by her." He headed to surgery, and I sobbed myself back to the waiting area. I turned the faucet off before I got to the kids, but Becca knew. I asked her and her boyfriend to go find a cheap hotel for us. Becca argued a little but soon saw the logic in the fact that we'd need a place to stay. And she was exhausted. She's good with emergencies, but not with hospitals. I guess I wanted to protect her some by asking her to leave. And, selfishly, I didn't want to feel as though I had to take care of her.

Before they started operating, they let me be with you in the hall outside of x-ray. After that, they took you away. I know that seeing me made a big difference for you. You talked in such a normal way, as if you weren't broken everywhere. We reassured each other that everything would be fine. Then off you went for four hours of surgery, and I waited in the surgical waiting room by myself. I thought of nothing but you and Devin. I paced. I watched TV. I tried to talk with other "waiters" but they were distracted conversations at best. Once I went outside in the front drive to pray and cry. I'll never forget my sense of dread when I looked up and saw a full moon. "Never have surgery on a full moon if you can help it," is always my astrological advice. So when Doctor Max came out and said you made it through the surgery, I was filled with joy and relief. He gave me a margarine tub with your rings and ankle bracelet and warned me it would be a long time before they would let me in to the ICU. And it was! I walked by the windowed door so many times hoping for someone to notice my need to be told something, my need for someone to come bring me to you. I asked anyone who went in and out of the room and was told, "It won't be much longer." But it was a very long time! I think waiting is the hardest part. Finally, at 7:30 in the morning, they let me in.

Gayle: What was it like in ICU?

Jess: Having never been in an intensive care unit before, I have to say it was otherworldly. First of all, it was hard to believe the reason that I was there. I kept saying to myself, "How could this happen to you and Dev?" And when dawn broke, I remember looking out the window with an incredulous anger. "How can they just walk around like it's a normal day? Why hasn't the world stopped? How can the sun be shining?"

When I first saw you, it was horribly upsetting. There were tubes everywhere. And machines were breathing for you and doing everything else you couldn't do on your own. But to be able to go to you and touch your face was all I needed. You were then, as you are now and always will be, my life. The kids come first, but they will go to their own lives. You and I are forever, for better or for worse. And so I stroked you and sang to you. You poor thing! When I wasn't singing lullabies, I was constantly talking to you, mostly telling you that Devin was alive and well. Soon I learned all your monitors and machines, and watched and listened like only an obsessive-compulsive can do. It proved most helpful in your stay in ICU to know the machines.

Gayle: What things became routine? What helped you to cope?

Jess: It's funny you should ask that, because I knew from the get-go that without rhythms and routines, I wouldn't make it. And I also knew that we had to create a semblance of normal within all that was not normal. I took a picture of Devin out of my wallet and taped it to the bed pole over your head so that it would be the first thing you saw when you came to. I didn't know at first that they were keeping you in a drug-induced coma. Your mom and dad got there at about 8:30 that morning. Your father was more outwardly emotional, and wasn't in the room with you as long as your mom and I. Sometimes he would drive home and she would stay in the hotel with me. We did a lot together. I made a routine out of getting candy bars at the gift shop with your mom, and she made a routine out of doing crossword puzzles and asking me to finish them. Your dad wasn't as steely as we *were. He had many more tears. We just showed up for work each day, and stayed late, sometimes very late. We went for walks to the pharmacy or some other store to get fresh air when they kicked us out, to do something for you. We bought more candy bars and lottery tickets. Losing the lottery became a routine. Joking about it was comforting. One time I made a bet with your mother that she would win something this time. When she didn't and I did, I won the amount of the bet, $2.00. So it was her win! In your room we made a routine out of brushing your hair, often finding and picking out the small glass chards that were left by the windshield.*

Gayle: Were there problems in the ICU?

Jess: Yeah! There was a big problem! You were there!

Gayle: You know what I mean.

Jess: Actually, it went very smoothly. They were so professional, so efficient, and so aware of the need to communicate to the patient as well as with the family. They couldn't have done a better job. Sometimes in the waiting room, however, we'd buzz the intercom and they wouldn't answer our call, or they would say that we couldn't come in now. What we discovered was that if your dad asked, our chances of getting in improved. So that became one of his "jobs". It must have been that deep, sexy voice of his.

You had one nurse who didn't use your name. She treated you like a thing rather than a person. I complained, carefully, to a doctor, and she immediately changed her way with you. She wasn't warm, but she at least treated you with respect and called you by your name as she did things to you. I guess the new school of thought is that even unconscious, there is a level of awareness on the part of the patient. It's about time!

Gayle: In retrospect, is there anything that could have made the waiting any easier?

Jess: No! Waiting is waiting. It gets a little easier with each surgery, but the fear that something might go wrong never changes. It's ever-present. All you want while you are waiting is for the doctor to come out and say, "She made it with flying colors!" Sometimes the results aren't always perfect in terms of the surgery itself, but we were all relieved that you'd "dodged another bullet" as your father was fond of saying. We were always a big group: me, your parents, my mother and stepfather, Becca, Larry and Gail, my brothers John and Tom, and later Devin. There were surprise visitors from home occasionally, like Ellie and Linda. They helped with driving your parents. Your dad's no spring chicken and had some issues with his eyes, so they relieved him when they could. Having family there is helpful. They don't need to say or do anything. It's just their presence and willingness to be supportive that made all the difference. There were fewer people a year later in the Boston waiting room those two surgeries, but that was okay. I had asked my mom not to come because I knew Fred was having some health issues and it was such a long trip. We probably gave the impression that we were waiting for you to finish your hangnail surgery. We weren't afraid to crack jokes and play games. It passed the time and made things feel more normal. We are a bunch of funny people. It would have been weird to sit in somber silence. And you wouldn't have received our best if we had not stayed "up". Thought is energy, and you deserved our best!

Gayle: What was it like when I was out of the coma but couldn't talk because of the tubes?

Jess: That was definitely a ten on my pain scale. You were frustrated beyond words, no pun intended, but it was one of the hardest things to see that you wanted to tell us something and not know what it was. We tried the picture boards the hospital brought in for you, but you had little patience for that, probably because what you wanted wasn't there. I couldn't wait for the tubes to come out, but it was two or three weeks before that happened. Once they took them out, you had problems and they put them back in. That was a rough day!

Gayle: Did you know what I wanted at times?

Jess: On occasion, but that was rare! We felt like we were letting you down. I was glad when that part of the ordeal ended and you could talk. At first it was just a whisper, then you graduated to a raspy, kind of sexy voice.

Gayle: What was it like leaving the ICU?

Jess: Scary! They took such good care of you, monitoring everything all the time.

With a regular staff I was afraid they'd miss something. I worried that when we weren't there, you'd need something but wouldn't ask for it. I know how you hate to sound like a complainer by asking for things. So, knowing your personality, I was afraid for you. For a few days you were in a cardiac care unit because they didn't have any available beds in the orthopedic wing. Then you were put into a room on 5E. You know I'll complain about that damned floor until I take my last breath. They were understaffed and didn't seem to be very attentive. I remember staying till one in the morning that weekend. That was where you were when you had trouble with breathing and Larry and I figured out that the water cup in the oxygen line was not screwed on tight. What a big smile you had when we finally fixed it. The nurses thought it was just that you were still having trouble breathing and told us to use that little exercise thing with the ball in the tube. But you were turning the colors of the rainbow, and they thought that was normal. Idiots! That weekend you were supposed to be resting up for hip surgery. So Monday morning you went down at about 7AM, and at 9 Dr. Hospodar came out and said he wasn't able to operate, that they were going to do some test to see what was wrong. Apparently the injury to your liver acted up and caused your gall bladder to malfunction. The next day we were in surgery to have it removed. The hardest part was that by the time you were strong enough for hip surgery, the window of opportunity had passed. It was a year or so later that Dr. Hospodar had to do a hip replacement. That was hard, and I know that if you'd been in ICU, you'd have probably had the surgery to fix your hip instead of replacing it later. So to this day, I curse the fact that you spent even five minute on that nasty floor.

Gayle: Once I was settled into the orthopedic wing, did things go better?

Jess: Some of the time. They were very compassionate and they kept you alive, but they also seemed understaffed. Meds came on time for the most part. The OT and PT were good, but so many bad things happened. It came as a shock! There was the time some whacked-out doctor told you on your first day out of the ICU and in the ortho wing that you were going home. And then he took you off Ativan. So you went from the maximum amount to nothing. That was a long night, trying to straighten out that fiasco. And you were in a boatload of pain on top of the anxiety that wasn't being properly medicated. "I'm going home?" you asked incredulously. "How can I go home?" You had ex-fixators, ropes and pulleys and a catheter. Unbelievable! But even more shocking than that was the night some man came into the hospital and tried to molest you and, when you screamed at him, he snuck down the hall and tried the same thing with an elderly patient. First of all, I couldn't believe that a thing like that could happen, and then I was stupefied by the response from security. Then there was the fire truck that someone parked outside in a courtyard and left running in front of the air intake vents. You were the first to smell the carbon monoxide, and they almost evacuated the hospital. Then there was the time when they left you with a morphine pump and no way to use it because both wrists were broken. And most times your food tray was brought to you and left for you to stare at until someone came in and you asked him or her to open things. We had to feed you for such a long time. But with all that went wrong, they still saved your life. And for that I was willing to let go of all the other things that happened.

Gayle: What was it like for you when I went from the hospital to the nursing home?

Jess: Well that was good and bad. It was good because it was closer, but the care was horrible. I thought the hospital was understaffed. The nursing home was ridiculous. Meds were often hours late, and that was with me chasing the nurse down and plaguing her. The noise and the smells were difficult. I learned to carry a small tin of Tiger Balm to put in my nose to help change the fragrance to something more tolerable, but there was nothing to do about all the wailing and screaming of the other patients. But somehow we managed to make it a home for four and a half months. The ritual decorating of the walls helped, especially bringing our garden in for you in picture form. It was better than nothing. And the Monday night suppers with the kids were great. You seemed to enjoy the gathering of your immediate family, the plates and silverware from home, and my good cooking. It was a big effort but with great rewards. Larry brought Devin for hours at a time. He would do homework, watch TV, or play on the new computer that we decided to buy for him. You seemed to like the idea of spending a little of the insurance money from the car on what I called "survivor presents." Dev wanted, as I knew he would, a laptop; and you wanted a bigger flat screen TV. That worked well because when you came home for your six-month stint in a hospital bed in the living room, it was nice to have a TV big enough to see from across the room. It was often all you could concentrate on. You weren't up for reading for a couple more years.

The last month in the nursing home was hell. I was so tired of it. I wanted you home so bad. I knew I could take better care of you at home. They brought a bed in for me because you were having so much trouble when I left that it was easier for them if I slept there. They didn't have to do much for you in that last month. Your mom and I were toileting you, and they loved my coffee. I'd stumble from bed, hair going every which way; run my fingers through the mess as I went to the kitchen. I'd make the coffee for the staff and for us. When it was ready, I'd bring two cups in to your room for us. You liked the morning coffee ritual a lot.

Gayle: And when I finally came home, how did it go for you?

Jess: Great. I had painted the blue living room orange and the TV room yellow to cheer you. I'd had the bathroom done over to be accessible, and built the ramp myself. Since I'd never built one before, I was a little worried that it might collapse and injure you further, so when it was done, I jumped on it, kicked it, and did everything I could to make sure it wouldn't fall apart. And I remember on a beautiful fall day, scratching my head and propping the boards higher, then lower. It just seemed that what was required by the local building code was too much of an angle. We didn't have the room for a straight shot at the angle I wanted, so I thought to build it with a right angle and a landing in the middle. That proved to be a wonderful perch for you to sit in your chair and sun yourself, or watch me garden or mow. I was sad and sometimes felt like I was letting you down in not having enough money to get some things. Then there was the tag sale to raise money for your chair lift. That was amazing. I still feel bad that it took years to widen some of the doorways so you wouldn't scrape your knuckles. Every time I see you in the kitchen, I wonder when we will be able to adapt it for you. But if I dwell on the sadness and guilt, it will never happen. I'm glad that we could afford horseback riding for a while. I wish insurance would cover it so that you could still go riding. It was such amazing therapy on so many levels.

Gayle: What was it like having Becca move out of the house?

Jess: I was happy and sad for her. She wasn't really ready to move out into her own apartment, but as she said, "There's no one home. I'm lonely and afraid." I felt like I was letting her down even though she was twenty-one and certainly capable enough. We both knew that I had to be with you. It was, at times, a matter of life and death. And the accident stopped all of our forward motion. She had experienced a trauma in her third year of college in Boston and had moved back home, gotten a job and was taking some courses when the accident happened. The amazing thing was that it didn't stop her forward motion until probably a year and a half later. Like me, she had a delayed reaction because there was no time to stop. We were needed. Becca was my rock for the first two months. She came to all the surgeries, took all the phone messages and talked with people. She was the "go to" person, holding down the fort. So after she moved, I was the lonely one. It made me sad not to have her there, but I never told her that I thought she shouldn't leave. That would have been selfish, and I really was glad she didn't have to feel guilty that she didn't do more for you when you came home. Devin was there for that, which was hard enough for him, but the age difference was great. Becca would have felt more compelled to get this, get that for both of us, and I was happy that she wasn't in the house for that. It would have been difficult to get on with her life as I thought she should. Getting you this and that and cheering you on was my job not hers. As for her being in her first apartment, I stole some time from you to go see her place, and tried to help her with little things. Later on, I made her a shelf unit and went on a few shopping trips, but it wasn't enough. And you weren't able to be a part of her first apartment. That was a great disappointment for her. And she tried so hard to find a first floor apartment. That meant it would be even longer before you could be a part of her newly found independence. What an effort you put out when you could finally do stairs! I was so happy for Becca and so proud of you. Well, I was also frightened that you'd hurt yourself, but there was no holding you back.

Gayle: What was it like having Lionel at the house working his community hours for us?

Jess: He didn't start for a while because he had had his own injuries and recovery time, but when he did, it was very challenging. I wanted to be mad at him, but when I looked into his eyes and saw another human being, I couldn't be mad. I felt it was only right that he do something for you, and often felt that 100 hours was not enough. As I put him on this and that project in the basement, I learned that he was a very capable young man. How could I hate him? I wanted to, but the more I got to know him, the more compassion I felt. But I couldn't come up to you lying in a hospital bed in the living room and say, "Hey, I really like this kid."

Gayle: Well, I remember how hard it was for me at first, but you're right. He was a good kid. I knew that in court when the judge wanted to sentence him to jail time. We had asked around about him and never heard anything bad, so I told the judge that I didn't think anything good would come of jail time. I could see Devin at seventeen maybe using poor judgment and causing an accident. I would hope he never does, but all I saw when I looked at this stranger who took so much of my life away was a good kid. I just hoped that he wouldn't disappoint me or cause me to regret my decision.

Jess: Judging from the recent communication that I've had with him, I think you made the right decision.

Gayle: Let's go back to you. How did you balance work and family with caregiving?

Jess: I'm not sure that I always did. There were many times where I collapsed in one way or another, but when I look back on what I've accomplished, it's pretty impressive. But when you're in the situation, it's just one day at a time, one hour at a time, one minute even. Being devoted to you helped. Having family and friends to lean on helped. I think every time someone went out of his or her way to do something, it kept me going. Every act of kindness touched my heart and helped me maintain my perspective—like when Jerilee (a client and friend of Gayle's) was going to pick up her son at the airport and stopped to give me a hug and a bowl of fruit, and when our chiropractor paid for three nights of my hotel stay, and when Chelsea called from human resources at work to see if I could use a crew at the house to help with modifications, and my cousin Nancy came and stayed till three in the morning visiting and shaving your legs, when Mel and Richard sent a card with "gas money" in it and later when you were home they sent care packages, when our friend Jane told us that she would take your case for free, when Molly in the ICU waiting room recommended I keep a diary, when the moms at Devin's school stocked our refrigerator, when your brother-in-law called every Friday like clockwork while you were in the nursing home, when Jamie (one of the hair dressers at work) came to the nursing home to cut your hair in bed, when Eileen (also from work) came and did crisis counseling, when various people closer to Albany offered their homes to me, and most important, when Jane told me I wouldn't make it if I continued to cling to the notion that the world is fair—these are a big part of what got me through.

I didn't go back to work for three weeks. I couldn't work until I was pretty certain you were going to live. One of my telephone clients, a physician, had asked for a reading in a phone message Becca told me about in the first week. After two weeks, I called her back and told her what happened. She was shocked and very sympathetic. I told her I'd like to try to do a reading for her but that she would have to be brutally honest if it was not up to par. We did the reading, and at the end she said, "Jess, you're more than on track. That was fantastic!" I will never forget those words. They meant that there was still a part of me that was intact, and it gave me the confidence to return to work.

I remember the first night back at work was a night I was giving the "Guided Imagery" lecture, and I had a few private sessions set up before that. I was going to get my vouchers when two women, a mother and a daughter I had worked with several times prior, came up from behind, slipped their arms in mine and the mom said, "We heard you've been having a rough time. We just wanted you to know that you and your family are in our prayers." They walked me to the elevator and both gave me tearful hugs. What a wonderful reception. So caregiving was made easier by good people and by returning to anything that resembled routine.

Gayle: Did people help enough? Who did and who didn't? And were you surprised?

Jess: I was surprised and saddened by those who did nothing, but this is not the place to complain. Those people know who they are. I want this to be a helpful book for those who have to go through what we went through with less wear and tear, so the one thing I will say is that if someone is going through this, they don't want meaningless offers of help. We needed real help. I would also tell readers to expect to lose friends and family. Some are not up for such a long haul, or are not sensitive enough to stick with being of service. It's hard if you've never been through a trauma, but it's important to prepare for the possibility that someone you love will let you down. I found the people who themselves had been through trauma were the most generous. And feeling sadness or resentment about those who didn't help, did nothing to move us forward or heal your pain. It was important to let go of the hurt in order to focus on the now.

Gayle: What was it like when you were on your own, taking me to the doctor or shopping?

Jess: I tried to take things slowly, thinking through the process of the slide board to get you from the wheelchair to the car seat. I had found those slippery nylon pants that helped so much with the transfer. My greatest fear was that I would injure you, but if I went slowly and thoughtfully, you seemed to be okay. You were, of course, nervous about being in a car. I was, too! I was ultra-careful not to step on the brake too hard. I remember when someone else braked and made a screeching sound; I thought you were going to die. You got pasty looking, then you got really red-faced, then you burst into tears. It's still hard when you or I are driving and trucks screech or someone ahead stops too quickly. It brings it all back for you. I'm not sure that will ever change.

Breaking down the wheelchair and lifting it to put it in the trunk of my little sedan was nasty. After a year of that, you didn't have to twist my arm to get me looking for a different vehicle. My legs were constantly bruised from leveraging the weight of the chair. We got a minivan because I could leave one of the seats out and tip the wheelchair's front legs up to get it in. What a difference! My legs and back were much relieved, however, my heart was sad about having to buy a minivan. It's not our style, but then I reminded myself that a car is just a tool, and we needed a wheelchair-friendly tool. The doctors' offices and the hospitals were always wheelchair friendly, but shopping was a different story. Stores should take a wheelchair through their aisles and see how difficult it can be to shop. I am always frustrated going down an aisle only to find that we have to backtrack because the next aisle or turn around area is too small. With all the people in wheelchairs, I still find it shocking and offensive, especially in national chain stores. I make it a point not to give them a penny more of my business in the future.

Gayle: What was it like when it looked like I might lose my right leg?

Jess: I just didn't give it space in my head or my heart. That worked well for me. And when we talked, I told you that you wouldn't lose your leg. Some days were challenging. The local doctor really thought that you had to remove the leg or die. I assured you that I would still love you no matter what the outcome. I kept reminding you that it was your spirit that I had fallen in love with, not your body.

Gayle: When I had the two surgeries and the month in rehab in Boston, how did you cope with all the driving and hotels?

Jess: There were certainly days when I couldn't believe that all this was happening to us, but if I kept my mind on the moment, it would lead to the next moment and eventually we'd be home again. Priceline.com was a miracle. We were struggling financially and Priceline always came in cheaper than affiliated hotel stays the hospital could offer. As for the driving, I like driving. But it did get old, fast. I'm used to you driving and me navigating, so I got lost a bit sometimes, but could usually get myself out and on track again without too much difficulty, even in Boston. Now that surprised me. One time I missed a turn and ended up in Waltham somewhere before I got my bearings, but I just followed the sun or the car compass. No problem. Seeing how lonely you were was hard. I would call you on the cell phone to let you know how many minutes before I'd be there, or when I had left to go to a hotel or home. I would call and have you listen to a moving song. My favorite was "You're Still You," by Josh Groban. It surprised me how often the stations played it at just the right moments.

Gayle: What was it like seeing me being lowered into a canoe at the rehab center?

Jess: Oh, my God! I thought that there could be no moment that would ever rival that one. You were doing a sport! And one you were good at before the accident. You were so scared as the Hoyer lift took you up and out of the wheelchair. I was grinning from ear to ear. Then when they lowered you into the canoe, it all changed. You were a new person. You were a part of your old self. That was one of the most memorable moments for both of us.

Gayle: And walking?

Jess: The first time I saw you walk was like the first day I knew I was in love with you. I watched you walk away from me all tall and cocky, and I was hooked. You weren't as cocky but you were pretty tall again. I remember the first time you stood up out of your chair at Dr. Hospodar's office. He got this shocked look on his face, stepped backwards, and then he said, "Jeez, you're tall! I had no idea!"

Gayle: What about the first time you saw me get on a horse?

Jess: I was proud, and there were tears in my eyes. Then, about six months into your riding, you began going up to Williamstown by yourself while I worked on the house. There must have been six rides I missed. When I went with you the next time, you blew me away. You were sitting up so tall in the saddle and looking like the cat that ate the canary. You had made incredible progress. I think you were starting to learn some dressage at that point. I remember one day running into a woman we have since gotten close to, Carol, and she asked questions about your accident and revealed that she was a nurse. Then she told me a famous quote that I had never heard before. It meant so much to me. "To ride a horse is to borrow freedom."

Gayle: Do you ever stop feeling like you have to protect me?

Jess: I think once or twice when I'd had a second glass of wine, but you don't really need that much protecting any more. Riding has given you so much stamina, balance, and strength. Except for the pain you're always in, it's almost like the old you at times. For a few minutes or hours I forget what happened. I'm sure you have moments when you're riding or in the kayak that you forget also.

Gayle: When did you stop jumping in alarm?

Jess: Did I? I don't think I have. I just don't jump as high.

Gayle: How has your life changed physically?

Jess: Well, my stress level took a leap. That's for sure. I did have that bout with my thyroid going over-active, then under-active, then leveling out about a year or two after the accident. My back hurts more. My wrists get very tired sometimes when I have to do hills with you in the wheelchair. I thought going down to and back up from the Rose Theatre at Shakespeare & Company this summer was going to be the death of me, but I survived.

Gayle: What do you do for yourself?

Jess: I go for psychotherapy, thanks to Jane (our lawyer friend) pushing me into it. I get a lot out of having fifty minutes to myself every couple of weeks. I liked it better when it was every week, but as life gets easier, insurance won't indulge me. I like disappearing into yard work, especially when I know you're out there with me. It's good for my soul. And I get a lot out of going to work, even though I hate leaving you. It almost always renews me. Sometimes I get lost playing games on the computer or working on making movies from our vacation pictures. Working on this book has been good. I love to write. And sometimes I can get lost in a good beer and a Red Sox game.

Gayle: Have you learned anything about yourself that you didn't know before all of this? How have you grown?

Jess: I never thought I could be this patient. It's never been a virtue of mine, but I've learned it in spades, and yet I've grown less patient with people who don't understand this new life of ours. Our life has changed dramatically since the accident. I've always been a compassionate person, but seeing the amount of pain you've been in, still are in, really takes me on an emotional rollercoaster. It's hard to watch and not be able to do much about it. Knowing that you have 123 places where arthritis has and can set in to cause you even more pain down the road is unbearable, and knowing even more pain is in our future as more surgeries are required. I've learned that my capacity for love is bottomless. I knew that before, but the last five years have truly put it to the test. I feel as though I was an unfired clay pot before the accident. The experience has annealed me in the flames, and I am stronger.

Gayle: This whole event has changed your life, your dreams. How do you cope?

Jess: As you know, I studied Psychosynthesis and Gestalt for two years and have worked with Robbie Gas who studied with Elisabeth Kübler-Ross who was the expert on death and dying. If I pay attention to the five steps of grieving[6] your losses and my losses, and even the losses of us as a family, I do pretty well. I still wake some mornings thinking, "This didn't really happen to us, and if I go back to sleep and wake a little later, my old life will be there." But unfortunately, I have to wake and accept what has happened because I need to go downstairs and let the dog out, put on water for coffee, and fix a tray with ground flax and applesauce for the Methadone-induced constipation that you have, a shot glass of glucosamine chondroitin to ease the pain in both our joints, juice so that you can take your pain pills, a few cookies or biscotti, and some fruit. Many mornings I admit to feeling quite angry. I'd like to kick the dog and throw the cat against the wall, but that's not me. But the anger is a deep part of who I am now. I think it's my inner teenager that hates all this because it's simply too hard, and it gets in the way of my becoming a famous artist or mystery writer or one of my other dreams. It's all too menial and hurts my wrists. Then my inner adult gets depressed because life is so freaking hard. I have to work, reconstruct a house, shop, cook, clean, and care for a person who shouldn't be doing many of the things that she does because she sees how much pain I am in or how tired I am and feels both guilty and compassionate.

A month ago, a colleague at work was hit by a truck and died. She was 45, the same age you were when the truck hit you. I didn't know her well, but I couldn't stop crying. So I have to deal with the fact that there's more to it than that. Her death is triggering some very personal feelings for me. I realized the

---

[6] Those steps are denial (this isn't happening to me), anger (why is this happening to me?), bargaining (I promise I'll be a better person if ...), depression (I don't care anymore), and finally, acceptance (I'm ready for whatever comes). If you don't know these stages, I highly recommend some reading or therapy.

other day after leaving therapy that my teenaged self thinks that death would be an easy way out of all this labor and emotion. But my adult self is ashamed that I would even think of suicide. And the hardest part of it all is that my inner child sometimes sobs and wonders, "Where will my dreams go if I die? And who will take care of my Gayle?" It's really a quandary some days! And I think that what gets me through the cacophony of my many-voiced choir is trying to get my wise self to conduct and bring those voices together into a more harmonious group. I am certainly not successful every day. I can get quite weepy, bitchy, and steely, but what I try to remember is that all of what has happened to me and around me contributes to the noble person that I am today, that I couldn't be me without all those experiences. And I know that the same is true for you. Perspective is a good strategy, too. I remind myself that you lived. You could have died. And by comparison to some, we have a wonderful life. We have a beautiful home. No enemy has burned it to the ground. Our children are relatively healthy and happy. A warring tribe has not killed them. I have a wonderful place to work and get paid well. I don't have to spend my days searching for food or water. So I try to be patient and take one day at a time. When I am at my worst, I try to remember and live by a Japanese poet's words, "My barn having burned, I can now see the moon."

I would suggest to other caregivers that you lean on others, and most important, lean on the person you are helping. It is disempowering for them to always be on the receiving end. Try to figure out what the other person can do for you and let them. I would also suggest that you find ways to stay who you were before caretaking took over your life. You need and deserve a normal life and a few normal routines. So ask someone to fill in for even an hour a week so that you can take a yoga class, a long walk, visit with a friend. You will be a better caregiver for the effort on your own part. Also, know that if you make mistakes, forgive yourself. Even the best of doctors and nurses make a mistake once in a while, and chances are you haven't had the benefit of their training. You nearly lost your right leg because I messed up and didn't know I'd run out of your antibiotic. And even if it was my fault and the infection went wild and you lost your leg, I wouldn't make it as a caregiver if I were wracked with guilt.

And remember that caregiving is for the long haul. You and I plan to live into our nineties. And we're not going to sit home and mope. We're going to travel. We're going to do sporty things. We're going to do as much as we planned on doing before the accident. I know that it will look and feel different, but it's going to happen anyway. We are two wild and willful women who aren't going to let circumstance totally dictate who we are.

Chapter 7: Gadgets, Gizmos & Helpful Ideas

Many of the things in this chapter may have been mentioned in prior chapters,
but for those who don't read every word, we thought it important to gather
all the helpful ideas together in one chapter for easy access.
And to make it even easier, key words are in bold.

While in the ER

The ER can be a very scary place. And you may find that it's not just the patient who is frightened. I remember one of my caregivers was overwhelmed with my injuries, and I had the presence of mind to help him to settle down. I just told him that he would be fine and to take it one step at a time. I know he felt calmer just because I was. **Eye contact** was important. I believe that Devin and I were treated better because we both made eye contact with our caregivers. I made it even more important when I asked a question. It's hard to lie when you're looking someone in the eyes.

I remember feeling more human **when the staff used my name**. I, in turn, reminded them of my son's name. And when I could, I asked their names. A willingness to use names helps personalize your experience. I know that Jess mentioned to a doctor while in ICU that a particular nurse wasn't using my name, wasn't talking to me when she did things. The doctor said that he would speak to her about it, and it changed immediately.

Jess did an interesting thing at home, just before leaving. She started calling people and telling them what happened but she only called certain people—her mother to take care of the animals, her brother to take care of her mother, a friend to take care of my parents, friends to help Larry and Gail. Later from the ER, she called one of our friends and put her in charge of **prayer and affirmations**. Our friend said later that she called or went to every church and synagogue in the Berkshires, called every prayer circle that she could think of, locally as well as nationally, and told the people she talked to, to spread the word if they could think of any other healers or groups.

In the ER, Jess was firm about seeing me. I was brought in by helicopter at about 7:30 at night. Jess, Rebecca, and her boyfriend arrived by car about 8:30 and didn't get to see me till about 11:30 p.m. She asked at least ten times, was told what was happening and that as soon as they could, she would be let in to see me. Finally, when they were done with x-rays, which took forever, she got to be with me in the hall. Surgery started at midnight, so we had half an hour together. It helped a lot. **Seeing someone you love before surgery helps** you feel more hopeful and grounded in your desire to live.

While your family is waiting in the ER, it is important to **maintain some normalcy**, physically. Much will be expected in the days, weeks, and months ahead. Jess sent Rebecca's boyfriend to the cafeteria for **protein**. They said they choked down a half a turkey sandwich and drank lots of **water**. At 11:00 PM, she sent them to find a motel and get some sleep. She knew she would need them the next day and wanted them as rested as possible.

While in ICU

It's very important for your family to **ask questions** and to know what procedures are being done. Everyone agreed that ICU was a frightening place. There are so many tubes and machines, other people making noises, machines making noises, and people running around. Often visitors get kicked out so that staff can do something they don't think visitors should see. If they don't tell you what, ask them. **Learn what the machines are doing and what the read-outs mean**. One simple thing that my parents and Jess learned was very important. **Watch the blood pressure monitor**. They knew that when mine started to climb over 138, it was time to call the nurse. Often it meant that I was having difficulty breathing because my lungs were filling with fluid and needed to be suctioned. They would chew their fingernails until the nurse did that and I calmed down. I'm sure the nurses appreciated their attentiveness, because it avoided a more urgent and tense situation.

Your family should alternately **take naps** so that someone is always a bit alert. **The more people you have, the better**. Jess said the ICU waiting areas were jammed with loved ones, some even sleeping on the floors.

One of the people in ICU keeping vigil for her father suggested Jess **keep a journal**. She said that there's no way you are going to remember everything, and she knew her father would grill her when he came to. She liked that it kept her busy and kept her from worrying quite so much. It gave her something to do when the nurses wouldn't let her go in.

A good friend whose husband is a surgeon told Jess to **bring snacks and goodies** for the staff. "They tend to remember you better," she explained. Jess would go to one of the discount stores and bring back big bags of nuts, pretzels, and fruit.

Restraints are hard for everyone to deal with when they are required. I didn't have the strength to move my left arm, but even with a broken wrist and drugged to the max, I would try to pull out the feeding and breathing tubes. They made me angry, and it made my family sad to see them. Jess would untie me when she knew she wouldn't nod off and just hold my hands loosely so that she could calm me. By then the nurses trusted her with things like that. And perhaps all the goodies helped, too.

I am an acupressure therapist and have always used **homeopathy**, especially **Rescue Remedy**. This is a Bach flower combination to help with mental, physical, and emotional shock. One of my doctors knew about it and allowed the drops after the breathing tubes were out. Although Jess didn't think of it at the time, there is a **Remedy Remedy ointment** that can be applied on the skin. We also wish we had known about **Arnica gel**. We discovered it a year later and it really helps with inflammation. **Arnica** and **Rhuta** are homeopathic remedies used for injury. Once the feeding tubes were out, the doctor allowed the Arnica and Rhuta tablets that dissolve under your tongue.

Another thing that was important was communicating with those who can't be at the hospital. My parents had an extensive **calling tree**, and Jess emailed daily "Gayle Updates" that family and friends truly appreciated. I know that the **calls and the emails** were important for my family to reach out and obtain the connection and compassion that they needed in order to get through our ordeal.

While in a Regular Hospital Room

Once I was well enough to be in a normal room, I learned how important it was to have someone **write down my questions for the doctors**. Then each time the team of doctors, residents, and interns come through, usually at some ungodly hour before your coffee or your family arrives, you have your list. If you are able to take notes, that's best because it's unlikely you'll remember or even understand the answers you get. They move fast and talk fast. If you blink, they could be gone. I wish I'd had a recorder that I could have listened to later.

Don't be afraid to **ask that things be adapted**. Nurses and CNAs are often pressed for time, and can't think of everything. One afternoon I was given a pain pump so that I could regulate when I needed more medication. The only problem was that I had no function in either hand. I tried pressing it with my right elbow, but that didn't work. It took me a while to say anything, because I didn't want to sound like I was complaining. After a few hours, a nurse came in to take my vitals and I told her my predicament. By then I was also frantic with pain and the nurse felt guilty, which made me feel bad, too.

After she pumped it a few times for me and found a way to adapt it, she talked to me about pain. This I found very helpful. She said that **you can't easily "catch up" on your pain**. If you try to be brave or, for any reason, don't stay on top of it, it takes a while to get back to a reasonable level and takes extra pain meds. There is a chart in most rooms so that you can tell them in numbers what you pain level is. Ten being the highest, I was at about a thirteen, I told her with tears in my eyes. Within a few hours I was back to what for me was normal for that time, between a 6 and an 8!

Unless your doctor says, "Under no circumstances should you move!" find something that he/she will allow you to move. **Movement is soothing**. Wiggle your toes, exercise in bed within the allowed range prescribed, but don't just lie there. I am a vital, fidgety, athletic person, and I was shocked at how quickly **muscles atrophy**. Down the road, I was even more surprised at how hard it is to bring those muscles back!

Drink as much water as they will allow. It is important for carrying away toxins, and it helps the veins to keep from collapsing as well as constipation. I was told that it would help when they came for blood, so I always drank a lot, but even more when I saw them coming. I also asked for a **warm cloth**, and learned later to **hang my arm off the bed**. The warmth and gravity would help my veins get a little larger and the "bloodletting" was much less painful. Doing some **deep abdominal breathing** also helped to relax me. That means when you inhale, you make a big belly, and when you exhale, you make a skinny belly. Before I learned these important steps, I would often get stuck twice or more before they could get a good blood draw from my vein.

Write down, or have someone else **write down, all the drugs you are taking**, what the dosage is, and how many times a day the drug needs to be taken. Ask if each drug should be taken with or without food. Most medications, whether Western, Chinese herbs, flower essences, or homeopathic, have a "best means of administering". For example, the homeopathic preparations are best taken under the tongue and a half hour or more before or after food, drink, and even after using toothpaste. Find out as much as you can so that your body gets the most out of what you take. I say a little prayer/affirmation with whatever I take, just as I would say grace before a meal. Blessing things raises their vibratory energy.

Now here's something that meant a lot to me personally, and it's a great story, too. Jess's cousin Nancy, who was in a snowmobile accident years prior to my disaster, came to visit me a few weeks after I was out of ICU. Not only did she understand what I was going through; she was also a woman after my own heart. We'd been commiserating for about an hour or two when she said to me, "Hey, girly. Those legs of yours are gettin' mighty hairy."

By then I knew not to take offense. I knew that she was going to offer to shave them, ex-fix, traction, and all. Now **shaving my legs** has always been a priority for me, so a month of growth was pretty depressing. But with all that my family was doing for me, I was hardly going to ask them to shave my legs. So

Cousin Nancy got started. We laughed and laughed till my belly ached. I think it took her about three hours and a dozen or more of those hospital throwaway razors, but finally I was shorn. How happy that made me! And what a great memory!

Washing my hair wasn't easy either. The CNAs were too busy to do things like that very often, and it came with a lot of begging. Between caregivers and Jess and Rebecca, I got my hair washed once a week. Yuck! And what a trick it was, relying on basins and bottles of water. If anyone could invent a more comfortable, more efficient way to wash hair while in bed, there would be many grateful patients around the world. Jess asked a friend who is a hair stylist from work to come in and cut my hair very short. It made everything much easier.

Decorating the room is also important. I felt so displaced, so homesick, so much in pain, that anything that anyone did to make that sterile room more like home was welcome. Even the smallest effort increased my level of comfort. When I first opened my eyes in the ICU, I immediately noticed that Jess had taken **a picture of Devin** and taped it on the traction bar over my head. A little further down the bar I noticed that she had also taped a picture of Rebecca. What a surprise! And what a comfort! Later, in a regular room, Jess cut out **pictures from magazines** and hung them in strategic places, for me to be able to see things that I love: the ocean, flowers, my family. Every card and letter was hung with surgical tape, which is in abundance and doesn't leave marks on the wall. Doctors and nurses remarked at how wonderful the room looked, but most of all they knew how much I was loved. Somehow, I think it affected my care in a positive way.

Bringing things from home is important. The first thing anyone thought of was my own squishy **pillow**. I believe that was Rebecca's idea. It smelled like home. When I mentioned that, Jess made it a point to bring frequent changes of pillowcases so it would still smell like home.

Cousin Nancy knew we were into feng shui, so she said she wanted to make me a **hospital quilt** with all the right colors and shapes. The best things for health are yellow, earth tones, and square shapes. The supportive color is red, and the shape is pointy. So Jess's cousin made me a quilt with yellow squares and red stars. Later she cracked Jess and me up by sending a card with one of every Ralph Lauren yellow paint chip because they were also the only ones at the time that were square. Jess proceeded to tape them to the bottom of my foot braces, the bed, the tables and chairs, and then challenged Devin to find them all. It was fun.

As you can tell, extended stays require a lot of **imagination**. There's only so much television a person can watch and at that point my attention span wasn't even up for half an hour of sitcoms.

Here are another bunch of helpful tips. Jess found the linen room right away and kept me in constant supply of towels and **johnnies**. As for johnnies, those oh-so-fashionable outfits that tie in the back, can be so starchy and rough. Jess would find the cart and run her hand down the pile of folded ones until she found the softest. When she wasn't around I got some pretty scratchy ones that came off as soon as she arrived.

We used a lot of **washcloths**. For some reason, a cool towel on my forehead was most therapeutic. Wiping down my skin and particularly my hands refreshed me. Placing damp, slightly wrung-out **towels on the heat vents**, which were always on the window ledges, seemed to help put moisture in the air. That helped because my throat hurt from the tubes. It was also nice not to get shocks from the static when someone touched or kissed me. Even in the summer, the air was terribly dry.

Rebecca and Jess **made johnnies out of several of my own tee shirts**. What a treat it was to wear my own clothes some days. Jess, who hates to sew, thought of this. She cut one shoulder and side along the seam, then stitched on snaps and later Velcro. There are some funny stories about the ones that had to be redone. Poor Jess is left-handed and a little dyslexic at times. But they had some good laughs over the mistakes, I'm sure.

Bed wrinkles are a hundred times worse than sock wrinkles, and if you can get anyone to pull on the sheets and sheet protectors, sometimes called "chucks", it's not only more comfortable but will reduce the risk of bed sores.

Help brushing your teeth is important if you have injuries to your hands, arms or shoulders. Since you are working with a toothbrush, toothpaste, a cup of fresh water and a spit basin, things can get pretty tricky. And if you spill, it could be a long time before anyone has the time to clean you up.

Fresh fruit and vegetables are a must. Albany's food wasn't half bad, and they had decent fresh fruit, but the vegetables were quite sad. By the time they were served, most of the taste, not to mention the **fiber** was cooked out of them. Frankly, I have found that is true with most institutional cooking. So if a family can supplement, they should. Be sure to follow any dietary precautions that your loved one has. Most of the **pain medications are constipating**, and when you can't walk, your intestines need all the help they can get.

Jess spent a few nights with me at the hospital. She was surprised that the staff removed the extra bed when I had no roommate, which was most of the time. She tried sleeping in the reclining chair in my room but it was horribly uncomfortable. **Improvising a bed** for herself, she pulled together three chairs, three pillows, and a flat sheet. She arranged the pillows on the chairs, tied the sheet around them, and then tied the sheet ends to the outside legs, in order to hold the whole thing together. I thought that was pretty clever.

Removing bandages can easily damage, even rip the skin. One of the nurses had a great solution: he brought in what looked like a lollipop wet with some sort of liquid antiseptic that he worked into my skin as he gradually pulled the bandage away. It was so much less painful when it was done that way; after a while I wasn't afraid to insist that all the nurses do the same.

While in the hospital, my doctor prescribed something called an **EBI bone stimulator**. It plugged into the wall and had a flat donut-shaped attachment that sat on my right knee sending **electromagnetic** signals to the bone to grow. It stayed there for ten hours a day. The amazing thing is that Dr. Hospodar placed a matrix for the bone to grow on and it did. I lost six inches of my right femur as a result of the accident and the device helped my bone to grow three inches along that matrix. I don't know what the record is for bone growth with this device, but I remember he was quite pleased with the three inches. Now I only need a three-inch lift on my right shoe. I don't know if they even make six-inch lifts. I feel blessed that such a device was available and that my doctor knew about it.

My family was so traumatized by watching what I went through on a daily basis that they could not focus on insurance matters or benefits. We missed out on eight months of **Social Security** benefits because the **social workers** were supposed to inform us of what might be available and never did. Or if they did, it was while I was napping. Finding your social worker is very important, and asking them to do their job is even more important! Perhaps one person who can stay focused and organized should take the job of finding the caseworker and asking what benefits the patient or you should apply for.

Examine your car insurance *before* **you get into, or cause, an accident**. We carried the minimum level of insurance required by law, a mere $20,000 in personal injury for myself and $20,000 for Devin as a passenger in the car. The car was totaled and so there was some money from that, but nothing more. Six months after the accident, when the hearing came up, a court assistant told us about the **Victim's Advocate program**. Jess put countless hours into getting the required paperwork together, and we waited an entire year only to be told that we would receive nothing. It wasn't until I was home from the hospital and the nursing home that the social worker with the visiting nurses association was sharp enough to tell us that we could and should have been applying for **disability** from Social Security.

Again, Jess spent hours on the paperwork. There were painful trips to a state doctor to determine that I was indeed disabled. It was an hour-long drive to see this physician. After several stressful months, I was denied because they decided I was an illegal alien. Good grief! More paperwork!

After Jess peeled herself off the ceiling, she made more calls and finally convinced them that I was indeed born and raised in Massachusetts. A year after the accident I started to receive disability. The same wonderful man who pointed us toward that, also informed us of an organization called **Ad Lib**. They determine how much help you need on a daily basis and pay someone to come in and cover those tasks as personal care attendant.

While in the hospital, I was put on a **Hill-Rom airbed**, which has a pump and redistributes the air wherever a pressure point develops. It was very comfortable and I managed to obtain one in the nursing home and a modified version of one when I went home. **Bedsores** are an ever-present danger to anyone confined to bed for a long time. I am convinced that the airbed was part of what saved me from this ugly fate. Don't be afraid to ask for a special bed that can help you be more comfortable. Or have someone like Jess who can badger the authorities for you like Shirley MacLaine did in the movie *Terms of Endearment*.

Of all the measures we thought of or were thought of by staff, I cannot emphasize enough the **importance of touch**. In the beginning I was so desperate for touch that I even longed for the caress of the thermometer as they passed it around my cheek and along the back of my ear. To all you doctors, nurses, CNAs, even the people who bring food and clean the rooms, I hope you really hear how absolutely essential touch is. That I should take some comfort in having someone come in and take my temperature means that many patients may be desperate to be touched, to be spoken to, to hear their own name. Even the best hospitals are noisy, bustling places where a patient quickly starts to feel lost and forgotten.

While in A Nursing Home/Rehab Center

Choosing the **right nursing home** is tricky business. We learned the hard way that many are desperate to put heads in beds. It can be a terrible burden on your family to listen to their sales pitches, visit a few, make a decision, and still feel that you ended up in the wrong place. We were troubled by the whole affair, and often you don't realize that you're in the wrong type of facility until you've been there for weeks. By then, it's too hard to move.

Where I stayed for four and a half months was not the best place for me. The nursing home specialized in Huntington's, and while I met a few lovely people with Huntington's, they require a great deal of attention. Without realizing it, I was competing for staff attention with them as well as with the elderly patients.

Nursing homes are filled mostly with the older people. I had just turned forty-five when the accident happened. I needed to mend bones, grow a bone in my leg, and try not to let my muscles atrophy. A month into my stay, Jess had to have a serious talk with the floor manager about my **diet** and getting them to serve more age appropriate meals.

I needed good **physical therapy**. My PTs needed to be imaginative and adaptive. Many questions need to be asked in deciding where to place someone, but the terrible thing is that most families don't know enough to ask the right questions. And often the patient is placed in the first empty bed despite your best efforts.

There's a lot of down time in a nursing home, so **bringing things in to stimulate the patient** is essential. Television is not enough. Visits are not enough. I often got tired from my visitors even though I loved having them come. Being on a lot of pain meds, it was hard to stay focused or know what to say. One of the best things I had was a **birdfeeder outside my window** and a mobile up in the woods across the little road outside my window. I spent a lot of time looking at them, and the birds that came to the feeder. They took my mind off my pain, my homesickness, and my sorrow over all I had lost.

Most nursing homes allow **visits from animals**, so we brought our dog. Everyone loved Ginger, and she loved the outing. She would visit with the elderly on the way to my room. The staff loved her. And she was a welcome reminder of my life before the accident.

Jess tried hard to keep our sense of family intact by **bringing in a home-cooked dinner for me at least once a week**. Devin and Rebecca came almost every Monday. We called it Family Night, and for me it was wonderful to have a good meal, to use **real cloth napkins from home and our own dishes and silver**. Often Larry brought Devin after school, and he would play games, watch TV with me, or go down to the library to do his homework. Just having him somewhere in the same building was a good feeling

As many people know, I call Jess "MacGyver" after an ingenious TV detective who always managed get out of a tight situation by making things with whatever was around him. There is now a show called *Royal Pains* featuring a doctor who does the same thing. The things that woman could do with a little cardboard, some plastic, and some surgical tape! She often took things that the nurses were going to throw away, knowing that they might come in handy sooner or later. She built me a **high-rise configuration on the rolling table** that all hospitals use. They had to bring me a second one for my meals because the first one was chock-a-block with her ever-growing inventions. She put my tissue box on edge to save room, taping it to the table so I wouldn't knock it over. She made **little holders** on the side and the top for pens, pencils, and toothbrush. She taped the phone onto another box so that it resembled a wall phone since I had trouble picking it up when it lay flat on the table. She created a **pouch for my hairbrush**, a hook for my EBI bone stimulator, and many more useful aids. Whenever she saw me struggle with something, she found a way to make it easier.

Find ways of **staying connected with friends and family**. Their lives are continuing and you want to try to be a part of some of it if you can. Larry and Jess would call me on their **cell phones** when Devin had a soccer game and give me a blow-by-blow description. It was like they were sportscasters and was a fun distraction. And Jess would take pictures and short videos for me to look at. Technology today is so amazing in how it can keep us connected. If only FaceBook had been around when I was going through all this. But cell phones and email were fabulous! Jess would call me from the garden and tell me what was blooming. And sometimes she would call me and turn up the radio for me to hear a song that was special to us. I loved it.

Try to **stay on top of the medications** that are being administered. Ask about dosage, and keep notes because mistakes can easily be made here as well. Jess was always **looking up the drugs she was unfamiliar with on the internet.** At one point, she realized that a new medication on my list was a duplicate of one I had been taking since the ICU. She brought it to the attention of the head nurse in the form of a question rather than an accusation. The nurse realized the error, called the attending physician, and the correction was made.

While in Transit to Doctor's Appointments & Emergency Runs

I had to be taken by ambulance from the nursing home to the doctor's office in Albany several times for checkups, and twice for emergencies. One of those times, a bolt in my knee came loose and had to be fixed. The pain was excruciating. The other emergency I no longer recall. But each time Jess and I went, she had to gather up so many things. It was like taking a baby on a trip. She had to **pack water to drink, pills, wash cloths, snacks, pads and diapers, wipes for toileting, and overnight things** for both of us in case I was admitted. These, along with her ever present backpack with cell phone, computer, and other necessities, were always with us.

Once we got to the doctor's office, finding **a room for toileting** wasn't an easy affair. It's not the kind of thing you want do in the halls, and I would hold it until we were out of the ambulance because there was always someone riding in the back with Jess and me. Remember that at this point I'm still on a stretcher and can't move enough to use a toilet. If we ended up in the ER, they had most of what I needed and a space where you could at least pull a curtain. Often at the doctor's office complex, we would toilet in a storage room or the cast room. Even after all I've been through, I'm still a very private person.

While at Home in a Hospital Bed

When it was time to go home from the nursing home, there were a bazillion things Jess had to buy, construct, or do. Our phones doubled as an **intercom system** when Jess had to go upstairs or outside for any length of time. I had to have a **bell to ring** when she was in another room and I needed her. I would have yelled, but my throat was still sore from the tubes and I didn't have my voice back yet. She had to have a **handicapped tub** installed, and **handicapped bars** in various places as I got more mobile. And of course, she had to build a **ramp** to get me in the house.

Jess remade an old dresser, putting wheels on the bottom and an extended tabletop like the hospital tables. Larry provided linoleum for the top so that it would be easy to clean when bathing me from a basin. The wheels seemed like a good idea but when she filled the drawers with towels and clothes and toiletries, it was too heavy to roll easily on the padded carpet. There was a bit of cursing until

Larry installed a hardwood floor. Before the hardwood went in, Jess needed to take off the wheels and replace them with flat disks advertised on TV for moving heavy furniture and pianos. My **dresser/table** glided easily along the carpet. Then she built a bookcase on the other side of my bed near the wall for everything else I needed. No more cardboard and tape jerry-rigging.

Bathing is hard to do in bed and pure torture when the weather is cold. My mom and Jess kept running back and forth, fifty times it seemed, just to keep the water hot. At this point I was trying to bathe myself as much as possible. It was part of my PT regime, and I wanted to be more independent, but it took forever! We often put **towels on the radiators or in the microwave** to warm them. I always asked to be dried off and rubbed vigorously, to help my circulation. I still wasn't able to move much.

Jess suggested that we spend a little of the insurance money on what she called **survivor gifts**. She knew exactly what to get Devin: a Mac Titanium laptop. He had it for two months before I left the nursing home, and I must admit to being envious on occasion. He was so proud and happy. He'd never had a laptop. For me, I wanted a **bigger television**. Since that was all I could do, she went out and got a 32" flat screen TV. We put it on the other side of the room, about 15' from my bed, and I could see it perfectly. She agonized over the 36" version, but after pacing off the distance, decided on the smaller one. She knew I would be upset if she spent too much.

Now this may sound odd, but the best invention my MacGyver thought up was the **toilet paper holder for the commode**. It took a few months before I was able to get up and use it, but it was ready when I was ready. Jess said she could just imagine me trying to have a private moment and having a spasm in my hand. She imagined great dismay as I might watch the toilet paper roll away. So she took duct tape and wrapped it around both ends of a pencil for the roll to sit on, then taped it to the side of the commode. I was so proud of her; I told EVERYONE!! I love the way **she anticipates what can go wrong**.

At one point Jess had to learn to give me IV antibiotics. We got so stressed over the littlest bubble for fear that it would go to my heart and kill me. Jess said,

"Can you imagine surviving all that you've survived and I kill you with a big bubble." It took about eight assurances by the nurses that small bubbles wouldn't kill me before we could relax. You can snap the tubing with your fingernail to make them burst.

Here's another great idea. When I started using a transfer board the last month in the nursing home, Jess went out and bought what we called **"slippery pants"**, men's sport pants which were made of nylon. The first time I got in a car, my dad was there to help. We told him to get on the other side of me and pull. I thought he was going to have a heart attack. The slippery pants worked so well that he had to catch me and stop me from sliding right out the other car door. The same pants were good for doctor visits since they had **zippered legs** and turned into shorts with just a quick unzip. Zipping them back on for pants wasn't as easy; still, what a great invention!

Another thing I can think of that might help other women is a **container allowing you to urinate in bed**. It was something that plagued Jess. She went online looking for things from camping and hiking stores. She experimented in the kitchen sink with hoses, funnels, and God knows what else, but this one stumped her. Finally Coleen, the head nurse, dug around in the supply closet and brought a tall container, much like the urinal a man would use but with a very different looking top. It was molded to a woman's shape, and although it was tricky the first few times, we finally managed to get it to work. And we still use it after some surgeries. Some nights I hurt too much to even transfer to a commode, let alone the wheelchair to go down the hall to the bathroom. So ladies, ask for this. It's a great invention.

It's also important for me to let people help me. Sometimes I don't need or even want help, but I know that the people around me often feel helpless and want to do something, anything. So **let people help**. Let them bring lunch on their way to you, let them fluff your pillows, or bring you some ice. Try to dream up anything just to let them help.

Through all the difficult times that you will have to go through, I cannot emphasize enough how important it is to **set goals, have dreams**, and most of all

make an adventure out of even the most mundane. When we have an out-of-town doctor appointment, it's not unusual for us to take a night in a hotel, order room service, do a fancy dinner out, go to the movies, take the scenic route home, go fishing at a lake we've never noticed before, sing outrageously loud in the car, or just act silly. And also, **make friends** wherever you go. Friends will go the extra mile for you, and a **smile** can change a day. It's up to you!

Chapter 8: The Details of My New Life

The Stair Lift

A one-story house would have been easier, but we live in a two-story house and could not afford to move, nor did I want to. I didn't want more change. This meant I would need a stair lift in order to get out of the living room and back into my bedroom. This was one of my most important goals after learning to walk again. In order to have my life back, I needed to return to my own bedroom. It's hard to feel normal, sleeping in a hospital bed in the living room instead of tucked away in your coziest space.

Stair lifts are very expensive. They can run anywhere from $2000 for a cheap one to $4000 and more, depending on the bells and whistles, twists and turns you need. Friends of ours got the ingenious idea to hold a tag sale to raise the money for my stair lift. We were already stretched financially by making the downstairs bathroom accessible and by the other things that insurance didn't cover.

What started as a simple tag sale grew bigger every day. It seemed our friends had boundless energy, and soon the tag sale was coming to life. Jess went out and solicited local business owners for a raffle. Their generosity was wonderful. Not only did we get gifts and services for the raffle, but also a rental company gave us a tent for the event in case of rain (and it did rain the night before as we were gathering things). Pasta's, a local restaurant, offered their parking lot for three days, and a car rental place let us borrow a truck to haul donations to the site.

One woman called to say that she had been preparing a gigantic tag sale for months, but when she heard about my fundraiser, she told her husband to pack the truck and start bringing everything to the restaurant where we were gathering things under our free tent.

It was a weekend I will never forget. The weather was perfect after a little rain the night before. I cried many times at all the people who volunteered to run the tag sale, and how excited people were to help. When folks stopped to look around, they almost always bought something. What made the event most memorable was that a dozen or more people bought something, then went home to find more things for us to sell. I was so inspired by everyone's generosity. Lynn, the owner of the restaurant, wouldn't take any money from us when Jess or Rebecca or my parents went to get lunch. In the end, we raised enough to buy a good quality stair lift and the lumber to build a walkway through the perennial garden wide enough for my wheelchair.

Wheelchairs

Now that I was upstairs, I needed an extra wheelchair. Jess tried several times to bring my chair up and down the stairs, but ended up so bruised that I insisted on getting another. We rented one from a local orthopedic and convalescent supply business, and ended up being totally ripped off. Jess thought the arrangement she agreed to was renting with an option to buy. After nearly a year filled with physical therapy, doctor visits, and surgeries, she finally had time to call them about the status of the chair. We were told that after paying $900 in rent, they wanted another $300 to buy the chair. Jess was furious. By then she had more time to focus on these kinds of details and discovered that we could have bought the same wheelchair, brand new, at BJ's or Costco for under $200. She talked with the owner insisting that he reconsider, but he wouldn't budge. To this day she still tells people about them. It's such a travesty that there are business people willing to take advantage of those who have already been so traumatized.

Since then Larry found that we could get a chair free from an organization in town called **United Cerebral Palsy. They take donated items and give them to people in need**. Jess called and got a chair the same day, which we were told we could have for as long as we needed it. We couldn't believe that a local business was willing to take $1200 for a chair they may have bought for $100 while a nearby organization was giving them away. We are grateful for UCP and now give them all the items we no longer need. Be sure to check in your area.

Shoes and Clothing

One of my favorite physical therapists, Roberta, told me about a place in Great Barrington called **Eagle Shoe and Boot**. We were delighted with how personable and helpful they were. Mike, the cobbler, was appalled at the poor quality of the lift from the same company that charged us $1200 for a wheelchair. His wife, Barb, showed us many name-brand shoes in stock for which Mike could **construct a three-inch lift**. There were some I wanted that he could not adapt and some he talked me out of because he thought I wouldn't be safe with such height. He took time to explain what he could and couldn't adapt and why. Since discovering them three years ago, I have had them put a lift on **dress shoes, riding boots, sneakers, dress sandals** and plain sandals for walking around the house. And in all these many years, not one of the lifts has failed, worn, or fallen off. What a difference from my first pair of shoes! I adored my shoe collection before the accident, and have shed many a tear since because I don't have the freedom to wear anything I want. I used to enjoy shoe shopping and it was often therapy when I was crabby, but now it's a chore. There are many shoes I want that I know Mike can't or won't fit for me. I may not be happy, but I trust him. There was one pair of shoes that he really didn't want to adapt for my daughter's wedding and I promised him six ways to Sunday that I would be very careful and hold Devin's arm all the way down the aisle. After much cajoling, he agreed.

It was painful to give away so many of my old **clothes**. Many dresses and outfits no longer looked attractive on my now-misshapen body. And because I was in bed for so long, I gained a lot of weight. Some of the **weight gain** was because I have yet to find an aerobic exercise that I can do safely. I can ride a horse. I can play in a swimming pool, but I can no longer swim because of my left shoulder. I can kayak gently for a short time. But because of the pain, none of these activities are aerobic enough to help me lose weight. And some of the drugs prescribed for me cause weight gain, adding to the problem.

If you find that you have to give away your old clothes, **don't forget to itemize what you give away** to Salvation Army or Goodwill and take it off your taxes. And don't forget to get a receipt.

I can no longer wear some of the long, flowing clothes that I used to wear because the skirts, scarves and shawls get **caught in the wheels of my chair**, or I roll over them, or they get dirty from the wheels moving against them. Even with guards, the wheels spit up mud and dirt.

Shopping is a challenge. I have been into several stores that use their one **wheelchair-accessible dressing room** for storage. If that happens to you, don't be afraid to ask them to move things so that you can try clothes on. If they want the sale, they'll accommodate you.

In smaller stores and boutiques, the sale items are often upstairs or downstairs. And these stores won't have an elevator. We found an amazing sale at a boutique in Maine, but the best deals were, of course, up a flight of stairs. Jess set me up in a chair at the bottom of the stairs, shopped for things she thought I might like for the kids, for her, and for myself. She brought them to the top of the stairs and held them up one at a time for me to see. After half an hour of this, she brought down the maybes for us to try on and make final decisions. Sometimes you just have to be creative!

Then there is the **emotional angst of being left behind**. As well intended as your shopping buddy might be in going up or down a flight of stairs to see if there's something you might like, you're often left sitting there. It's lonely, boring, and awkward being left behind.

Grocery shopping in big stores is impossible when I'm alone because I would have to get the wheelchair out for myself and wheel it to and around the store, but I can't do that. When I am on my own and happen to be having a good day, I can find a small grocery store or market and walk in with my sticks. I can pick up a few things in the time my body will give me; but if there's a line at the register, I'm out of luck.

Thresholds and Other Wheelchair Obstructions

If you have never been in a wheelchair, it's hard to understand all the problems that arise. Our house downstairs wasn't too bad after we removed the carpet with its thick pad and had Larry install a **wooden floor**. Fortunately Larry owns a flooring shop, so we could buy flooring as we could afford it and he would gift us his labor. Thick padding makes it nearly impossible to maneuver a wheelchair. It's even difficult for someone to push the chair. Years later, I qualified for a power chair which probably would have worked on the **plush carpet**.

Two of the **doorways downstairs were only thirty inches wide** and I often scraped my hands or knuckles on the doorjambs. Last year Jess hired a contractor to change one of the doors to a thirty-six inch pocket door. My knuckles are happier now.

We have yet to be able to afford to make the **kitchen handicapped-accessible** but hope to some day soon. Because of this, I only cook once in a while. It is exhausting to stand for long periods of time in order to work at the counter or wash dishes at the sink. Someday, we will be able to put in **lower countertops and a low sink** for me to use from my wheelchair. It's difficult to open lower cabinets from a wheelchair because you're in front of them and the wheelchair is in the way. We have to look at roll-top and sliding-door designs, which unfortunately are more expensive than regular cabinets. The **toe kick at the base** of the cabinets also needs to be higher to accommodate your feet while you are in the wheelchair.

The upstairs of our house was even less wheelchair-friendly. There were **inch-high thresholds** into my bedroom and the hallway. Jess didn't have much time so she cut pieces of clapboard and duct taped them on both sides of the thresholds to make a smoother ramp up and down. All the doors upstairs are thirty inches wide and difficult to maneuver through without scraping my knuckles at least once a week. We had to take the bathroom door off and replace it with a pocket door because it would not open fully, which made the opening smaller because the door and hinges were still in the way. Every time I was in a hurry, the bathroom door would bite me.

We have a very wide hall upstairs so we hired people to bring up the washer and dryer. I don't spend a lot of time downstairs because it takes too long for the stair lift to go up and down, nor could I carry the baskets of clothes. So now I can help to do some. It's amazing what a difference it makes to have the **washer and dryer closer to the bedrooms.**

Curbs and Rough Terrain

Even though life in a wheelchair is easier than it used to be years ago before they installed so many ramps and curb cuts, there are still times when you just don't want to go the extra half a block to get to the next curb cut. Jess tends to get impatient and has gotten very good at **"jumping" curbs**. She tells me to lean back, shifting my weight to the back of the chair, then she pushes down on the handles in order to lift the front wheels onto the sidewalk from the road. As I shift forward she lifts the back wheels up onto the curb. It's a smooth move we have developed over the years. I'm just not certain how much longer Jess will be able to do this.

When I got my first chair, I told them I needed to get onto the soccer field. What I got was the closest they could come to an **all-terrain wheelchair**. Often to get to one of Devin's games, we have to go over some pretty bumpy fields. Jess quickly figured out that **the chair goes better backwards**. We may look silly at times, but when it comes to getting to our son's soccer games, we'll do just about anything. Sometimes Larry or another dad will jump in and offer to push. They tend to figure they can do just fine moving forward, but if we hit a big enough bump, it could bounce me right out of the chair, or worse, the chair could stop dead while I keep going forward. Sometimes they'll just lift the front wheels and power me through the grass. That's a little scary, so don't be afraid to speak up if you don't feel safe with the way someone is pushing your chair.

I have been asked many times why I didn't get a power chair. My answer is that I'm afraid of getting weaker than I already am. Lately, however, I have used the power chairs at BJ's and Costco. They offer more freedom, and give Jess a break. It's not easy pushing a wheelchair with one hand and pulling a cart full of food with the other. Since getting the power chair, Jess and I could have an easier time shopping, but insurance doesn't pay for the **ramps and lifts** it takes to get the chair out of the house and into the car.

Shopping and Other Outings

I must say that I was shocked when I started shopping from my wheelchair with Jess and the kids. There are **surprisingly few stores that leave enough room for a wheelchair between the aisles**. I can't tell you the number of times that Jess had to back up the chair because we'd go down an aisle, turn a corner and not be able to go any further. We've had to move things when we could, but sometimes what needs to move is simply too big to move the two or three inches needed to slip through. We tend to avoid places that aren't wheelchair friendly. It's our money and we can chose to support the more considerate stores while boycotting the rest.

One time the kids took me to the mall to Christmas shop for Jess. It was exciting, to say the least. Rebecca pushed me fairly fast and often came close to bumping me into busy shoppers as well as a few counters. Devin preferred a faster modality and often got up on the back of my chair for a free ride. Although it was fun, it was also hair-raising. When someone is pushing you, you put a lot of trust into their hands. One time Jess let go of the chair completely when she saw a blouse she wanted to look at more closely. What she didn't realize was that the chair didn't stop when she let go, and I didn't realize until I was ready to crash that she wasn't pushing anymore. "Jess? Jess? Where are you?" We laugh at it now, but it was scary, and I was pretty mad at her. It's okay to get mad at the people you love when they do things that frighten you.

Hotels and Motels

Jess and I will never forget the first time we stayed at a hotel. It was in Boston for a doctor's appointment prior to the surgeries that saved my right leg. We got to the desk to pick up our room key and were told that we were in a **handicapped room on the seventh floor**. The look on Jess's face was priceless. She was stunned. "Excuse me," she said politely. "Did you say the room is on the seventh floor?" The man smiled and said yes, not knowing what the problem was. "What does a person in a wheelchair do if there's a fire?" Jess asked, dumbfounded. The man didn't know what to say.

The next morning I woke up to a very tired partner. She had spent most of the night figuring out how she was going to get me down the stairs in case a fire broke out. She said she wasn't going to go to sleep until she had it figured. I think it involved bed sheets and a couch cushion. She was going to tie me to the couch cushion then wrap another sheet around the cushion and pull me down the stairs as if I were in a sled. Ya gotta love her!

A Mile in My Shoes

One day early on, I asked Jess to **spend a day in my wheelchair**. As perceptive and compassionate as she can be, there's nothing like the real thing. Of course she agreed, and then was amazed at all she learned. And she was surprised at how much she hurt by the end of the day!

It would be a dream of mine, now that I am in a wheelchair, that everyone spend some time in one. Store owners should tool around their shops in a chair if they want us to patronize them. And I would want hotel and motel designers to think a little more carefully on **what floor to put handicapped rooms.** Not everyone in a wheelchair has someone to help push, and getting out in case of fire is a significant consideration. We always bring a portable shower stool because not all motels have **shower benches**. The handicapped rooms aren't always as nice or as spacious as the regular rooms, so we now take a normal room on the first floor and adapt it to our needs.

Restrooms, despite code, are often difficult. It's harder when the door to the stall opens inward. Just imagine. You roll in with your chair, the toilet is there, and the door is beside the wheelchair against the wall. It's rare that there's enough room to push the door shut. So now you're facing the back wall. How the devil are you going to get on the toilet from there? It was nearly impossible in the days when I had to have the wheelchair leg extensions that stick straight out. Jess had to take them off and put them back on after leaving the stall. Also there's often not enough room to maneuver your wheelchair around to lock the door. Sometimes the **toilet paper** holder is too low and getting the paper off the roll forces you to go beyond your hip precautions if, like I do, you have a hip replacement. **Flushing the toilet** is almost impossible when it's low and far away. Most unimpaired people flush with their foot, but I can't do that. So the auto flush is a boon to folks in wheelchairs, unless it's a super flush. One toilet in a restaurant was so powerful I thought for sure I was going to get sucked right into the bowl. What an unpleasant thought. Luckily, Jess is almost always there to woman-handle the chair as needed.

Many people assume they will never be in a wheelchair, so they have no reason to care whether or not we can maneuver in the world. I never thought I'd be in a chair, but here I am. Perhaps because I had a brother with Down syndrome, I am more sensitive to people who are differently-abled. Now that I am disabled, I am even more aware of the potential problems. When you see a person in a wheelchair, move out of the way. It's easier for you than the person in the chair, with a cane, or a walker. **Make eye contact**. It still surprises me how rarely people are willing to look me in the eyes. Children stare, but adults look away. Help if the person is struggling, but be willing to back off if they don't want help. Have compassion. Hold the doors for them. Try to remember that there is probably no one who has asked to be in a wheelchair. It's not where anyone wants to be. It's not a happy place.

Insurance and Other Possible Benefits

We had many problems dealing with the insurance companies. The first problem was with the car insurance we had. Without considering what the ramifications were, both Lionel's family and ours had purchased the **minimum insurance** required in Massachusetts. What many consumers don't understand is that in the case of an accident, everyone who sustains bodily injury receives only what they've paid for. In our case in 2001, the minimum per person was $20,000! Trust me when I tell you it's not enough!

The problem is that this is **rarely explained** sufficiently to the consumer. Perhaps I should have realized that $20,000 would amount to pennies in comparison to the actual cost of co-pays and missing work, but I did not. We have since raised our coverage to $150,000 per person. The surprising thing is that the premium is not significantly higher. We have told all our friends to find out what their coverage is and increase it if they need to.

The next issue we encountered was not so much an insurance issue as an administrative one. My caseworkers in the hospital and the nursing home failed to inform Jess, my primary caregiver or even my parents, that we should get started on the paperwork for **Social Security Disability Insurance**. Because of the extent of my injuries, it should have been apparent that I was unlikely to return to work soon, if ever. Therefore, the caseworker should have started that process. Jess was trying to keep me alive and advocate for me medically. She was certainly not in any state of mind to think about such things. That is what caseworkers get paid to do.

Eventually the Visiting Nurses Association made their first call to our home. Their caseworker went through a checklist of the benefits I was entitled to and asked what we were getting. He was shocked that we had not already applied for Social Security Disability. He immediately gave us phone numbers and paperwork to get us started.

Getting SSDI is not easy. Many people who deserve it are denied, so we went into the process with trepidation. I had three separate appointments with physicians and administrators before they would agree I was entitled. At that point in my recovery, each time I had to get into a car and travel any distance was exhausting and painful. We were still using a slide board to get me in and out of the wheelchair to the car seat.

Once approved, we had already missed nine months of benefits. Coverage was not retroactive. Another month was lost due to foolish administrative mistakes, mistakes that we often wondered whether they may have been intentional. After being approved, they sent a letter of denial because they believed I was an alien. Now, that could have been funny if we weren't so desperate. It took several phone calls and faxes for Jess to convince them that I was indeed born and raised in this country. Soon after, the checks started to come in, but not for the month that I was considered an alien.

Then there was the **victim's advocate program** that we only learned about the day of the court hearing. Jess spent over 120 hours on those applications over a course of a year. She would submit the paperwork required, and then they would ask for more. One time they simply asked for it to be presented in a new way, so Jess had to take time to do it all over again. We're talking pages and pages of receipts for things we paid for out of pocket. It all seemed rather capricious but typical of government assistance. So remember, **keep all your receipts!**

After Jess got all the paperwork that they wanted, redoing it twice, we were told it could take a year before a decision was made. And so we waited. Almost a year later we were told that we would be getting some benefits. Jess bought a bottle of champagne, of which I could only drink a small quantity because of my drugs; nonetheless, we celebrated. This windfall could have meant anywhere from one to five thousand dollars. We were excited that we would be able to dig out a little from our accumulated mountain of debt.

A month later we still had not heard from them, nor had we received a check. Jess called to see when we would be getting our aid, but apparently there was something else wrong with our paperwork. We had been denied.

We were stunned again. Why had they not called us to tell us of the reversal? Jess called the office several times but to no avail. Because something was not properly documented, they reversed their original decision to help us. We felt beaten into the ground. We had spent nearly two years on this and had done everything as we were told, even doing it over completely when told to. Jess wrote several letters and made more phone calls. She can be a very direct and formidable advocate, but finally even she gave up. Our lawyer jumped into the fray, but all our work came to nothing. True to character, I was sad and Jess was livid. We were both blown away by the wasted efforts as well as the capriciousness of the bureaucracy.

The caseworker from the Visiting Nurses Association also urged us to call **Ad Lib**, a non-profit organization that pays caregivers to help disabled people with things that they cannot do for themselves. Health insurance only covers so much for so long, and you have additional needs they will not help you with at all. That is where Ad Lib comes in. A nurse came to the house to evaluate what I couldn't do for myself, and the organization pays for several hours every week for me to get help. Each year I am re-evaluated, and the benefits either go up a little or down a little according to my abilities. I am most grateful for this wonderful program.

My **health insurance** was excellent where it came to covering their portion of hospital, medical, and nursing home bills, but the co-pays on a million or more still add up to a lot of money. After four years, **Medicare** became my primary insurer, and I must say they don't cover half of what Blue Cross once paid for. I am grateful for what they do cover, but it is truly frightening when I think about what the future may hold. I know that over the years I will need joint replacements at the very least and I pray that Medicare will cover what I need. **Mass Health** is the secondary insurance and will not pay for out-of-state office visits or surgeries. Unfortunately, my doctors are out-of-state and I have to pay the expensive co-pays. This puts a strain on our finances, but it is important to continue to have Dr. Hospodar oversee my care. Future surgeries will require that I find a surgeon in Massachusetts who will work on me.

Most of my **problems with Medicare of late are with medications**. There are certain meds that are effective, and for no apparent reason, my pharmacy often informs me that Medicare will no longer pay for the one that works best. It took nearly a year of letters and calls from my doctor, filling out forms, and unleashing my beloved upon them to get a particular drug that helped with my stomach issues, most of which were caused by taking so many anti-inflammatories and narcotics. I was forced to suffer through six months of giving four other medications a try before they *finally* **wrote an exception** and allowed me to return to the drug that was effective. I think the clincher was when Jess told them that I had just seen a doctor who suggested that I needed my colon removed. She explained that soon I would need an invasive, expensive procedure to allow the bile to drain from my stomach and that if that didn't work, there was probably a gastric surgery in my near future. She said, "You can spend a little more money now, or a lot later. Your choice." Finally they saw her logic. My stomach and I were quite relieved.

Where my health insurance stumbled was with **outpatient physical therapy**. Because the PTA at the nursing home filed fraudulently for more hours than he actually performed, and because he often wrote in his reports that I refused therapy, the provider was under the impression that I was not a good risk. The truth is that I never refused therapy in the nursing home.

Partway through learning to walk with my outpatient PT, Tootie, the insurance company decided I was no longer going to get benefits. When she called them to argue, a representative told her that I was a "black hole" and would never walk. Tootie sunk her teeth into that poor woman and set her straight. It also helped that Tootie had read all of my records and was aware of the lies that were in them. She pointed out that some of the activities and exercises the records showed that I had done with the nursing home PTA were actually not possible at that time. There was a brief review and a terse apology. So it's important to have **good advocates** who are willing to argue for you. If your insurance doesn't think you want to get better and aren't willing to put in the effort, they apparently have the right to refuse you coverage.

A physical therapy that they would not cover was the two years of equus therapy. Even though **horseback riding** gave me strength, stamina, and the ability to walk short distances with some degree of grace, it is **not a covered benefit**. I have been fortunate to have parents who help out from time to time. I don't know what we would have done without their help.

Getting My Driver's License Back

That old phrase, "adding insult to injury" is the most apt way to describe getting myself behind the wheel again. Even though I did not cause the accident, in order to get my license, I had to be tested by a special physical therapist, have my doctor write a letter to the Massachusetts Registry of Motor Vehicles stating that I was healthy enough to drive, take five weeks of driving lessons, get my learner's permit again, pass the written exam as well as the road test, and pay out a boatload of money. This is something that may vary from state to state, but bears mentioning here because the whole process shocked and insulted me. So if you are in an accident and it takes a bit to get back to driving, be prepared to jump through some hoops. It made me angry, being required to take classes over again. The teacher was the same teacher I had when I was sixteen. And I know that the young man who caused the accident did not have to go through the same hoops that I had to go through before he was allowed to drive again.

Learning Patience

Knowing your limitations and restrictions is important, but it is equally important to stretch your limits. It is a **constant balancing act** and one I am not always successful in achieving. I have been competitive in golf, volleyball, and canoe racing, so working hard and stretching my limits was easy, but it was often painful. I have always been very **tuned into my body**, but on one notable occasion I went too far. We were going to a soccer game and the field was down a steep hill. Jess wanted to drive around, but I wanted to try walking it myself. Reluctantly she got behind me, holding the waist of my jeans as I inched my way down. I did fine on the downhill stretch, but coming back, I tore some muscles in my leg. It truly shocked me. It also made me angry that something that seemed like it should be so easy could have done so much damage. My doctor explained that the muscles in my right leg were not all attached in the proper places and that they needed to be babied a bit. I was sent to bed for another eight weeks. He would have done surgery to fix it, but because of the dormant infection, he did not want to risk it.

The biggest change as a result of the accident is **how long everything takes**. I thought I was patient before the accident, but I have become even more patient. On a bad day, however, patience does not come easily. I used to run to reduce stress. Now I can't run. I have to walk. Walking is slow, especially with my altered body. My stair lift is slow. Wheelchairs can get you places fast, but I don't have the strength to make it go fast. Getting dressed and undressed takes longer. I am often late and trying to rush because I have forgotten to allow enough time. Everything takes more time than it used to. Showering takes forever, especially after a surgery when limbs need to be protected from water. And I can do none of this without help.

I'll never forget the first time I was able to take a shower again. It took half an hour to put plastic over the places that couldn't get wet and tape the plastic to my body. Then there was the time at the rehab center in Boston when my PT said we were going to make brownies for Devin. It took us two hours from box to baked. Part of that was because I had to rest. It was unbelievable! I cried from the pain of the effort. I cried with frustration for how long it took. And I cried for joy over being able to do something for my son. I told Devin when he came to visit to eat them slowly because of how long it took me to make them.

All the things we used to take for granted now take serious **preparation, thought, and effort**. I can't just run out and get milk whenever I want to. I have to think things through. If I am going to be alone for any part of a day, Jess and I need to figure out what things I may want or need to do and set up for it before she goes. If I drop something or forget something, I'm in a quandary. Should I wait until Jess gets home and ask her to get it? Even the extra thought takes time.

I have discovered that it's important to work on **patience and acceptance**. This is my life now. Nothing can undo the moment in time that changed my life so dramatically. This is where I am now and who I am now, and now is all I have.

Surgeries

Double your fluid intake two days before a surgery in order plump up your veins and be fully hydrated. The night before surgery, it's good to **have a big meal** including proteins and complex carbohydrates similar to the preparations of an athlete. **Post surgical nausea** can be lessened by eating hard candies just before the cut off time. The extra sugar helps with hypoglycemic nausea. I also take **Rescue Remedy and Arnica** for bruising the morning of surgery. If your surgery is later in the day, you may have to ask for **ice chips** if you want them. Staff doesn't always offer them. **Prior to IVs**, you can ask for a shot of novacaine if you find IVs to be painful. **Bring your "as needed" meds**. Often I wake from surgeries with a migraine. By the time a doctor sees me, then prescribes medication, and the pharmacy delivers, I'm a wreck. It's important, however, to tell a nurse that you need to take what you've brought from home due to possible complications and interactions.

We often **book a hotel for the night after a day surgery** when out of town because things don't always go smoothly. On many occasions, we have used that extra night and more. I don't want to drive two hours back to the surgeon if I have complications. And always **pack extra clothes!**

Chapter 9: The Healing Power of Kittens

While I was still sleeping in the hospital bed in our living room, Jess came up with the idea that kittens would be a wonderfully healing experience for Devin and me.

I was uncertain about the added responsibility, but she can be persistent. "There's nothing like litter-mates to bring a smile to your face," she said. Jess's cat of eighteen years had died a year before the accident. Devin had four cats at his father's house including the fully-grown kitten that we got him when he was six. We were a one-animal family at the time of Jess's suggestion.

When I finally agreed it might be a good idea, Devin turned inside out over the thought of kittens in his life again. That settled it. Off we went in my wheelchair to the rescue center. It certainly was easier than the long process we went through looking for our dog, Ginger. There were no kittens at the shelter the first time we went, so we waited two weeks before trying again. This time we had several to choose from. But there were only two choices if we wanted litter mates. As a matter of fact, there was the mother, the father, and four kittens all waiting impatiently for someone to choose them. There were two boy kittens and two girls. We wanted to take them all.

Devin, Jess, and I played with them for at least an hour. Devin was in love; Jess was melting. I knew we'd be going home with kittens soon, and it would be either the boys or the girls. The more I watched them, the more I liked the boys. They seemed more interested in my wheelchair than their sisters. One of them got my attention, growling over a piece of cardboard he was playing with. I thought that was pretty feisty. He was a gold tiger with a white belly and white markings on his face and paws that made him look a lot like our dog. Jess and Devin were getting very cozy with his brother, a black and white tuxedo cat. I liked that they were so different, and yet similar. They had the same markings except where one had black, the other had gold.

And so the decision was made. We paid our money and were told they would be neutered and we could pick them up in a few days.

We went to the pet store and spent way too much money, but it was so much fun! At that point I mostly went out for doctor appointments and surgeries, so this was a treat. I loved how happy it made us all. Choosing kittens was making us feel normal again, a regular family doing regular things. We could hardly wait the three days until they were ready to come home.

I love to research things, and so one of my purchases was *Cats for Dummies*. By now my ability to focus was improving. So I started reading up on how to introduce the new kittens to our dog, how to care for them and how to train them. I was learning as much as I could, and grateful for the distraction from pain. Soon we went to get our new family members. My son has always been an animal lover, and at the time was considering becoming a veterinarian. As we got in the car to go to the shelter, I thought he was going to burst with excitement. I have always seen him as Tigger[7], bouncing and jumping and skipping, but since the accident he'd been less bouncy. Nothing could stop him now! Kitties!

Once they got used to the downstairs, they started the sibling kitten routines that Jess had been talking about, which neither Devin nor I had ever experienced. They ran. They jumped. They flew through the air. They hunted each other. They laid in wait. They ambushed each other, often in midair. They rolled together. They bathed each other. They fell asleep together. And we laughed so hard at times, we nearly peed in our pants. It was wonderful, and we desperately needed the laughter.

We named them Champagne and Caviar, something of an affirmation of future abundance. And Ginger learned to respect and tolerate them. Often one or both would curl up next to me and sleep. It was comforting to feel their softness and listen to them purr.

Being more used to dogs growing up and not knowing any better, I taught them to fetch. Later, upstairs in my own bed, it became routine to toss the play toy from the bed. They would catch it in midair, six feet off the ground, twisting and turning, and still land on their feet. I was rapt. Now I had something other than TV to keep me company when Devin was at school and Jess had to go to work.

---

[7] A character from the Winnie the Pooh stories by A. A. Milne.

Chapter 10: Equus Therapy

The Horses in My Life

It was my first off-premise PT, Tootie, who told me, "You will walk. And you will ride a horse." As an avid athlete, she had been severely injured during a basketball game. She reached a plateau in her healing until she was encouraged to do PT on a horse. "That's what got me walking again. And that's what got me to change my major from pre-med to physical therapy." She talked at length about the therapeutic benefits of horseback riding. I had ridden some when I was younger, but after that, only once as an adult. I had surprised Jess on one of her birthdays with a family horseback riding adventure. Rebecca, Devin, Jess, and I went for a memorable trail ride in Lenox. But I told Tootie I wasn't certain that I could do it. As she reassured me with each session, Jess was busy making arrangements up in Williamstown for me to start.

I was nervous when I first arrived at the barn of Equus Therapeutic in March 2005. My throat was tight and my heart was pounding. Would I be able to stretch my legs over the width of a horse? Stretching even a little still hurt, and once I got up, I'd probably be up there a while. Would these men, Joe and Mark, even be able to get me on? Would I be able to sit upright long enough to relax? Would it be fun? Or would it hurt too much? Had I gained so much weight since the accident that two men wouldn't be able to get me on the horse? And how the hell was I going to get off afterwards? I was sure that I would be embarrassed by my new heft and not want their help, but I certainly couldn't get off by myself. I was frantic.

When I met Joe and Mark, my first instructor and my side-walker, I was impressed with how quiet-spoken and down-to-earth they were. Each one had a child who had used equus therapy for years, which taught them the value of using horseback riding for physical and emotional therapy. Joe's daughter had spina bifida, and Mark's son had had Down syndrome. Joe later told me that Mark's son had died not that long ago.

With much trepidation I let Jess push my wheelchair up the special ramp of the indoor ring. Then I stood, positioning myself next to Saint, the horse they'd chosen for me. Joe instructed me to face in the same direction as the horse. He stood at Saint's head as I grabbed the saddle, picked up my right leg, and gingerly swung it up and over. Mark held the lead rope and gently guided my leg around the horse. Saint stood perfectly still.

Oh, my God, I thought to myself; I was on! But, holy smokes, I was so high off the ground! As Saint took his first steps, so did I...towards a feeling of independence. As I was led round and round the ring, I began to hope and dream that someday I would take control of the reins and move through space, not on my own legs, but at least according to my own will. To turn left or right as I chose, to ride through the woods as I used to hike, enjoying the sounds of the birds and the wind through the trees, the smell of decomposing leaves or blooming flowers. Oh, how I missed these things! I had almost given up on them. Years later I met a woman at the Williamstown stables who shared a famous quote attributed to a Helen Thompson which matched my emotions in that moment: In riding a horse, we borrow freedom.

Joe asked me to be aware of my body, so I quieted my inner exuberance and began to focus. I was shocked. Everything felt wrong. Though it had been three and a half years since the accident, I was still very physically compromised. My legs felt as though they were crammed into and past my joints. My arms felt pinched and short. My trunk felt stiff and unyielding. And it all hurt!

Saint continued to walk with Mark leading. As instructed, I paid more attention to my body and not my emotions. I was sure I would fall off. I didn't seem to be able to move in harmony with his gentle sway. I took a big breath in and a long breath out, forcing myself to stay aware of the big, strong-muscled creature beneath me. I felt that I could trust this horse, and over time we developed an understanding. We trusted each other's patience, but as those first few minutes passed, it took all my concentration to get my legs to let go of their tension. I kept reminding myself to keep breathing, one deep breath after another, to keep myself from tensing up. Slowly and painfully my leg muscles relaxed, easing their way into a longer, looser state.

Saint was a big barreled old stallion. I felt like I was mounting a house instead of a horse. He was stable and strong. In some ways I was like a child, having to be helped on and then to be helped off him. And like a child, I was both frightened and exhilarated. I was smiling so hard my cheeks felt like they might break; yet at the same time the panic was almost overwhelming. His matter-of-fact, sturdy, nurturing manner was the perfect antidote. He felt parental, which helped me feel safe, and I knew he would stay with me no matter how many feelings I experienced.

In the beginning I was afraid of many things, but I knew he wouldn't let anything happen to me while I was on him. Later they explained that it takes a special horse to become a therapy horse. They need a smooth gait as well as being emotionally stable. Joe called it being "bomb-proof". Saint was clearly that kind of horse.

It took two or three sessions to let go of my emotions and tension enough to relax into Saint so that I could enjoy the therapeutic benefit of his movements. Instinctively, I closed my eyes, not realizing it was an important technique to get new riders attuned to their bodies and the horse. At that point, I was still out of touch with my body. Movement of any kind was still so painful, and I knew it would take quite some time before I could truly enjoy the movement.

Because there was only a blanket between Saint and me, I began to notice the places where my body touched the warm creature beneath me. Just as when I took my first steps, I felt like the Tin Man from Oz. All my former grace and flow was gone. My bones did what they were supposed to do, but with little muscle awareness. Now as I relaxed more, the movement of the horse began to move my body. Awareness slowly began to return to my muscles, my nerves.

In the beginning, riding was tearfully exhausting. After each session I was in such pain that I had to retreat to my bed for two or three days, sleeping and taking extra pain meds. Sometimes my ride lasted only ten minutes before Joe made me get off; he said I couldn't control my body enough to stay on the horse any longer. After a month or so he introduced the saddle. It was a special saddle with extra long stirrups so that my legs could be nearly fully extended. Ordinarily riders are seated with their legs bent, pulling tight with their calves, but my legs and my knees could not bend in that way.

Over a period of three months, I was able to ride longer, depending on the day and how I felt. I had built up enough endurance to ride for half an hour, but some days I would tire after only ten minutes. My strength waxed and waned for the next three months. It took six months before I could consistently stay on for an hour. Even after two years it was painful, but totally worth the effort!

Riding has given me back much strength and stamina. It has helped my balance, and my walk is no longer the Tin Man walk. Some of my old athletic grace has returned. The horse is the only animal that can replicate the human gait for its rider. Along with all the physical benefits, there are also neurological improvements that come from riding. Add to that the emotional benefits of bonding with another living being. I could say much about the joys of bonding with a horse, but Linda Kohanov is more eloquent, describing it in The Tao of Equus.

> .... to horses, emotion is neither good nor bad; it's simply information. As animals that are preyed upon in nature, it behooves them to know when another herd member is feeling afraid or playful, angry or in pain, depressed or content. Though they ultimately strive for wellbeing in their relationships, horses don't consider so-called positive emotions any more important than the negative ones humans routinely try to suppress. To these animals, the ability to intuit fear in a distant herd member and act on this feeling without hesitation is a lifesaving skill. Their innate aptitude for resonating with another being's trust, joy, or confidence is a life-enhancing skill.

When I was young, I went to a horseback riding summer camp. I loved every horse I encountered just because they were horses and I was horse crazy, but I didn't distinguish one from another. Now, here at Oak Hollow Farm, I was again involved with horses, but in a different way, and for such a different reason.

After any trauma, trust is a huge issue. Week after week, I was developing not only trust in my horse, in my instructors, and my body, but also trust in the world.

It was ridiculously hard in the beginning. Even now, after riding for two years, it's only in moments that I am able to lose myself and just enjoy the ride. In those moments it is thrilling, and yet relaxing at the same time. Those fleeting moments give me a nostalgic glimpse of who I used to be. There is a comfort in recognizing an old friend, me. Anyone who does something well knows that moment in time where you forget yourself and your surroundings fall away. Whether it is that perfect swing in golf when you hit the ball just right, or a good move in a chess game, there's a feeling of glowing from within. Those moments where everything flows harmoniously are truly stunning. Since the accident, those moments for me are few and far between. Before the accident it was easy to lose myself in the sensation of movement when I was skiing or canoeing, golfing or dancing, or simply taking a lazy walk with Jess and our dog.

When Joe left Equus Therapeutic and turned me over to Linda, my next instructor, he emphasized how important it would be for her to keep an eye on me. I was apt to overdo if given half a chance. Linda took that challenge and many more since she became my instructor. She was careful to stretch my legs once I mounted the horse. If she didn't, the ride would be much more painful.

It is important for me to clarify that in riding horses as therapy, you don't have to have the strength to ride non-stop for the entire hour. You may be paying for an hour, but some of that time is spent perhaps brushing down the horse, having the saddle put on, getting on the horse, and stretching before riding. This stretching can be done both on and off the horse. Like a PT session, each riding lesson is broken down into segments. Some segments are for building strength, some for relaxing and letting the horse's movements massage your body, some time for active stretching on the horse, and some time spent on endurance conditioning while actually riding. The advantage to being on horseback is that your "chair" is always right underneath you.

With the improvements in my abilities, I was given a new horse to ride. Mirage was almost as tall as Saint but not quite as wide, thus I was able to begin to wrap my legs around him in a more "proper" manner. Mirage was also younger and more spirited than Saint. It was harder to maintain balanced and continuous contact with him as I rode. As my legs rose to the challenge, he became more aware of what I was thinking. He could tell when it was time to work, and he stepped out with more confidence in me, his ward. As the pain in my legs quieted, I was able to attend to the rest of my stiff body. I closed my eyes and became aware of each and every area that was not moving with Mirage. Intending to move with, not against him, I allowed his more powerful muscles to teach my body. My shoulders fell away from my ears, and the sensitivity in my hands increased, becoming aware of his mouth. I was trying to maintain a constant yet gentle and equal contact so that these could also communicate with him. Last to respond was my spine and my buttocks, both of which needed to relax and find our mutual center.

This all took time and trust. On good days, I seemed to be able to get past my limitations and focus for moments at a time on talking with Mirage via my posture, my balance, my hands, my legs, and my intent. When I was successful, it was magical.

Once I developed a relationship with Mirage, it felt different than with Saint. Saint had been like a kindly parent, but Mirage and I felt like friends. I could communicate with him better. I could telegraph my messages through my thoughts and my body, and by then I was more relaxed, more confident on a horse. Also I may have had more mental static in the beginning when riding Saint.

By the time I moved on to Mirage, I was able to stand for a while and brush him. That helped make the relationship reciprocal. I wanted to get to know him as a personality, and I wanted to be sensitive to his needs before I got on him. I believe that he's another sentient being, not a tool like a car. Mirage was very sensitive. That was obvious from the beginning. He had good days and bad days just like me, and I wanted to know his mood before I got on him. I needed to help him help me, and I still needed so much help.

Between Saint and Mirage, I rode a mare named Charm a few times. We never made much of a connection, and I didn't trust her much. When Mirage first came to the stable to be boarded, his owner watched me ride Saint. Apparently, she thought I had "soft hands" and asked Linda if she would let me ride him. Although he was not a therapy horse, it was a good match. He was bigger and fit my body better than Charm. When I first saw Mirage, he seemed very gentle and accommodating, but also a little sad. Figuring out his sadness would be a wonderful challenge for me.

When I first rode him, I was able to walk up the short ramp by myself and get on while Linda held him in place. Because of his size, he was harder to mount, but once there, I felt a difference right away. I wanted to pat him, take care of him, and develop a bond. And I could now. I was stronger and a better rider. I was certainly less afraid. I was ready to give something to the horse instead of just accepting the help he gave to me.

Over time I grew to recognize his moods. Definitely he preferred being outside to being in. He wasn't in very good shape in the beginning, even starting to get a bit lazy. So I was able to push us both. Now that I was stronger and more in charge, I loved to ride.

Once when I was riding Mirage in a group lesson with three other women, Charm decided to come close, perhaps to settle a score with Mirage. Normally Mirage would have given it right back to her, I was told later, but as Charm approached, I felt him spread his legs slightly and settle into the dirt floor of the indoor ring. Linda yelled to Charm's rider to steer her away from Mirage, but it seemed that he had made a choice on his own. To my amazement, and to Linda's as well, he had decided to protect me by not moving. He was going to take whatever Charm had to dish out: a kick, a bite, whatever came his way. Mirage dug himself in, almost as if he was clutching the ground with claws that he did not possess. He'd never felt so stable, almost bullish. Our bond deepened that day. Linda was thrilled by what she had seen, because it meant that she could trust Mirage more with other Equus riders. She was thoroughly impressed.

Mirage wasn't perfect. Like any horse, he had a few bad habits. His favorite one was to let me know when he was done working by trying to scrape me off, using the wall of the barn. But now I was confident enough to tell him, "No! I'm in charge." Those moments actually empowered me. I felt less like a victim and started realizing that I was regaining a will of my own.

Though Mirage was a great ride at the time, he didn't give me the thrill that I got with Sweet Pea, my third mount, because I felt he needed so much emotional attention. When I was no longer riding Mirage, however, he would come over to the fence when he saw me pull up in the car. Like old friends, I'd go to him and we'd exchange pleasantries for a few minutes. He deserved the attention; it was while riding Mirage that I fell in love with horses again. He helped me create a new pathway in my new life.

When I started riding Sweet Pea, I got a different ride from a very different personality. Linda Carman, a reporter for a north county weekly and also a rider, recognized my joy as well as my hard work in this quote. "A handsome woman on horseback, her face alight, neatly turns the rangy dark bay with a long white blaze on his nose around a series of orange cones, then across rails on the ground. Her steering is deft, and the horse walks, then trots, then walks again, in response to her cues."

I must have begged Linda for six months before she would allow me to ride Sweet Pea. Like Mirage, he wasn't a therapeutic horse, and he certainly wasn't "bomb-proof". He spooked easily and was a little unpredictable. So Linda hesitated, wanting to make sure I wasn't reaching beyond my abilities at the time. I'm sure she was considering my safety and the liability of the owners of the barn.

Sweet Pea handled very differently than Mirage. His mouth was much more sensitive to the signals I sent him through the reins. If I told Mirage to go left through the tension in my hands while my body's tension or my legs were communicating to steer right, he would get confused by the mixed signals. Sometimes it made him rebellious and he'd try to scrape me off. At other times, he would just stop in reaction to my mixed signals. Sweet Pea's reaction, in contrast, would be to dance around with the confusion, get upset, prance, get spooky, and frantically toss his head.

When Mirage pushed my leg up against the wall, it was annoying and uncomfortable, but with Sweet Pea I could end up on the ground. So in order to convince Linda I could ride him, I needed to become a better rider. That was my new goal.

I worked my fanny off, literally, before Linda was confident that I wouldn't be giving Sweet Pea all kinds of wacky, mixed signals. I started reading Linda Kohanov's two books and other books about horseback riding. I watched a video of Gawani Pony Boy to learn more about how to communicate with horses. I tried to become something of a horse whisperer. And I worked my body beyond its limits so that soon I was to have the leg strength to be better wrapped around Mirage. As time went on, I gained more muscle in my arms, my legs, and my core. Finally I was strong enough that if Sweet Pea, the horse I so desperately wanted to ride, decided to go left when I wanted to go right, I would be able to keep my seat. The last thing anyone at the farm wanted was for me to fall off or be thrown.

The day Linda said I could ride Sweet Pea, I was as nervous as a cat. She had built him up as kind of a scary, inscrutable steed. But my fears did not deter me, nor did her discouragement. Just because something is scary doesn't mean I'm not going to do it. If it's my next step, I am willing to push myself. And I had faith that Linda wouldn't let me ride a horse I wasn't ready for. By then she could see I had outgrown Mirage.

The first time I got to ride Sweet Pea, he was all saddled and ready to go. Linda had ridden him for a while before she let me on him. I was disappointed not to commune with him first with the brushing and chatting as I was accustomed to doing prior to riding. I had watched her ride on many occasions to see what I should look like when I got on him. I had touched him and talked with him, so we weren't total strangers.

Being around horses is one of my favorite things, and yet often they bring up a lot of uncomfortable feelings. Sometimes I felt envious watching Linda ride Sweet Pea. They looked so natural together. But then I can get envious watching someone walk on television or at the mall. I get envious of able-bodied beings on a regular basis. I would have loved to have had a horse to ride when I was an able-bodied person. I know that my passion for horses as a child wasn't just a passing fancy. I had years of loving horses from afar before finally letting it go when it didn't seem as though they were going to be a part of my life. And then when they were, there were many feelings that came up when I rode: envy, fear, and frustration. I was anxious to get good enough to ride on the trail without being led, or to ride in the ring without Linda watching my every move, always ready to catch me. She was wonderfully protective, but I longed for the day when she wasn't, when she would believe that I was accomplished enough to ride with her.

Obviously, if I were to have an accident on the horse, it could be horrible. If I fell, I might have titanium sticking out all over the place. Even a minor accident could end in the loss of a limb. It wasn't a pretty thought. And being on a trail is less predictable, more risky than riding in the ring. There is a risk to just about everything. Who knew that better than I?

In the beginning, Sweet Pea did not stand still very well. As soon as he felt my weight descend on him, he started to head off at a fast walk, ignoring Linda who was trying to hold him back so that I could get settled. He was so kinetic; he just wanted to go! Even though we were now more used to each other, I could feel him holding back with every fiber of his body because he knew he was supposed to, but he still wanted to step right off and go, which would be fine for an able bodied rider.

I fell in love with Sweet Pea when I first saw him. He was a beautiful, tall, mature horse. He was well muscled with shiny black hair that was so soft. His ears were perky. His eyes were kind and alert, and he had a white stripe down his nose. His step was exuberant. He was a good match for me, or at least the person I was and was still trying to be. Despite my handicaps, I often felt kinetic like Sweet Pea. And I missed being able to do something about my kinetic desires. I was such a bouncy person, and the personality of this wonderful horse beneath me was a perfect fit.

What I gave him in return besides a lot of love and attention was a determination to communicate with him the best I could. I tried hard to send clear messages with my body. I worked to become better at being a good passenger, letting him know that if he was nervous about something flapping in the wind, I'd give him a moment to figure it out instead of forcing him to move on and bend to my will. I aimed to understand him and allow him the space to explore his world. In return he gave me back a bounce in my step and a quickness of mind that matched me more closely in personality than Mirage. He rewarded me with a wonderful ride. And he stayed more centered and stable under me than he does with Linda. He seemed to sense that she could handle his moods, and that I might not be able to. Linda was impressed with how gentle he was with me. All the things that she warned me about, he didn't do with me.

Once, Linda had a student from a local college with her who was writing a paper on equine therapy. They watched as I tried to get the halter on Sweet Pea. He did his usual trick of raising his head as if to say, "I don't really want to work now." I said out loud, "Now, Sweet Pea, you know I can't reach that high, and if I try it will hurt me. Please put your head down so that I can get your halter on." As he lowered his head, Linda said to the student, "See that! I told you!" And the student smiled and agreed, "He's putty in her hands. It's amazing!"

I didn't make a big deal out of it, because it was no more than what I would have expected with my children. I just expected him to do what I asked and rewarded him with love when he did. It's not that he was a perfect horse, either. He shied with me at times, and also sidestepped once in a while, but now I could hold my seat.

Taking It Deeper

Since starting to ride two years ago, I've done a lot of reading. Especially interesting to me were the Gawani Pony Boy books and videos. He is a well-known horse whisperer who has a very special understanding of the language horses use. These videos are of him working on the ground instead of riding. Much of his communicating is with posture, eye contact, turning away from the horse, and moving his hands. I have certainly learned a lot. I learned that I didn't have to be fully able in my body in order to communicate with the horse. It can be as subtle as a look, a thought, the way you turn your body, how you present what you're thinking and feeling that gets a horse's attention. Being with a horse is so much more than what you see in Western movies, although I must admit to watching as many as I can to admire the horses and observe the way they are being ridden.

With all that I have read, however, my life with horses has changed dramatically since reading Linda Kohanov's book *The Tao of Equus*. I've always sensed that horses can give me more than "a ride around the track." Being a psychology major and doing feng shui and energy work, I look easily at the subtle energy behind things. I've always had animals in my life, and now with horses I want to embrace as much of this experience as I can. Her book has taught me to embrace myself, my emotions, and to watch how the horses react to me. For me, horses are a mirror into my soul. They have shown me the places where I hurt, where fear and anger still affect me consciously and subconsciously. They show me where I carry joy. Linda Kohanov has shown me how much more they sense than I ever could have dreamed.

Before I read the book, I was not aware that anyone was matching people and horses as a means of doing psychological trauma work. At Equus Therapeutic, the instructors worked on the physical plane primarily. I talked a little with Linda about the psychology of horses and tried to get her to read some of *The Tao of Equus*, but at that time there was only so far she could go with some of the theories, because her background was very traditional. I was pleased that she was open at all.

Kohanov says that many of her clients have feelings or thoughts that they try to dismiss, including random intuitive hits about the horses. She suggests that they go mingle with the herd, then write down some of those passing thoughts and feelings, no matter how weird they may seem. Later, participants in her workshops gather to share these seemingly random thoughts and often discover that these are real experiences that have happened for the horses. Realizing that the horses have communicated to them is powerful for those who attend her workshops.

In her second book, *Riding Between The Worlds*, she discusses how feelings are not necessarily the reality of the moment, and that some of the things you feel are not necessarily coming from you. This is my experience as well. I am a strongly emotional person with a deep connection to my insights as well as the thoughts and feelings of others. Some of it is my training as an acupressure therapist where I've become attuned to my client's inchoate feelings; some is from feng shui training that teaches sensitivity to the energies swirling around you. So I am very sensitive to my immediate environment. Kohanov believes that people can be affected by their physical surroundings, or may have intuitions of something that has happened when somebody new enters the room. Emotions are contagious, she writes; the panic attack you just felt may belong to someone else, though you may take it into your body as if it were your own. In that moment in time, it is real for you. So there is a need to learn to differentiate between your own feelings and those that may be in the air, so to speak.

A good example of this is an experience I had recently with our cat. Kiwi was lying on the bed with me, and we were both in a very quiet space. Jess slammed a door downstairs. I felt the cat twitch and then tense as the instinct of fight or flight ran through her body. I had my hand on her and felt instantly cold and clammy. Then I felt a metallic tension go from my hand up my arm and into my shoulder before I recognized that it belonged to my cat. I was able to stop it at my shoulder, but I noticed that I wasn't able to let it go easily. No matter how many times I said to myself, "Let it go, let it go," it didn't stop. I actually had to remove my hand from the cat, put it on my shoulder, and massage it until I felt the tension and the cold recede.

So my experience with animals is changing. Since reading Linda's book, I absolutely believe that when I climb on a horse, they know what I've been through. And they know how I am in the moment. I believe that it is all transferred information. And in the same way, whether I'm consciously aware or not, I know what the horse has been through and what his mood is in the moment. But receiving and knowing what to do with that information takes much practice, and it is helping me deal with my PTSD.

When Linda Kohanov works, she often allows participants to take time matching up with horses. They have a say, but in some instances, it is the horse that has already chosen the person. The person is responding to the horse's choice. And more often than not, the horse and the person have similar things that have happened in their lives.

So I am now trying to become more aware of my emotions and those of the horse. Being present in that way has become a huge part of my healing. I understand that I don't need to take on the emotions of everyone around me, that I have a choice in the matter. In the same way, if the horse is in a bad mood and I'm in a good mood, I don't have to relinquish my good mood to his bad one.

Recently I tore a muscle in my right leg, the one with the dormant infection. Because my surgeon did not want to risk waking the infection, he opted not to repair it with surgery. Instead, he sent me to bed for two months. Having to give up riding for that length of time made me sad, and also nervous about the time lost. I knew how hard it was going to be to start up all over, rebuilding the muscles that I worked so hard to build. It was painful and exhausting enough, the first time around. And the daily effort of getting dressed to ride, driving the half an hour to Williamstown, passing the site of my accident, getting out of the car and perching on the back of it to get my boots on and properly laced, then getting across the uneven ground all the way to the barn—I'm tired before I even get on the horse. But knowing that riding has improved my body in every way, I know that it is worth the effort. I have had a goal from the beginning: to walk gracefully in spite of the three-inch discrepancy between my two legs, the constant pain, and the fused bones in my right foot.

I know that I will have to start off slowly, rebuilding. I can't return to twice a week right away. I know that riding is good for my heart and my high blood pressure and all the things that stink because of this sedentary new life of mine. Also, my mood changes when I'm riding. It gets me out of the house, and I can feel more independent. I miss the horses on the days I don't ride. Sometimes the only ones I see all week are Jess and Devin, maybe Devin's best friend, the dog, and the cats, and sometimes Becca. It makes for a very small, sad world, and I'm not a small, sad person. Yet, since the accident, there is a part of me that is reluctant to extend much beyond that at times. It takes so much energy to do any more. It also takes courage.

I am proud of having survived the accident, and I am proud of all I have accomplished. It's taken me a long time to be able to say that. But my body still embarrasses me. I know that it's nothing that I caused and therefore shouldn't embarrass me, but the truth is that it still does. I don't want people to notice how hard everything is for me. And even though nothing happened to my face, I still feel disfigured.

Dreaming

For a few years, I dreamed of owning or leasing a horse one day so that I could grow more intimate with a particular horse. It would have been like having another close friend. In reality, it would be too much extra work for Jess and more money than we have. And sadly, I have had many setbacks since then and have not ridden in many years.

I don't believe horses look at me as though I'm disabled or disfigured. They simply accept. And I know that if I rode more often, I would get stronger, not just physically, but emotionally as well. In my wildest dreams, I'd have a small, low-maintenance home with a barn close enough to the house that I could get there in my wheelchair. I would have two horses and enough land, maybe near a national or state forest, so there would be plenty of room to ride. I'd want it to be in the Southwest where I could ride year round. Many classes here in the Berkshire winters are cancelled because it's too cold for the horses.

Maybe that's why I watch so many Westerns, because that's what I want. I want to get on a horse and ride a long way, as I used to be able to do on walks and hikes and riding my motorcycle. I miss that freedom. I don't get outdoors enough and I miss that, too. There are days when I sink into a kind of agoraphobia, where leaving the house, even leaving my bedroom, is difficult. Riding a horse is like going for a walk with a friend, one that I can trust, and one that is as excited to explore our surroundings as I am. A horse can take me places that my legs can no longer go.

On the jacket of *The Tao Of Equus*, there's a picture of Linda Kohanov's horse Rasa with her front hooves up on the steps of her house. They are greeting each other at the front door. That was my dream.

A Visit To The Epona Center

For our fifteenth anniversary we traveled to Linda Kohanov's, where Jess had made arrangements for me to work with one of her staff for three hours of groundwork with a horse. She also arranged an hour with Linda just to talk. She wanted it to be a surprise, but she's not good at keeping secrets. Apparently it was difficult to arrange while we were visiting our daughter in Tucson for a week, but she did it, and we had a life changing experience there in Sonoita, Arizona.

When we arrived, we were greeted by Denise, a soft-spoken yet tough woman who would facilitate my ground work experience. She spent an hour talking about the accident, my limitations, and what exactly the Epona experience was all about. Jess and I went over all the handouts together. We asked a few questions, then Denise took us out into a fenced-in area where there were several red metal enclosures. She explained that my selection process might take a while and not to hurry it. She asked me to close my eyes and get a sense of each horse. I did that and figured out which horse I wanted. It was a process of elimination at first. One horse just wanted to chat and have fun, but I was on a deeper quest. The next horse was too sleepy and seemed content just to nap. His name was Harley, and Jess has pictures of him lying on the ground snoring. It was the funniest thing I'd ever seen! The next one seemed too skittish around my wheelchair. The one after that wanted something from me, but I wanted more of an equal exchange to occur.

Finally, I felt good about a very large, sturdy, black draft horse named Kairos. Denise had me approach the horse's pen and stand outside it to commune directly. I felt as though he was safe and we could share something, though I wasn't sure what. I was also aware that this horse truly choose me, as Linda expressed in her writing. So it definitely seemed like a good choice both ways, but it wouldn't be until I was done that I would know the reason. Denise gave me permission to go into the pen on my own. I got up out of my wheelchair and slowly moved into his space. She and Jess watched as I approached him. He was munching grass when I put my hands on his side. He lifted his head and gently brought it around me like a hug. When he blew air out of his nose, I knew he was relaxed and I could relax with him.

The next thing he did was nothing short of amazing. With his head curled around, he brought it down to my left leg and "lipped" me from boot to hip. I don't know any other way of describing it other than "lipping" because it felt like a series of kisses or bites without teeth. It was so intimate. Then he did the same on my right, which is my more injured side. He seemed quite interested in my right foot, staying longer there. This is the site of my most recent and quite complicated surgery. Then he "lipped" my ankle and leg, stopping for a little while at my knee, or lack thereof, before "lipping" up to my hip. When he was finished, he blew out another relaxed snort and went back to eating.

It seemed he noticed my differences and accepted them. It didn't feel like we were quite done yet, so I simply stood there trying to process the tears welling up in my chest. Then I became very aware of a tightness in my chest and a stricture in my throat. Since the accident, I have had trouble swallowing and breathing. Kairos lifted his head and moved slowly to his water trough. I watched as he lapped at the water, but then he did something I've never seen a horse do before. He lifted his head and swallowed slowly as if to allow me to study the muscles working in his throat. I was fascinated with the ripple of musculature as he swallowed. I felt a release and an awareness of the need to forgive my body. I knew then that I could learn to trust it again. I hugged him and walked away.

I settled back into my wheelchair, and Denise asked how I felt and what had happened. I could tell before relating my experience to her that she was quite moved. She said she felt as if there was a protective bubble around the four of us and said that she had never experienced that sensation before. She asked Jess if she had been aware of it, and Jess said that she felt as though we were being watched over. Later, Jess said that she had been in tears several times while observing from my wheelchair, and she confessed that when she saw his sturdy legs, she welled up with tears, thinking, "Oh, no! Not this horse! You'll be jealous of his powerful legs. They're so beautiful."

When Jess mentioned that to Denise, she smiled, saying, "It's so interesting to see the process of selection, knowing the horses as I do. You can't tell by looking at him, but Kairos has nerve damage in his legs and some trauma or abuse." Both Jess and I were astounded at the accuracy of our pairing. It was exactly as Linda's book suggested. Kairos had picked me.

After lunch we had an hour with Linda, who was under pressure from her publisher and pinched for time. She looked at me and asked matter-of-factly, "What can I do for you?"

"Nothing, really," I replied. "I just wanted to meet you, and thank you for saying so eloquently all that I have been feeling from the horses in my life."

Despite the pressure from her publisher and upcoming deadlines, she quickly relaxed into a wonderful three-way conversation. She showed us the artwork for her upcoming horse power wisdom deck and book, *Way of the Horse: Equine Archetypes for Self Discovery*. At one point Linda said, "You don't have to answer this, but I have questions about the pain you've been through." She related that her mother had recently died from cancer, and she couldn't fathom the pain she knew her mother had experienced. I explained how there were not enough pain pills in the world to take away the hurt, that sometimes it's just something you have to accept and relax into. She listened intently, then asked if we had a chapter in our book on pain.

"There will be now!" Jess replied. We laughed. How could we have overlooked how helpful it would be to the reader to devote a whole chapter to pain? Whether concerned with their own or the pain of others, certainly a reader would benefit from this type of focus. Pain is such a large part of trauma.

We all seemed to sense when the hour was up. We were getting ready to leave Linda to her work when she invited us to see her new colt. I went with her in the golf cart while Jess followed, shooting pictures all the way. We were introduced to Merlin, the papa, and to the proud mama Rasa and her beautiful horse child, Indy, short for Indigo Moon. She told us about the birth and how powerful it felt to be present for it.

We must have spent another hour ooohing, aaahing and photographing her new colt, but finally it was time to go. We left feeling changed. The experience at the Epona Center was enriching beyond words. I was floating, taking in my experiences there. Though the evening was extra painful because of all the effort, when we drove away from the center, I felt no pain.

Horses and Insurance

This chapter on horses would be incomplete without some discussion of the limitations of insurance. We have tried several times to get my insurance to pay for horseback riding and have been refused. We understand that if this is going to change, it will have to go through the same process that chiropractics and acupuncture went through to become therapies covered by insurance. Riding is a legitimate therapy and should be covered as such.

Nothing has given me the strength, the balance, the stamina, or the workout that equus therapy has afforded me. All my injuries limit what I can do for exercise. I can work out in water for no more than fifteen minutes before I am exhausted. I cannot swim because I cannot raise my left arm; without the full range of motion I sink. I cannot walk for more than five or ten minutes depending on my pain level each day and the stability of my knee and foot. Before beginning to ride, I could walk only for a minute or so. And with the leg-length discrepancy, even with shoe lifts, it still wasn't pretty. Riding has loosened my legs and hips as well as strengthening them. Now I walk with almost no limp, amazing everyone I know. I owe it all to the horses and my own hard work. Yet this one, best therapy is the one I am least able to pursue. We hope this book can help promote change regarding insurance.

Recently I worked with an old friend, Reba, who is the head physical therapist where Jess works. This meeting was not covered by insurance, either. After describing what was broken and my progress to date, she explained that walking would be half workout and half pain. The way she explained it is this: The body can't take weight-bearing exercise without the strength to bear the weight. I asked her to repeat it so that I could take it in again with my eyes closed:

The body can't take weight-bearing exercise without the strength to bear the weight.

When she said this the second time, my body recoiled with the memory of the so-called therapy provided at the nursing home. At the time, I completely lacked the strength to bear my own weight and yet I was advised to do just that. Reba told me to continue riding horses as much as I could afford, then taught me several exercises to do with the stretch bands in order to build more strength. Some exercises I had already been shown by other PTs that insurance had paid for, but there were many others that were new. She was wonderful, and gave me more hope. At some point, I should be able to work out on a bike at home in between riding sessions. A recumbent bike would be good to start with, she explained, but it won't be aerobic until I can work on an real bike outside.

I look forward to more ways of getting stronger. I know, however, that no matter what kind of bike I find, it will never offer the emotional connection nor the spiritual healing that I get from interacting with horses.

Chapter 11: Pain

When I try to describe the initial pain of the accident, it becomes clear that the English language is completely inadequate. There are no words to describe those intense and horrific feelings, but I will do my best. The pain of the accident itself, the car piercing my body, the bones breaking through my skin, the ribs crushing my lungs, followed by the desperate need to breathe and the panic of not being able to take that much needed breath, the need to try to move and knowing that I couldn't because I had literally been pierced by the car, are all agonies that were like a bee-sting times a million. The pain was sharp. It felt like glass breaking within my body. There was nothing dull about the pain. That and the desperate, unfulfilled urge to reach Devin, blended into a cavernous, echoing shriek from which I could not escape. The weight of the car on my chest, the tissues needing to explode with pain of injury, the lack of air, all rolled into one enormous, ongoing scream, a scream which had a life of its own and seemed as though it was trying to engulf me. To this day, nine years later, I still feel my body screaming in a never ending need to be heard.

There is a certain level of pain at which your senses become completely overwhelmed. Your body comes to your rescue by going into shock and, for a short time, you feel little or no pain. Immediately after the accident, while Devin and I were stuck in the wreckage, fear kept our adrenalin pumping and our experience of pain less important than being rescued. Devin was afraid the car was on fire, but it was actually the powder that's released from the air bags that looked to him like smoke. He was wounded and anxious, aware that his mother could not breathe, yet during all that trauma, our body chemistry took care of us. Devin doesn't remember being in pain, even with ten breaks in his arms and legs and a broken nose and wrist. Larry and Jess recall him needing pain meds for a week after he came home in two casts, but Devin doesn't remember it. I remember hearing the sirens and a voice of someone who was getting oxygen on me, and as the adrenalin ebbed, the pain began to take over. Linda was not the only one to ask, "In that intense state of pain, were you aware of what was going on around you?" I know that Linda wanted to know if her mother, with all the pain she was in as she lay dying, was aware of her being there.

I was afraid of dying. Death seemed inevitable, and I was certain that it could happen at any moment. My body seemed to disconnect from my mind, and I felt a shadow of sadness replacing my body. I have more memories of that than of anything going on around me. I felt pain around leaving my family, and that emotion was stronger than anything that was happening to me or anything that people around me were saying. The pain tried to make me lose consciousness. It kept trying to make me let go, beckoning me towards death. I was afraid that I wasn't going to make it, and I whispered it only to Jess.

I remember feeling surreal during the rescue process, in the ER, and in the helicopter. My mind seemed to go somewhere else, like that feeling just before you go to sleep where everything is echoing. You're aware of what's going on around you, people talking, commotion, but I couldn't really focus. Maybe the brainwave frequencies slow down. That's what it felt like when the car had me pinned. I was aware of people around me. I was aware of what was going on in the rescue process, but it didn't feel like it was happening to me.

People tell me that I was talking to Devin in the ER, even joking with people, encouraging my helpers. I was very focused. What I remember most was the feeling of the echoing, intense screams which I had to push away from myself in order to answer a question or talk to my son. There were times when I could will myself to override the scream, especially to find out if he would be okay, and there were moments when I could not manage this at all.

Even though the pain today is not as bad as when the accident first happened, I still have glimpses of it, which is difficult because it scares me. It brings me back very quickly to June 3, 2001. Let's say today my knee is particularly painful. I might take a step and feel an incredibly sharp pain that threatens to make me lose control of my leg. The pain will sear through nerve endings and take my breath away. Sometimes, it has the power to take away any awareness of what I am doing in a moment. My surroundings then become a backdrop to the flashback of moments during the accident. It triggers the flinching memory of pain as well as actual, in-the-moment sense of pain. So while I'm in physical pain, I am also in emotional pain which increases the depth of the abyss I find myself in.

Jess and I had a very interesting conversation recently that caused me to ponder the subject of pain and memory. The doctors put me into a drug-induced coma in the ICU so that I couldn't experience the fullness of the pain that I was in, and also so that I wouldn't move my broken body and do further damage or disturb the healing process. My body was still experiencing pain or at least discomfort. We know this because as Jess was watching me, my facial expressions would change and my body would move some, especially when my blood pressure rose. Despite the drugs, my body had to heal itself and my brain still had to direct that process. On a cellular level, the body uses the experience of pain, sending signals to the white blood cells and platelets and the various glands even if the drugs kept my brain from remembering. I believe that the body is incredibly wise, that it has wisdom beyond what can be measured scientifically. So it makes sense to me that my body has a memory of the pain that I still have to deal with in some way. I still have losses to mourn, anguish to capture in words, even if the drugs masked some of the awareness of trauma so that my brain would not notice and record those memories. I don't know exactly how it works, but I am certain that at some level all was noticed and felt.

Part of my work, perhaps for the rest of my life, will be to try to heal some of those lost memories which a well-meaning medical system imposed upon me, yet which seem to impede my ability to mourn, to accept, and move on, which I believe to be the natural healing progression after trauma. I want to deal with the sadness of letting my family down, the frustration of trying to come to terms with this life-changing event. Part of my inner work is also to heal the pain of letting myself down. There is a constant danger of allowing the pain to become who I am, and I want to prevent that, to prevent the pain from dictating what I do in life. Of this I am certain: I am so much more than what happened to me.

While I was in the hospital, their staff tried to get me to use a simple pain scale from one to ten. They wanted me to give them a number, where ten was the worst possible pain and I need you to get me more pain meds, while one meant I'm just fine and dandy; let's play cards. But I was mending in so many places, I often felt like my knee was a ten, my chest was a five, my elbow rated a two, and my foot was at least a nine. Instead of giving them the single number they wanted, it made more sense to take inventory. Then there were times when I wanted to say I was at a twelve, because there was no measure for that amount of pain. "I'm off your damned chart," I'd be thinking. "I'm in so much pain I don't know what to do! I'm speechless! I can't give you a number! You don't understand this pain, and I don't understand this pain! Just shoot me now!"

I am sure that the number system is an attempt to take a logical measure of pain in order to help determine whether to administer pain meds and how much, but there is nothing logical about pain. Emotion plays a huge role! Caregivers need to know that. It was difficult to pin down because pain changes all the time. Three minutes ago I might have been at a six, but now I'm off the charts and no one is answering my call bell.

With that much pain coming from so many places in your body, what you end up with are waves of agony constantly washing over you, then backing off a little before engulfing you again. I can only guess that the body sends out its own pain killers, but sometimes they aren't enough to subdue the pain, and the meds aren't enough either.

My experience of pain in the hospital was much like the weather here in the Berkshires, or as we locals call the "Berzerkshires". If you feel okay now, wait a few minutes and you will feel very different. At times pain came blowing in like a nor'easter, in sudden gusts and with mercy toward none. It came in waves of intense, I-don't-think-I-can-stand-another-second-of-this sensation, then subsided a bit, only to return. I think that most people experience pain that way. The body tries to adjust to it physically and emotionally. There are moments where you struggle to rise above it, and moments when you just don't have the strength. Pain is different for each person depending on past experiences of it, depending on their threshold. Even this threshold can change from experience to experience. If the pain in my knee is at a "6" and I start worrying about the possibility that my infection may be waking, all of sudden the "6" may start to climb to an "8" simply because of the anxiety.

It felt like the pain of a difficult childbirth, but in childbirth you at least come out on the other side with a beautiful baby and the pain ends eventually. After injuries like I sustained, there was no baby and the pain didn't end.

I sustained 123 breaks and fractures and, as many physical therapists reminded me, that means there are at least that many invitations for arthritis to set in. As anyone with arthritis pain from any old injury or from aging joints knows, people adapt so they can continue doing their normal activities. I myself have few good body parts left that aren't in pain. Everything hurts, almost every day, but as the weather changes, the amount of my pain often increases.

The word "pain", interestingly enough, may not actually mean the same thing to the reader that it does to me. People often think of pain as something small and discrete, like when a child hits their shin against a table, a sharp pain, maybe followed by an ache for a short time, and then it heals and is gone, pain followed by healing, which never bothers you again. Maybe it brings with it certain feelings—stupidity, clumsiness, resentment or vulnerability—but these are fleeting and disappear as the wound heals. But chronic pain is an entirely different species of animal. The pain I experience feels like a rawness, a swelling, a pressure at the site of the old injuries, almost like a Charlie horse. It feels hot, and is often accompanied by a certain amount of panic, a sense of being claustrophobic inside my own skin. This pain predictably worsens with every dramatic drop of the barometer, or every time I do more than I should at any particular moment.

We've done some research about weather and climate and their relationship to pain. Doctors still argue whether or not the weather influences pain, but there is no doubt in my mind after living with this body for nearly nine years post-accident that whenever there is a sudden change in barometric pressure, I'm in a significant world of hurt. Temperature and dampness have much less effect on my well-being.

Picture a balloon. When the barometric pressure is relatively stable, say in the thirties, it pushes down on the balloon, thereby holding it in place, keeping it the same size. But when the barometric pressure drops, the balloon expands because there is less outside pressure to hold it in place. Cells are basically balloons filled with water and various bio-chemicals. If cells are already inflamed, as many of mine are, then those cells are like small balloons which are slightly over-inflated to begin with, and their skins are already stretched and under pressure from the inside during ordinary conditions. Now remember, pressure outside the body changes with the weather. When the external pressure drops, each cell, muscle, joint, or tissue begins to expand; when external pressure rises, the opposite effect comes into play. These movements, the expanding and contracting with weather changes, causes the nerves to fire and trigger pain. Slow changes are more bearable, but the sudden ones can be excruciating.

We have been studying barometric pressure changes in the United States, and it is said that Hawaii and San Diego have the smallest degree of barometric fluctuation. We have read that some places in Arizona are relatively steady as well. Having visited Tucson and Linda's center south of Tucson, we decided to track barometer readings in some of these places. What we discovered was that while the barometric pressure was fairly steady in Tucson, it was actually steadier in the town of Sonoita where the Epona Center is, over a three-month period of time. Sonoita is more mountainous, greener than Tucson, and may get some of the air patterns from San Diego. This research may cause us to change where we plan to live someday in order to be less effected by the weather, though we've yet to track a full year. We have no idea what it's like during the monsoon season in the Tucson area, so we're not putting our house on the market yet.

My dad gave me a stick carved from hemlock. Mounted outside my bedroom window, it's an old fashioned way to track barometric changes. When pressure is high, the stick curves to the sky, and when the pressure starts to drop, it begins to droop. When it's moving, you know I'll be taking extra pain meds. When I hurt from contracting and expanding muscles through normal use, it's only certain muscles that hurt, but when it's the weather that's causing the expansion of tissue, it's ridiculous. Everything hurts!

When I'm hurting, sometimes moving gives me relief. Simply lying there rocking or thinking, "Oh, poor me!" doesn't help much. Yes, sometimes all I want to do is lie there in bed because I hurt so much, but I know things may feel better once I get moving. Some of the pressure seems to be released or smoothed out somehow through movement. Maybe fluids drain out of the joints as they move; I'm not sure of the exact mechanism, but I know what it feels like. As I lie there, it feels like I'm becoming a larger, tighter sausage. My limbs are heavy, more difficult to move due to stiffness. My chest feels weighted down and each breath is shallow. If I try to pay attention, I feel frustrated, distracted and fuzzy minded. Gentle stretching movements seem to help more than energetic, jaunty movements. Anytime the movement you are doing is enjoyable, which for me would be playing in the water, riding a horse, or pulling a few small weeds, those few moments of getting lost in the activity, or as athletes say "getting into the zone", are worth a lot on a day when you're in a lot of pain. And so, any day I'm in a boatload of pain, I don't particularly want to get up and go ride a horse. But that's when riding gives me the most benefit. Not only am I moving this ridiculously painful body and dispersing some of the hurt, I'm getting lost in something I love. That distraction is worth its weight in gold.

Distraction is a big factor when it comes to dealing with chronic pain. If you are constantly aware of every bad feeling in your body or your spirit—feeling your pain as well as feeling bad that you are in pain in the first place—you are not going to thrive. You may survive, but you will not thrive, and thriving is a choice you have to learn to make. I am not advocating that you ignore the pain. I've had to learn to strike a balance between being aware of my body and the messages it has for me against the need to move away from my body. Anything that you like doing can function as a distraction.

Often nights are the worst time for me. There are not as many distractions as there are during the day, unless you live in New York or Las Vegas and have the energy to chase the bright lights and excitement. Outside of the 24/7 metropolis, when it's two in the morning and the whole house is asleep, or the night staff at the hospital is less attentive, you're going to experience more pain.

When I am at a high level of pain, television is my best friend. I enjoy the familiar voices of shows like *M.A.S.H.* or *Law and Order* that have been on forever. They allow me to fade out. If something grabs my attention, that's great, but otherwise it's a simple distraction. The more pain I'm in, the more I prefer reruns.

Reading a book at a high level of pain demands too much focus, even for someone who loves to read. I have always been able to get lost in a good book, but since the accident, reading is often too hard. It requires concentration and effort on a day when the pain has already raised my stress level and I am exhausted. Movies are often a good distraction, but when my pain level is high or even moderate, I miss too much and can't enjoy.

Music can be a wonderful distraction, too. It opens my heart, but when I connect emotionally to the music, it can connect me to emotional pain that I may or may not be prepared to deal with when I'm already in too much physical pain. This is something that Jess was not aware of early on. We both love music, and she loves making me tapes and CDs, but the emotions the songs brought up were often overwhelming. She was certain the music would be soothing, and was dismayed to see how often it was not. Now we both understand that when my body is at a fever pitch, music only stimulates sadness or the mourning I still have to do. Also, it reminds me that I can no longer dance.

Emotional pain is as real as physical pain. I received no help with it from the hospital, and little help at the nursing home until Jess paid a therapist to come and visit. I found it shocking that in the hospital there was no recognition of the trauma that I had just gone through, nor the loss of my routines, my work, my family as I knew them. I was going through life-altering changes and many more were on their way, but no help apart from drugs was offered for those crucial recovery issues.

I did meet once with a psychiatrist while in Albany because in transferring me from ICU to a regular room, they took me off Ativan, an anxiety medication, without telling me or my family. This traumatic withdrawal, described in an earlier chapter, was not the biggest issue I needed emotional support to cope with, but it did show me that I needed help with my anxiety. To this day, I am looking for ways to deal with the pain of my life changes. I need some ideas and a lot of coaching to help mourn the tragedy that has happened, to mourn the loss of many parts of my body, to mourn the loss of so much of my life. I need help to identify my fears and face them. The mother I wanted to be, playing soccer with my son and doing so many other things, had died in the wreckage. It seemed that all my dreams were gone. Certainly there is no way to dream while you are in pain. And it was impossible to dream while I was struggling to save my leg, and when I was in agony trying to learn to walk; merely surviving took every bit of energy I could muster. I wasn't certain I would even be able to walk. My sporty life was gone. Would I ever run, bicycle, dance again? There was so much that I needed to talk to somebody about and still do.

I needed someone other than family to talk with, because I felt that I needed to put on a brave face for them. I worried constantly that something I said would make them sadder than they already were. My family was overwhelmed, dealing with their own pain and fears. I didn't want to add mine to their mix.

When I was in the nursing home I asked if I could see a therapist. It seems to me I should have been assigned a therapist like I was assigned a doctor to oversee my physical care, but instead I had to ask. The man they sent was completely inadequate. He had no suggestions, no message of hope, no ideas on what to do to feel better. His continuing response was to say, "Oh, my God! Oh, my God!" This was certainly no help. After three sessions I asked him not to come back. He was making me more depressed than I was before he entered my room. There was a woman there, Chris, doing research for her thesis. She came to see me twice and was compassionate, and actively listened without looking like she was overwhelmed. After two sessions with her I felt more optimistic, that is, until they told me she left the facility. That was when Jess decided to hire Eileen, a psychotherapist with expertise in trauma counseling and other modalities.

One of Eileen's first suggestions was that I draw and color what my pain would look like. Art therapy often sounds trivial to an outsider, but this assignment felt quite helpful. It offered a good creative distraction as well as a way for me to express my feelings. The drawing also allowed me to become an observer of my pain instead of allowing it to consume me. At that point in the nursing home I was unable to sit up, and it took three or four people to move my body for toileting and bathing, so the pain held a lot of power over me. Later she did several sessions of EMDR, Eye Movement Desensitization and Reprocessing, which made use of the link between the emotional system in the brain and eye movement to help defuse trauma. She explained that EMDR had been used successfully with war veterans suffering from post-traumatic stress. It helps desensitize a person to their trauma so that the triggers for PTSD are less powerful. I must say it did help me. We worked on the sound of helicopters, which had been a daily sound at the hospital for two months. The sound triggered the memories of being close to death and feeling alone on the way to the hospital.

Eileen helped me move along in my daily life without being quite so skittish, but I still needed more. When I went home, my life was filled with bathing, toileting, going to doctors, going to PT, leaving little time or energy for therapy. We had several sessions at home, but they were taxing physically and financially. She charged me less than she should have, and for that Jess and I were grateful, but still there was a point at which we could no longer afford her help.

At present, I have the time to see a therapist once or twice a month. It is paid for by insurance and is helpful, but in a way, it's too little too late. I need insurance to provide a therapist who has some experience with other survivors of major trauma. If I could find such a person close to home who is covered by my insurance, I would be on the phone making my first appointment immediately.

As for products, I have found many things that are helpful. Liquid glucosamine chondroitin is a godsend. The pills gave me some relief if I kept the daily dose at fifteen hundred milligrams, but we have read that the body doesn't absorb it that well when in pill form. The liquid seems to get to the source of the joint pain in a much more effective way. I don't need anti-inflammatories every day like I did in the first year, but I still need them often enough. They are difficult on my stomach, but there's no getting around the need. It seems to help when I change my script after about six months. Perhaps my body gets used to one kind of anti-inflammatory after a time, and it doesn't seem to be as effective. I have daily complaints from my tummy and work with my primary physician as well as a gastroenterologist.

Three years ago, we discovered MonaVie. It's a juice containing nineteen organic fruits as well as the much touted acai berry. The blend called Active has additional glucosamine added to it. After three months of drinking four ounces a day, I began to notice a difference. I began to drop down from my 1800 milligrams of Motrin. Within six months I was able to stop taking Motrin on a daily basis. Now I only take anti-inflammatories when the weather shifts and the barometer drops. I find also that MonaVie helps with my drug related constipation as the four ounces is supposed to be the equivalent of thirteen serving of fruit and vegetables. My GI tract will attest to that. I have to say that this juice is a blessing!

Arnica gel works very well for acute pain. It is a homeopathic product that you rub into the joints and muscles. Devin and his soccer buddies even use it for injuries on the field as well as pain after practices and games. Tiger balm worked a little better for me than typical pharmacy muscle rubs and patches, but then I discovered the arnica gel. It works better than anything else. Sometimes when I'm not in acute pain, I will have Jess take a wooden spoon and rub cinnamon oil into my joints and muscles. You have to be careful to not get the oil in your eyes. It does burn a bit. This was recommended by my Vietnamese herbal physician who lives in Bennington, Vermont. I have been going to him for more than ten years. I also use the microwavable hot packs. They give some relief as well. And on the few occasions when we have access to a whirlpool, I find that very soothing. Definitely, massage is helpful, but it's not covered by insurance. I rely on Jess and, once in a while, Devin or Becca. When the pain is obviously due to swelling from over doing something, ice works best. I find twenty minutes on and twenty minutes off is a good schedule. Sometimes it takes three or four hours of ice to truly make a difference. Also, remember to protect your skin from the ice or the heat. Both can be damaging.

And, of course, there are the drugs like Oxycontin, Methadone, Morphine, and others for physical pain. Then there are the drugs for nerve pain like Neurontin and Klonopin, drugs like Flexeril for the muscle spasms, and Ativan for anxiety. I seem to tolerate physical pain more than I can tolerate anxiety. So many people, myself included, worry about becoming addicted to the drugs. I may be considered addicted to Methadone at this point, but I'm not going to worry about that. If I think about it more, I guess I'm addicted to everything I take. But if I'm to get out of bed at all, I need these drugs. In the beginning, I was very afraid of getting addicted. Before the accident, I was most uncomfortable taking medication of any sort for any reason. I would always consider an alternative, something holistic like acupressure or massage, homeopathy, or anything else before taking pharmaceuticals. Well, I learned that when you are in as much pain as I was and still am, your body cannot be fighting that pain all day long. That's no kind of a life. And it's wearing on the body in so many ways.

One thing that I learned that everyone should know is that you can't play catch up with pain. In the first few days out of ICU, I was set up with a pump for morphine, then the nurse disappeared. Not only did I have no way to press the pump, but I had no way to press the call button to point out this mistake to the nurse. By the time Jess got there, I was out of control, and it took hours before the drugs got my pain to a manageable place.

Then there was a time later in the hospital when I thought I could tough it out and didn't press the newly designed pump. I ended up again struggling so much that they couldn't give me enough to make the pain subside right away. So it's important that you keep up with the pain. It is proven that patients end up taking more meds overall when they try to "catch up" rather than if they had administered small doses over a period of time. I learned quickly that it was indeed more effective than trying to drown the pain in a large amount of meds which often they can't administer because of potential dangers. I think that the pain itself creates a tension in your body which can restrict circulation and increase blood pressure. Pain can also lower your resistance to infection, and can lead to many other problems.

Pain can be very damaging. They used to think that it was a subjective thing, and it was not easy to get pain medication prescribed. The attitude was, so you're in pain, so what? Suck it up! You're injured or sick. You have to expect pain. Now they want to know how much pain you're in. They want to manage it. Even in terms of patients' rights, you now have the right to not be in pain if medication can alleviate it.

I remember when the bolt in my knee backed out while I was in the nursing home. That was horrible, and that kind of pain threatens to make you black out, to cause your body to shut down. I was quite happy to be given drugs then, and the doctors and nurses were extremely worried about the amount of pain I was going to be in until they were able to get me on the operating table. They were wonderfully compassionate and caring.

There were times after coming home that I became concerned with the amount of drugs that I was on, and I was worried that I was becoming stupid. I know at times I was a little more forgetful on narcotics, but I am also more forgetful when I'm in pain. I've come to the conclusion that it's the circumstances of my life that have dulled my ability to concentrate at times. It's not the drugs. My primary physician described it well. He said that if all of the pain medication is being used for pain, there is nothing left to make you stupid. That helped me a great deal to have it explained in that way, and it made perfect sense. There are days that I have to take two or three extra pills, and no one around me is aware that I'm on that many medications because they are all addressing my pain. I still sound and act quite myself. I think that everyone's experience around pharmaceuticals will be different, and addiction is a real concern. I have worked with a pain specialist in Albany and doctors at a local clinic. I would highly recommend this kind of help.

Note to the reader: As you can imagine, this was the most difficult chapter to write. What we do often with my story is make a tape which Jess then transcribes. As I talk, she keeps me rolling with questions that disappear when she transcribes. Usually she cleans the chapter up, does some rewriting and spell checking, then reads it out loud to me once through just to get the flow. Often we are both in tears in the middle of that first read. Then she reads it to me another day or prints it out for me to make changes, corrections, and additions. Well, this chapter didn't go that way. Jess read it to me "raw" meaning she didn't do any restructuring or rewriting first. We had our usual tears and more, so the reading took a lot longer than other chapters, but when we were done I said, "Oh, my God! That's awful!" Jess agreed that it was weak but thought that everything was there and that it just needed to be rearranged. She also said that it seemed that the chapter on pain rose and fell and meandered much like my experience of pain. I so wanted this chapter to help people like Linda Kohanov, who struggled with what she witnessed as her mother lay dying, understand the intensity of it. And I wanted it to help all kinds of people, people who haven't experienced this, people who have, doctors, nurses, and caregivers of all kinds. And so we wrote and rewrote until we felt we had captured what we were looking for.

We are just everyday folks who want to reach out and share our experience. Our hope has always been that this book would help people of all kinds. It has been a difficult process and often we've gotten frustrated with how long it has taken. We are not published and experienced writers. And so much interrupts the process of writing. Things have happened in our lives, our children's lives. Family members have been hospitalized and some have passed since we started this. This journey of our lives takes so many twists and turns.

I can remember Jess saying, "Okay. Let's finish the book by Christmas…let's finish it by the fourth anniversary of the accident…let's finish it this month." And here it is fast approaching the ninth as we bring the writing to a close. Some people have been so generous with their time in giving us interviews, and a few bowed out. That was an interesting dance to watch. I think we were most impressed with Lionel's willingness to be a part of the book. We had hoped that he would, because he was a major part of this journey, having caused the accident. And if anyone should ever be in that terrible position, we hope that they read that interview. It is brief, but it's powerful. Everyone needs to heal!

Chapter 12: Defining Moments

The small storefront classroom is filled with fifteen or more teens slouched in chairs and on the two window ledges. Several of them turn to watch the two women approaching the door. The instructor, a slender woman in her late thirties, holds court. "Okay, people," she says, "Gayle and Jess are here to talk about Gayle's accident."

Gayle holds Jess's arm with her left hand, a walking stick in her right. She smiles as she makes her way to the front of the class.

"Cell phones off, please," the instructor reminds the young audience.

While the room full of seventeen-year-olds put away food, phones, and notebooks, Gayle greets Karen, the owner of the driving school in Adams. When the teens are settled and quiet, Jess speaks first.

"I'm Jess and this is Gayle. We've been coming here for three years to share Gayle's story with each class of new drivers. Karen believes that real people telling real stories will have a greater impact on you than watching a few movies about accidents." Jess looks around to make sure she has everyone's attention. "Because of the injuries from the accident Gayle was in, it's an effort for her to leave the house and come here. When she showers, she has to sit on a bench for most of it. She takes a stair lift down the stairs. And even though she walked in with quite a lot of grace and only a walking stick, don't be fooled. Every step is painful. And most of her time is spent in a wheelchair." Jess pauses to make eye contact with several of the teens. "And yet it's an effort that she knows is well worth her physical pain." She pauses to look around again. "I'll be passing pictures around as she tells her story. Please keep them moving so that everyone gets to see them. Some of you may find them difficult to look at, so feel free to pass them to the next person."

Gayle smiles as her partner speaks, then tilts her head as she hears her say something she has never said before. "In every life, there are defining moments. With every class, Gayle's hope is that something she shares with you may turn into one of those defining moments."

One teen catches Gayle's attention, focusing for the first time that evening. Others sit up, attentive to what might come next.

"It's good to be with you tonight," Gayle begins. "I don't know if Karen mentioned to you that my son, Devin, who was also in the accident, is here tonight to film this presentation. I'm sure that his presence will make this more emotional for me than usual." She pauses, already beginning to choke up. Jess has moved to the back of the room, holding the photographs and is smiling at her. "Over eight years ago, Devin and I were struck head-on by a young man only a few months older than you. It was graduation time. He'd been partying the night before and was heading home after eating lunch in Williamstown with a friend. He fell asleep behind the wheel of his family's truck. Devin and I were heading to his school in Williamstown to get his French book. Devin was only twelve years old. It was a beautiful Sunday afternoon. We thought we were just going for a nice ride." Fighting back another wave of tears, Gayle pauses to take a sip of water, then continues.

"I was only a month out of the nursing home when I had to appear in court to testify against the guy who hit us. Picture the scene: I am in a wheelchair with an IV and still quite drugged. As you will see in the photos going around, I have metal on my left leg and left arm. I'm still a mess and in a terrible amount of pain. The judge called on me to read my victim statement, and I asked if I could read it directly to the young man. The judge agreed." Gayle picks up some papers and begins to read.

As she reads, several of the students tear up. And then it happens. As she looks at one of the girls in tears, an image comes to her.

That very girl is driving her parents' car from one graduation party to another. The car is packed with kids. Loud music pours out of the open windows. The smell of beer is pungent. The girl starts to drift into the opposite lane. No, she suddenly realizes, that's wrong; the car should be on the right-hand side of the road. Scared, she pulls back hard on the wheel. The vehicle over-reacts, nearly skidding off the road. But it doesn't; the car stops just short and sits there, askew on the shoulder.

None of the kids even seem to notice. They are singing and shouting, having a good time. She pulls out her cell phone and calls a friend to come and pick them up. The partygoers protest, but the girl is scared sober by the near-accident. She turns around and looks from one to the next. "In my Driver's Ed class I saw pictures of a terrible accident and got to meet the woman who was hit. I'm not about to let the same thing happen to us."

The vision surprises Gayle, but she doesn't let it interrupt her presentation. After taking another sip of water, she begins to talk about her injuries. Some of the photos stall while a student studies the mangled vehicles. Suddenly another image appears.

The teen with the baseball cap turned sideways has matured into his mid-twenties. He is an EMT at the scene of an accident. While all around him, the older EMTs rush around to administer to the young woman who has driven into a tree, this young man throws himself belly down on the hood of the car and reaches in through the shattered windshield. He gently takes the woman's face in his hands, forcing her to make eye contact. "You're going to be okay," he assures her. His compassionate gaze calms her down and the screams subside. "I won't leave you," he says. "Breathe with me."

Moved by these visions, Gayle remembers the EMT who kept her conscious when she was trapped by the crushed car. Shaking her head, she looks over at her son who is fussing with his movie camera. She smiles at him and thinks to herself, "Look how much progress we've both made since then."

A hand goes up in the front.

"Yes?"

An athletic-looking boy asks, matter-of-factly, "Did you die?"

"I believe I died a few times," she informs him.

He raises his hand to follow up. "Do you remember anything?"

"I only have a vague memory of the details. Most of what I remember is how easy it is to die. I never thought that it would be like that, but choosing to live was very challenging. In some ways, it would have been much easier to relax and slip away. I also recognize that not everyone has a choice." She looks into his eyes to catch his reaction and another vision comes through.

He is playing football in college. It has been raining for a while. He goes down field for a pass, and just as his fingers touch the ball, he is tackled before he can get a grip. He hits the ground with a sickening crack. His back is broken. A quick fast-forward, and she sees him in a wheelchair, paralyzed from the waist down. He holds a full bottle of painkillers in his hand. He looks at them, considering. But in his head he hears Gayle's warning, "It's so easy to die." He grips the bottle in agony, and thinks about all the people that would be affected by his actions. Finally he screams "No!" and empties the pills into the toilet.

"Do you hate Lionel?" asks a girl sitting in the back.

"No. I do not hate him. He was just a kid, and he made a mistake." She pauses, then takes in a deep breath. "Do I hate what happened to me? You bet I do! But Lionel didn't seek us out with the intention of hurting us."

A young woman looks directly at Jess. She tosses her curly brown hair out of her eyes. "How did you feel about Lionel and the judge's ruling?"

Jess frowns briefly. "I wanted to hate him. Look what he did to our family! But if Gayle could forgive him, what purpose would it serve to go against her? You know, to stay angry with someone for what happened in the past is exhausting. I had so much to deal with, in the hospital and later at the nursing home, just to help keep Gayle alive and relatively comfortable. I couldn't afford to be angry." This seems to surprise many in the class. "Later when I got to know him, I actually liked him. That was difficult. And at the time, the ruling seemed fair, but now I wish the judge had done more."

Gayle interjected, "Yes, we wish the judge had made him send me a Christmas card every year, or pay me ten dollars a month for the rest of his life. I just don't want him to forget what happened, because I can never forget."

Again Gayle flashes into what seems to be a future scenario for this curly-haired teen.

The setting is a courtroom. The teen is now in her fifties and she is the judge. She is about to rule on the assault of a rapist. Before she speaks, her eyes fill with tears. Her memory of the driving school class is as clear as if she were still that teenager. She knows what is expected, what ruling is conventional, but she cannot force herself to say the words the defendant wants to hear. In a fit of rage, he stalked and nearly beat to death the man who raped and murdered his wife. He fully expects to go to prison. But the judge seems to have something else in mind. "I see no benefit in sending this man to jail. You are hereby sentenced to ten years of community service at a women's shelter. You will report to a parole officer for those ten years. It is the hope of this court that something good can come from this and that you will make better choices in the future." The gavel slams and the woman walks out of the court.

Gayle is a bit stunned by the power of this last vision, but in front of her is another girl timidly raising her hand. She has to bring her attention back to these kids who seem to need her now. "My aunt died in an accident two years ago," the girl says in a whisper.

Gayle tears up, but says nothing. Her expression communicates empathy. The class is silent for a few moments, and then Gayle prompts her. "Do you want to share more about that?"

The young girl shakes her head no. "That's okay," Gayle reassures her.

The evening is coming to a close. Jess goes to the blackboard and writes down their cell phone number. "How many of you have someone to call if you get in trouble and need a ride home?" asks Gayle.

More than half the class raises their hands.

"How many of you have two people you can call?"

A few hands go down.

"Now you have another number to call. Jess and I will go out and get you, no questions asked." Most of the class takes down the number.

Karen goes to the board to add her number as she does every month. In less than an hour, the feeling in the room has changed from playful and curious to deep and thoughtful. The change is palpable. Gayle looks out at the young people, once again pleased with her choice to open up the wounds, to share the painful experiences of the accident and her life since then. She smiles at the class, though her body is beginning to tire.

"I have one more piece to read to you." No one looks bored or anxious to leave. "I promise it will be short. It's a letter I wrote to my son on the fifth anniversary of the accident. I had so much to say to him that he did not want to discuss. He had moved on. I was happy about that for him, but for me, I had so much still in my heart. And so I wrote this letter when he was 17; the same age Lionel was when he fell asleep while driving, the same age that you all are now."

Five years, an anniversary to be celebrated. It has been five years that a moment in time has stolen from us. Here I sit in a self-pity party that is overwhelming. I am a goal-setter. I have been working so hard to see just how far I could get. How far could I push these injured legs, arms, this injured soul? I was told that I would not walk, that I might not be able to use this left arm of mine, that I would lose my right leg. I had hopes that far exceeded what my doctors would warn me of. I am sure they were erring on the side of caution, but I would listen, and then say to myself, 'We'll see about that.'

Five years ago on a day similar to this, you and I were wrapped in one another, aware of every breath, every sound, every nuance that could communicate how we were feeling. I could not help you with my hands; my legs could not pick you up and take you away. My hands could not even touch you and brush the glass from your face or the blood from your wounds. My lips could not kiss the spots that hurt you, kiss your fear away as I had done only a week before. I was helpless in so many ways. But my words and my voice could tell you that I love you … before, then, and now.

I am sorry that I could not keep this from happening. I am sorry that I could not hold you when you were in pain. Know that with every breath, every thought, my body and my soul were reaching out to you to comfort you. Through my words and my voice, I tried to comfort you, to console you, to keep you from being afraid and from feeling alone. I told you everything would be okay. It was. Nothing was ever the same, but everything is okay.

I love you.

Devin ducks his head, slightly self-conscious, as everyone in the room looks his way. Some of the teens smile at him. Others seem thoughtful. Karen wraps up the evening with a few closing words and then approaches Jess and Gayle to thank them. Jess replies to her, but Gayle is still looking thoughtfully at the departing group of kids.

The curly-haired girl pauses in the doorway to look back. Gayle acknowledges her with a small movement of her head. The younger woman stands in the exit hesitating between two worlds, indoors and out, past and future. She blushes and her hand rises up, offering a small wave goodbye. Another girl tugs impatiently on her sleeve, pulling her toward the parking lot. The young woman smiles once more at Gayle who moves slowly towards the door. Gayle holds her arms out to the girl. They share a quick embrace. The teen whispers, "Thanks," then turns on her heels and moves ahead to catch up with her friends. Gayle's legs ache and her right knee catches for a moment as she moves back towards Jess and Karen. The scene shifts for one last time that night.

Jess is standing off to the side talking to a high school principal in an auditorium where Gayle has delivered her message to hundreds of teens. There are at least thirty lined up waiting their turn to shake her hand, thank her, or hug her. Gayle's face is soft and her expressions are lively as she continues to share her experiences and her feelings about what could have brought her to a very different future than this one. It is clear in this vision of the future that she has found the true purpose of her accidental journey.

December 13, 2003

Ordinary Day
By Jess Kielman

With you
by my side
watching TV
nothing special
after a day together showing our jewelry
at a gallery in Housatonic.

Pride in listening
to you
tell new friends
about your new life
about how you were pinned
behind the wheel of your car
about how you watched
death beckon
again.

With you
while by your side
the machines
clicking and beeping
and humming their rhythmic chorus
and breathing for you while you slept.

Joy in looking over
at you today
tears like the tide
rising in your eyes
your memories, your insights
of how easy it was
to die
and how hard it is
to live.

Lying by your side
resting with you after an ordinary day
the TV a little too loud
your hand reaching for mine
knowing that you lived
to have an ordinary day
is nothing if not
extraordinary.

Epilogue

Every inspiring story, whether fiction or non-fiction, should have an engaging and uplifting ending, and an ending that ties up all loose ends. Although Gayle and I worked hard to create such an ending, it may be misleading. What our ending does not address are the many hard truths that some of you who have been victims of trauma need to know and consider as you navigate your own personal journey. Here are some of those hard truths.

Yes, Gayle had the choice to live or die, more than once, but not everyone has that choice.

Yes, Gayle can get out of her wheelchair and walk for perhaps five minutes, but every step is painful and wears out her already damaged joints.

Yes, Gayle gets Social Security, but it was a struggle to get it, and it's a struggle to keep it. As soon as someone reads this book, they may report to the powers that be that Gayle can walk and talk and should not continue to receive benefits. We know of such a case where a young boy is being denied benefits because of an article written in a newspaper about his courage in the face of debilitating brain cancer.

Yes, Gayle gets Social Security, but it is not enough to live on. She lives in constant fear of what her life will be like if I should be disabled or die.

Yes, Gayle's insurance has paid for most of her hospitalizations and doctors, but the co-pays have been staggering over the years. And two surgeries were "deemed" unnecessary and not covered at all. You can be certain that they were indeed necessary. It has been and continues to be a part-time job for me to make all the phone calls to insure that bills get paid. Furthermore, there are many other things that were entirely necessary that were not covered by insurance.

Yes, Gayle received money for her wrecked car, but not enough to purchase a new one that would accommodate a wheelchair.

Yes, Gayle was granted 100 community hours with the teen who caused the accident, but it was a drop in the bucket considering the extent of the damage done.

Yes, Gayle got insurance to pay for the helicopter ride that saved her life by bringing her to Albany, but it took two years and over twenty phone calls to get it paid.

Yes, Gayle got fantastic physical therapy, and most of it was paid for by insurance, but because of some dishonesty at the nursing home, her insurance did not want to allow her to continue with PT. One of her therapists went to bat for her and succeeded.

Yes, Gayle had the pleasure of riding horses, and it was the physical therapy that got her out of the chair and walking short distances; but it is not a therapy that is approved by insurance.

Yes, Gayle can move around the kitchen enough to make a sandwich or some brownies, but we have yet been able to afford or find financial assistance to get a fully wheelchair accessible kitchen.

Yes, Gayle recently got a power chair, but the most important part of it for her, the power lift to get her up to the height of our non-compliant kitchen counters, was promised but not included. I called often, but to no avail. A few of her PTs have also called with no results.

Yes, Gayle has a power chair, which is supposed to make her more independent, but insurance does not cover the ramps to get it out of the house or the lift to get it in and out of the car.

Yes, Gayle beat an infection in her right leg and it was not amputated, but it can awake at any time and for any reason.

Yes, Gayle has wonderful family and friends who are supportive, but they do not know many of the difficult details. She refuses to let on for fear of depressing or overwhelming them.

Yes, Gayle had several opportunities for lawsuits, but they take time, energy, and money. Our decision was always to move forward instead of living in the past.

Yes, Gayle has beat all the odds, but she is frighteningly close to the limits of what medicine and surgery can do for her. The next time her hip or her shoulder dislocates, or a joint wears out totally, she is facing fusion or amputation unless medicine makes great strides in the next few years. At present her left elbow is broken in two places and we are awaiting surgery. And with each surgery, there are complications such as infections, constipation, breathing, and liver damage due to all the medications.

Yes, Gayle and I wrote a book, but it took years of reliving all the experiences. It took a lot of courage to take this project on in the midst of surgeries, bed rest, and PT.

Because both Gayle and I are optimists, we were reluctant to include this section, but without it, we felt that we had omitted important information. In the first several years, Gayle thought that if she worked hard enough, she would get better and have her former life back. Unfortunately, that is not the case. Many people who have been injured never regain what they had or who they were prior to their injuries. When that happens, we feel it is important to mourn what you have lost in order to begin to create your new life. Whatever your journey has become, know that we are here to support you in any way we can. Please do not hesitate to reach out beyond reading this book.

Blessings,

Jess Kielman

Reading Resources

What struck us in the beginning of our journey was the scarcity of supportive groups, reading material, government assistance, and help of any kind other than medical. It seemed we were so alone and yet it was difficult to believe that there was little out there in the way of help. With accidents and injuries happening all the time, it didn't seem possible. There was a plethora of books for cancer survivors, alcoholics, and those who have lost loved ones. Since the summer of 2001, more has been written. We hope this list of other books is helpful.

Any of the Christopher Reeve books are both informative and deeply moving. Several of Gayle's acupressure clients knew both him and his wife quite well and kept Gayle updated on his condition. When Gayle was at the rehab center in Boston for a month, she could feel his presence nearly every place she went. She was inspired by all that he was able to accomplish after his trauma of falling from a horse. She was inspired by what he was able to endure and devastated when she heard of his death. As the caregiver, I identified with his wife Dana, and shed many tears when she also died years later. When I think of the heroics it takes to endure what he and Gayle went through, I am moved most by this particular quote of his:

"A hero is an ordinary individual who finds the strength to persevere and endure in spite of overwhelming obstacles."

Christopher Reeve's books:
Still Me (July 1999)
Nothing is Impossible: Reflections on a New Life (April 2004)
Don't Lose Hope (September 2005)

There is a practical, hands-on manual that guides victims through the maze of recovery. It is entitled *Surviving an Auto Accident: A Guide to Your Physical,*

Economic and Emotional Recovery, and it is authored by Robert Saperstein & Dana Saperstein (March 1994). Topics covered in this book include the experience of an accident, the injuries involved, the psychological trauma, how to heal economically, and how to deal with the legal end of the trauma.

Car Accident Secrets by DS Publications (January 2005) is a step-by-step instructional manual for those who want to avoid the expense of a lawyer in settling their claims with the insurance companies. It is a very detailed book and a good assist for those who choose this path; but it is totally "nuts and bolts" and doesn't address the emotional part of an accident.

Crash Course: A Self-Healing Guide to Auto Accident Trauma and Recovery by Diane Heller, Laurence Heller, Diane Poole Heller, & Laurence S. Heller (January 2002) deals in detail with the process of healing the trauma of auto accidents. Topics include boundary rupture, somatic therapy, and ways to deal with trauma without "re-traumatizing" the victim.

Waking the Tiger: Healing Trauma by Peter Levine and Ann Frederick (July 1997) is a classic. It deals with trauma of all kinds and is a must read. Some of the topics include the trauma vortex, the healing vortex, immobility response, Pooh Bear, Somatic Experiencing, and much more. To say that Dr. Levine is innovative is an understatement. I found his techniques for dealing with the stuck energy involved in trauma to be both compassionate and constructive. He talks about how trauma is "frozen energy" as a result of being "too civilized" thereby denying and/or trying not to experience the emotions surrounding trauma. *Waking the Tiger* is for survivors of accidents, disasters, war, and traumas of all types. He helps identify and explain why trauma victims may experience anxiety, depression, unexplained physical pains, and seemingly unrelated illnesses. "When people have been traumatized, they are stuck in paralysis—the immobility reaction or abrupt explosions of rage." - Peter A. Levine

The Body Remembers: The Psychophysiology of Trauma and Trauma Treatment by Babette Rothschild (October 2000) is similar to Peter Levine's *Waking the Tiger* in that the author acknowledges the body-mind connection of trauma. She gives examples of her work with trauma victims and goes into detail about how PTSD (Post Traumatic Stress Disorder) is not about the past as much as it is about the present emotional content of trauma and how to deal with its triggers.

90 Minutes in Heaven: A True Story of Death and Life by Don Piper and Cecil Murphey (September 2004) is an interesting and inspiring read. Because I have heard Gayle tell of her own near-death experiences and have witnessed her struggle to reclaim a life after being so broken in an auto accident, I have nothing but respect for Don Piper's story. His retelling is striking.

A Special Note From Gayle

I would like to express my desire to continue sharing beyond this book. If you have questions or just want to share something with me, I welcome the connection. My email address is gayle.andrew@gmail.com and my mailing address is P.O. Box 449, Lenox, MA 01240. Because of difficulties with my wrists, I do not check my email as often as Jess does. So if you don't hear from me as soon as you would like, her email is: jess.kielman@gmail.com.

Notes

Notes

Notes

Index

A

B

C

O
Oxycontin, 257

P
Pain Pump, 195
Pain Scale, 248
Panic, 39, 143, 166, 228, 238, 246, 250
Physical Therapy, PT, 36, 61, 62, 70, 76, 78, 79, 83, 85, 89, 90, 98, 115-124, 132, 133, 135, 156-158, 170, 179, 202, 209, 220, 222, 226, 245, 255, 271
PICC Line, 82, 163
Priceline.com, 186
PTSD, 90, 238, 255, 275

R
Ramp, 3, 73, 80, 92, 122, 139, 181, 204, 212, 213, 227, 271
Rehab, Rehabilitation, 15, 61, 65, 82-88, 101, 158, 186, 187, 210, 222, 273
Rescue Remedy, 194, 222
Rhuta, 194

S
Slide Board, 185, 217
Social Security, 79, 80, 159, 169, 200, 217, 270
Social Worker, 79, 158, 200
Stair Lift, 99, 208, 209, 212, 221, 261

T
Therapy Horse, 125-127, 228, 232
Tiger Balm, 180, 256
Toileting, 81, 181, 204, 255

Deep Blue Press

P.O. Box 449, Lenox, MA 01240

Made in the USA
Lexington, KY
04 January 2011